ARMS and the MONK!

Arms

and the

Monk!

The Trappist Saga in Mid-America

by

M. M. Hoffman, Litt.D.

WM. C. BROWN COMPANY
Publishers
DUBUQUE, IOWA

4169

Author of:

ANTIQUE DUBUQUE: 1673-1833

THE CHURCH FOUNDERS OF THE NORTHWEST:
Loras and Cretin and other Captains of Christ

THE CENTENNIAL HISTORY OF THE ARCHDIOCESE
OF DUBUQUE: 1837-1937

THE STORY OF LORAS COLLEGE

YOUNG AND FAIR IS IOWA

"St. Benedict intended the Holy Rule to serve
as a guide in the Military Service which the
Monastic Institute is, and where those who are
called to that service are trained to fight *under*
our Lord Jesus Christ as King and Captain."—
Abbot Maurus of Mount Melleray.

"We place, O Lord, on the head of this Thy
Abbot and warrior, a helmet of defense and salvation to the end that having his forehead en-
nobled and his head safe-guarded by the *horns*
of both testaments he may appear terrible to
the enemies of the truth, and by Thy grace be-
stowed upon him, he may prove a robust champion against them."—Prayer from the Blessing
of an Abbot.

Nihil Obstat:

ANTHONY KREIMER, Ph.D.
Censor Liborum

Imprimatur:

✠ HENRY P. ROHLMAN
Archbishop of Dubuque

May 15th, 1952

FOREWORD

No other monastery has had a more inspiring, a more soul-stirring existence than New Melleray at Dubuque.

Over a hundred years had passed and no one had written an authoritative history of this Iowa Trappist house. Something had to be done about it. Here was a story of the austere, spiritual soldiers of Christ, a most unique one, with sparkling annals and moving, melancholy chapters, growing cobwebby with oblivion, and threatening to remain forever untold. Pious disquisitions on the Cistercian life at New Melleray had appeared, and spiritual treatises, pamphlets, booklets, even magazine articles embellished with splendid photographic studies, had often touched on the richly mystic existence of the contemplative sons of La Trappe in the midwestern countryside. But no pen had ever traced out its definitive history.

Brilliant writers as well as profound students at our universities pondered the matter but they all side-stepped the task. They were intrigued, and there is no doubt about this fact: the interest in the great Cistercian order today is extraordinary. In the summer of 1950 and not long before his death James Norman Hall, co-author of *Mutiny on the Bounty* and author of other gripping tales, spent a few days of rest and reflection at New Melleray Abbey. He became interested in the snatches of the fascinating stories he listened to about the humble Trappists and toyed with the idea of writing their legend, but went no further. No son of the Church was he, and as a stranger to monasticism he was diffident about making such an attempt. One wonders what this captivating chronicler of the sagas of the seas would have made of the saintly saga of the Iowa prairies.

This present attempt is not an historical study of the Cistercian way of life with all its religious and devotional implications. It tries simply to be an honest and straight-forward history of New Melleray, striving also to retain, of course, those spiritual undertones which form a part of it. It is as far as possible a faithful reflection, without any exaggeration or distortion, of the old and grand Trappist cloister and community that for over a century has been sending up from the

vii

Mississippi valley its prayers and penitential works to the throne of God for all mankind.

A major part of it has been garnered from the old manuscripts of the monks themselves. Much more in the form of letters has unfortunately disappeared through fire. Father Benedict Cowles, O.C.S.O., assembled materials during several years that proved of invaluable assistance. Brother Timothy Westemeyer, O.C.S.O., a son of the Iowa country and with kinsmen, near and distant, in the Cistercian order since time immemorial proved to be a veritable mine of Trappist information. Only through their encouragement was this task commenced and only through their help has it been completed.

                                                    M. M. H.

CONTENTS

CONTENTS

ARMS and the MONK!

DRAMATIS PERSONAE

This is the story of New Melleray, a cloister of contemplative life in middle America. The monks of this house lead silent existences based on a philosophy of life and eternity which is being examined with a new, an awakened, interest in every part of the United States.

This story started in Iowa in 1849. It had a long introduction in Europe, Canada, and eastern United States before that. Its American chapter is now well over a century in length.

Ten miles from Dubuque over a concrete stretch of the Old Military Road and two miles through a beautiful forest that has been set apart for a State game preserve, pious monks live in seclusion. A building of mediaeval Gothic — white stone walls, a gleaming slate roof, arched windows, and spires — crowning a hill backed by trees and green fields: such today is the Iowa monastery of Our Lady of New Melleray. Within yonder walls men are living in 1952 by the old sixth century Rule of St. Benedict.

New Melleray is but one of the flowers in the blossoming Cistercian garden in the United States. A little over a hundred and twenty years ago a brilliant Frenchman visited this country and wrote his findings in a famous book that is still studied today, *La démocratie en Amérique*. Baron Charles-Alexis de Tocqueville held that democracy could exist only by seeking a moral support in religion. He saw the Catholic immigration from Europe beginning to arrive on the western continent. He asked, somewhat fearfully: "Can the Catholic Church, accustomed to exist under royal European auspices, prosper or even survive in the free atmosphere of the young American republic?"

Would that de Tocqueville could behold the answer today: the healthy growth of Catholicity and the efflorescence in this last cycle of time of its spiritual and mystical orders. The astonishing growth of the Cistercian order in America in the last score of years is part of that answer. In the nation which has the highest standard of living in the world, where comfort and even luxury abound on every side, where education and science and progress flourish as nowhere else on the globe, the austere orders like the Trappists, — like the brethren of New Melleray —, grow with an ever more irresistible appeal to the gallant youth of the land.

The truth of the words written by the Pope of Catholic Action, Pious XI, less than thirty years ago has finally been reaching the hearts of men. Speaking of the contemplative monks he said:

From the earliest times this mode of life, most perfect and most useful and more fruitful for the whole of Christendom than anyone can conceive, took root in the Church and spread on all sides . . . Since the whole object of this institution lay in this — that the monks, each in the privacy of his own cell . . . should fix their thoughts exclusively on the things of heaven — wonderful was the benefit that accrued from it to Christian society.

This story starts, as we said, in 1849. A small company of Irish Trappist monks, assiduously fulfilling the duties of prayer and penance for the benefit of Christian society, entered the upper Mississippi valley in that year. Other groups of Europeans were welcomed here contemporaneously with the monks. There was a cluster of Hungarian followers of the liberal aristocrat, Louis Kossuth, who opened up a farm colony in the youthful state of Iowa. Farther south from New Melleray and across the Mississippi on the Illinois shore came Étienne Cabet and his "Icarian" Utopians from France. They, too, had communal ideals like the Cistercians to the north of them. They had ideals of equality and especially of equality of property. "Was not Jesus Himself an Equalitarian?" they asked. But they were materialistic communists, who did not try to dominate human passions and greeds. They came into Iowa and gradually disappeared, long after the earthly paradise of pleasures and temporal riches at which they aimed had burst into thin air. The communal life founded at New Melleray in 1849, based on that of the first Christians who were of "one heart and one mind," had been the life of the Cross and the thorny Crown. It lasts today, and stronger than ever, it now buttresses the bastions of Western civilization against the new and far fiercer communism which is Sovietic and atheistic.

Shortly before the French Icarians there had been another semi-communal religious body located on the Mississippi shores opposite Iowa. It was that of the Mormons, calling themselves "Latter-Day Saints," but its members had already left for the Salt Lake of Utah.

Yet strangely, long before all these, there had been Trappist monks in the Mississippi valley. Most of them were Frenchmen who had fled from Emperor Napoleon's persecution in Europe, and after tarrying in Pennsylvania and Kentucky, had settled at Cahokia, Illinois, near St. Louis. Here in 1809 they erected with patience and toil their monastery near a cluster of huge Indian burial mounds. This site of their long vanished, log-cabin cloister is known today as Monks' Mound. Here they starved and worked and built and prayed for four long years and finally began to flourish. Here, among the Indians, they wanted to build an Indian school, and one of the brothers, the intrepid Dom Urban Guillet, went to Washington to confer with a senatorial committee about it and to obtain title to lands for its support.

These monks of Our Lady of Good Counsel monastery among the Indian graves and mounds, were edifying the white settlers and the red savages by their lives of privation and penance. Then their crops failed; then the War of 1812 with England broke out, and their own Trappist oblates and their helpers were summoned to defend the border from British-led Indian attacks by way of the great river; and then, worst of all, the dread cholera struck them, and poor and emaciated by their previous sufferings, many of them were laid low by death. And finally in 1813 their illustrious leader, a great Trappist name in Europe as well as in America, Dom Augustin de Lestrange, asked them to close their brave little foundation, and those who were left of the community ultimately returned to France.

For a decade previous to 1849 there resided in Iowa as bishop of the Dubuque diocese — an immense diocese that stretched all the way north to the Canadian border and all the way west from the Mississippi river to what is today Montana — a saintly man with a Cistercian soul. One of his books printed in Paris and donated by him to the New Melleray monastery library a hundred years ago today, shows on its musty title-page: "The Monasteries of the Order of La Trappe, by Clement Tallon." Clement Tallon, the author and an official of the French government, had two brothers who were eminent Trappist monks, and all three were nephews of the Iowa bishop. Related by close ties of blood to the Trappist brotherhood, the bishop was far more closely allied to it in spirit. It was his fond prayer all during that decade that his diocese should some day be blessed with a monastery of that holy and penitential order.

Bishop Mathias Loras had been born at Lyons just as the Revolution in France was rushing to its climax. He was but an infant in his mother's arms when she pleaded with the tyrant Couthon for the life of her husband, a wealthy aristocrat and counsellor of Lyons. But Loras *père* was in the very first group to be guillotined in the Square des Terreaux, and a few days later the same fate overtook two of his sisters and two brothers, one of the latter being mayor of St. Cyr. In all, seventeen persons of the Loras family lost their lives for their political and religious convictions.

Classmate and close friend of Jean Baptiste Vianney, the canonized Curé d'Ars, in his youth, Loras became after his ordination a professor and then the president of the large diocesan seminary of Lyons. Abandoning what promised to be a brilliant church career in France, he came to America to labor as a missioner in the forests and everglades of Alabama and Florida. Now, working heroically on the prairies and the rivers of his far-flung northwestern diocese, he intensified his anchoritic life of sacrifice and lonely poverty until his very soul was become that of a Cistercian monastic.

On a hot July afternoon in 1849 Bishop Loras' cup of spiritual joy was filled to overflowing. In his modest brick house, the "episcopal mansion" of Dubuque, he was entertaining four Trappist brothers, travel-stained and weary from long, arduous journeys. Next to him sat his vicar-general, a successful missioner among the Iowa Winnebagoes, the Abbé Joseph Cretin, — also an illustrious exile from France. Cretin's uncle had been guillotined in 1793 on the same platform that received the blood of Loras' father, and a year later his mother had been imprisoned by the revolutionists.

Opposite the purple-soutaned bishop sat the bearded and white-robed abbot of Mount Melleray Abbey in Ireland. Dom Bruno Fitzpatrick was a young man still for he was only thirty-six years of age. The son of a successful Irish physician, he had been educated in France, and after his ordination to the priesthood he had entered the Trappist order in Mount Melleray. His great talents as well as his zeal and holiness were so marked that in the spring of 1848 he had been elected by the community to become the third abbot of their foundation. Until his death in his eighty-first year, he was to be the leader of both these Cistercian communities, the one in Ireland, the other in Iowa; he was to bring them up the mountain of toil to success only to go down with them into the forlorn valleys of vicissitude. But always he emerged the victor — the victor over famine, impoverishment, disaster and the evils of a sinful world.

Dom Bruno was flanked by two remarkable monks of his order. Father Clement Smyth and Father James Myles O'Gorman had both been educated by Protestant — principally Anglican — teachers, because the prescriptive laws of England made it penal for a Catholic to teach school. Both men were graduates of famed Trinity College of Dublin. Father Clement Smyth had been president of the Mount Melleray Seminary and was now selected by Abbot Bruno as the prior of the new American venture. Father James Myles O'Gorman was a bit of a blue-blood, of "Castle Irish" extraction. His mother, Alicia Myles of Tipperary, was a daughter of Major Myles and was a convert to the Catholic faith. Her brother had become a man of some military renown, the Major-General Sir Edward Myles of the British army, and it was he who had arranged for his nephew's complete education at Trinity College.

Behind this trio of choir brothers sat the brown-clad lay brother, Ambrose Byrne, referred to repeatedly by his prior as a "man of judgment and prudence." Brother Ambrose was an agriculturist and a geologist, and because of his knowledge and wide experience in these capacities his advice was relied on in the selection of land and water sites for a Trappist institution in the new and strange American wilds.

On that July afternoon of 1849 the plans for the foundation of the new monastery were discussed and the terms agreed upon in the unpretentious mansion of the bishop of Dubuque. These were the founders of the New Melleray Trappist institution: these tonsured Cistercian monks with the bishop and his vicar. The bishop's dreams for his diocese and the abbot's hopes for his monks were at last to be blended. Smiles were on their faces and their hearts sang happily the praise of God. The fertile land of Iowa so generously donated by Mathias Loras was to be tilled by the horny hands of pious Trappists, and on these rolling prairie lands was to be erected the Iowa Trappist house of God. And out from the ancient Scriptures seemed to come the words that day to these Cistercians newly arrived in the Mississippi valley:

For the Land, which thou goest to possess, is not like the land of Egypt . . .

But it is a land of hills and plains, expecting rain from heaven.

And the Lord thy God doth always visit it, and His eyes are on it from the beginning of the year to the end thereof.

If then you obey my commandments, which I command you this day, that you love the Lord your God, and serve Him with all your heart, and with all your soul:

He will give your land the early rain and the latter rain, that you may gather in your corn, and your wine, and your oil,

And your hay out of your fields to feed your cattle, and that you may eat and be filled.

Beware lest perhaps your heart be deceived, and you depart from the Lord, and serve strange gods and adore them;

And the Lord being angry shut up heaven, that the rain come not down, nor the earth yield her fruit, and you perish quickly from the excellent land, which the Lord will give you.[1]

At the end of this signal meeting Bishop Loras tendered to the monks his hand and his heart as simple and Cistercian as their own. Simple Trappists! They were to live with other simple brethren in a secluded Iowa monastery, in silence and solitude, and every day they were to pray and to meditate and to work with their hands in Iowa soil. Yet they knew they were rich for they all possessed Christ and they understood the depth of His Love and the infinity of His Mercy.

[1] Deuteronomy, Chap. II.

Not so did the world understand it.

Exactly seven years before this meeting at Dubuque, the English-man, Charles Dickens, stood on the bank of the Mississippi river at Cahokia, Illinois, three hundred miles to the south. It was a muggy day in July, 1842, as he gazed across the scrub-studded prairies at the Indian burial mounds. He asked the meaning of the name, "Monks' Mound." Then the world renowned but still young novel-ist listened with contemptuous curiosity to the tale of the Trappist monks from whom Monks' Mound took its name just as it has been here recounted: how there in the lonely wilderness some thirty years before, the sons of La Trappe had painfully built their log monastery and had spent their time in prayer and in silence and in labor for the Lord; a number had died of the disease called the cholera and the remaining members had later returned to France. Dickens' re-action was that of the coldly fashionable and unbelieving world ex-pressed in his ill-tempered remarks: "What fanatics! What gloomy madmen!" Nearby in the Mississippi was Bloody Island, so called because hot-blooded duellists had sought its wooded shade to shoot each other to death. Coupling the passing of these young blades of St. Louis with the deaths of the monks, Dickens sneeringly announced to the world of his day that there was no great loss to the community and no "very severe deprivation" was wrought to society.

The Trappist brethren at Dubuque would have been the first to admit that they were peculiar. For the same book of Deuteronomy quoted before gave the divine answer for them:

> Because thou art a holy people to the Lord thy God. The Lord thy God hath chosen thee, to be his peculiar people of all the peoples that are upon the earth.
>
> Not because you surpass all nations in number, is the Lord joined unto you, and hath chosen you, for you are the fewest of any people:
>
> But because the Lord hath loved you and has kept his oath. . .

What a muster of souls with significance fraught for the future was this meeting of 1849, attended by four of these Dickensian "gloomy madmen!" Probably nowhere else at that period of the American Catholic Church could be found a group of six church-men more able, more cultured and, above all, more courageous. A remarkable fact that should not be overlooked is that five of these gentlemen, — then or later of prelatial or episcopal rank — were destined to play an active part in and leave an important impress on American history and American Catholicity in the Northwest. Loras, the intimate friend and counsellor of the two United States senators from the young state of Iowa — Generals George Wallace Jones and Augustus Caesar Dodge — was the only one at the time of this meeting who already reigned over a diocese as its episcopal shepherd. Just a year later Joseph Cretin, the Dubuque vicar-general, was to be appointed by Rome as the first bishop of Minnesota with his see city at St. Paul. Dom Bruno Fitzpatrick was a mitred abbot and for many future years his sparks of zeal and wisdom were to fly from Ireland's Mount Melleray to bishops, abbots and monks in America. And within a decade Father Clement Smyth was to become the second bishop of Iowa, and Father James Myles O'Gorman was to go to Omaha as a bishop, to be the Vicar-Apostolic of Nebraska, the only instances in history where Trappist monks became bishops of American dioceses.

The story of the Iowa monastery of the poor men who labor in New Melleray started in 1849. This Iowa start, however, was only a milestone along their dauntless march of achievement. Of the previous milestones that led up to 1849 we must record a few words, for the graphic background of these Cistercian Bayards —truly, *chevaliers sans peur et sans reproche* — will illuminate the thrilling events that, decade after decade, were to follow.

II

MONTE CASSINO TO IOWA

· · · · · · · · · · · · · · ·

The six men who gathered in the little Dubuque episcopal mansion on that summer afternoon of 1849 — Dom Bruno and his three monks, Bishop Loras and Abbé Cretin — were, as time was surely to prove, the actual authors and fashioners of the Iowa Trappist institution. Others gave of brain and brawn, of toil and suffering, to its construction and development, but it was to the vision, the enthusiasm and the generosity of these six gentlemen of Christ that New Melleray Abbey owed its successful, albeit oft tottering, beginnings.

Today, crowded as it is with novices and professed monks, with its many spiritual activities and temporal labors, New Melleray is a veritable powerhouse of prayer and penance. Yet a century and more ago it was a dangerously weak and tottering institution which these six men had to guard and to guide lest it plunge into the abyss of disaster that ever yawned at its feet. The agonizing events before 1849, and similar events in its history long after 1849, when the founders had already long been called before their just but merciful Judge, were of such a precarious and menacing nature that as one gazes back through the perspective of time he gains the vivid im-

9

pression that only through a miracle of God has New Melleray survived to become the divine powerhouse it is today.

As late as 1892, when the Dubuque abbey was well over forty years of age, a learned professor of history writing under the auspices of the State University of Iowa and still conscious of this hazardous Cistercian venture, stated that "it is not unlikely that this (foundation) may find its isolation fatal, and that it may prove to be the first and last Trappist Abbey west of the Mississippi." Looking back today we dare to say: Unfounded fear! Monks are indestructible! Yet thanks entirely to the omniscient God Who guided it, New Melleray Abbey is now well started on its second century, possessing greater vigor and promise than ever, and three more Trappist foundations flourish west of the Mississippi; one in the Ozark hills of southern Missouri, another in the Wasatch Mountains of Utah, and the third in the Pecos Valley at the foot of the Sangre de Christo Mountains, outside Sante Fe, New Mexico.

The 1849 meeting was but an early milestone in the development of the stirring story of the Iowa Trappists. Already they had travelled thousands of miles by land and sea, by lakes, canals, steamboats and stagecoaches, to reach their goal of an American foundation. Already they had encountered disappointments and losses, opposition from American bishops, suspicion from priests, hostility from some of the laity, and ridicule even in the Catholic press of that day. The atmomosphere of Know-nothingism and Nativism, rampant among the non-Catholic masses in the '40s and the '50s of the last century, made the road hard and life acutely arduous for these foreign White Monks. Among the cultured and educated classes, there was not the ignorant hatred of the masses towards them and their ideals, but something worse: a cold contempt for contemplative piety, a cynical disbelief in all that stood for supernaturalism, a subtle but assiduous attack on faith in the Christian dispensation. Who better than Emerson, the poet of contemporary agnostic transcendentalism could voice that attitude:

> "I love a church, I love a cowl,
> I love a prophet of the soul;
> And on my heart monastic aisles
> Fall like sweet strains and pensive smiles.
> Yet not for all his Faith can see
> Would I that cowled churchman be!"

The patient, heart-breaking struggles and travels of the Irish Cistercians up to this year of 1849 would form, in their description, a classic Odyssey of their own. But they were merely the prelude of a great drama. The grand saga of epic disasters and long-drawn battles against varied catastrophes was to be carried on until well into a new century.

These monks of our story have been called, it will be noted, Cistercians and Trappists as though the names were synonomous and interchangeable. A short glance into the long panorama of their monastic background will clarify the mind of the curious reader. We will now leap back, therefore, for just a moment to the rising of the curtain on our story's very beginning.

The fierce military conflagration about the hills and walls of Monte Cassino monastery in 1943 and '44 made the Western world, at least, again conscious of St. Benedict and his monks and their heroic work started there in Christian antiquity. Now happily in 1952 arising again from the ruins caused by American soldiers and British bombers in World War II, Monte Casino still stands after fourteen centuries as the historically focal point from which the streams of Benedictine contemplative life began meandering through the civilized world.[1] Benedictine monks, ever since 529 A.D., went to various wildernesses in Europe, — (and only in the last century to Africa, America and Asia) — built their monasteries there, cultivated the land and applied themselves to the sciences and arts. Benedictine monks are members of a community of men, leading an austere and contemplative life apart from the world, under strict vows, and in accordance with the Rule of St. Benedict.

Besides the contemplative orders such as the Benedictines, there are active religious orders: such as the orders of the friars — the

[1] Winston Churchill questions in his memoirs the value of the Allied bombing of Monte Cassino monastery in Italy during World War II. The wartime British prime minister declares: "The monastery did not contain German troops but the enemy fortifications were hardly separated from the building itself . . . On Feb. 15 therefore, after the monks had been given full warning, over 450 tons of bombs were dropped, and heavy damage was done. The result was not good.

"The Germans had now every excuse for making whatever use they could of the ruins, and this gave them even better opportunities for defense than when the building was intact."

Incidentally, Monte Cassino Abbey will now have inscriptions on its new bronze doors to symbolize the five destructions since its foundation fourteen hundred years ago. One panel will picture a steel helmet, an aeroplane and a giant bomb.

Franciscans, Dominicans, Augustinians — or such societies as the Jesuits, — whose members take care of the sick and directly feed the poor and teach children in school, and even conduct parish work. It is true that the contemplative orders often do some of this work indirectly, for much of their material goods goes to the poor and they assist other charitable activities. But their primary work is spiritual: it is prayer and meditation and austerity. In a world which knows nothing of prayer and austerity, it is these orders who pray for the world and all those in the world who have neglected prayer.

As the centuries rolled on some of these strict orders grew weak in their primitive discipline and fervor. Reforms had to be instituted to correct their laxity, caused sometimes by their landed possessions and wealth. When the laxity of the Benedictine life of the tenth, eleventh and twelfth centuries is spoken of, it must be immediately understood that this did not mean grave disorders or corruption, but a too easy and free interpretation of the strict Rule of St. Benedict.

One of these marked reforms occurred at the turn of the twelfth century under the great monk, St. Robert, who founded what he called the New Monastery, at Citeaux in France. And from Citeaux is derived the name of the Cistercian order. A little later under St. Bernard of Clairvaux, the Cistercians became probably the greatest contemplative order of all times. Within fifty years this order had five hundred abbeys, and later numbered in the thousands its monasteries and convents.

Then again decadence descended upon part of the order. Although riches and great properties led to laxity in numerous places, there were many abbeys where there was no diminution in fervor, fasts or fortitude. And so in the seventeenth century the Order of Citeaux was divided into two Congregations, the Cistercians of the Common and the Cistercians of the Strict Observance, the latter adhering strictly to the Rule in all its phases.

But what of the name "Trappists?" We are now coming to that.

There had been for a long time an abbey in northerly France called La Trappe. It was an old, old Cistercian abbey going back to the year 1140 A.D., and because both of its prominence and its robust growth it became widely known as La Grande Trappe. In the seventeenth century a zealous abbot who had been a rich and reckless rake in his youth tried — and succeeded in a large measure — to reintroduce profound piety and severe austerity in the Cistercian order. His movement was called the Great Reform. So great was the fame of holiness under this Abbot de Rancé that men like Bossuet, the celebrated French pulpit orator, and King James II of England came to La Trappe to make spiritual retreats. As these reforms introduced by de Rancé at La Trappe began to spread through all the Cistercian houses of the Strict Observance, the name Trappist everywhere accompanied them and it is by this name today that the White Monks are popularly known.

There is just one more remarkable Trappist besides de Rancé of whom a word must be said here — because of his influence on the Cistercians during a critical period of world history, because of his pioneer American venture, and because one of his followers actually visited the Iowa area in the year 1817.

Father Augustin de Lestrange, usually known to history as Dom Augustin, was the young novice-master at La Grande Trappe when the thunders of the ugly French Revolution began to roar over Europe. More sagacious of the horrible future than many of his elders he led a group of Trappists out of France to sanctuary in Switzerland; most monastic institutions were destroyed and the remaining monks imprisoned or liquidated. In the old ruined Carthusian house of La Val Sainte in the Swiss canton of Fribourg Dom Augustin opened a refuge for many Cistercians who "liberated from monastic despotism" by the revolutionary fanatics still craved their Trappist way of life. He and his community then started a new Reform with a capital R, one of the most drastic ever attempted and going far beyond the normally austere Rule of St. Benedict. One example of many severities: they renounced even the rough straw mattress allowed by St. Benedict and slept on boards.

Under Dom Augustin La Val Sainte soon became an abbey, and under this amazing human dynamo of saintly zeal it started to found new Trappist houses, all with his severe Reform, in many parts of Europe: in Spain, in Belgium, in Holland, in Italy, in England. Came Napoleon: and he reached out his grasping Corsican hand to La Val Sainte to seize the handsome, adventurous and devoted Trappist who defied him. But Dom Augustin swiftly led his groups of followers to short-lived foundations in Germany, in Austria, in Poland, and finally in Russia. For years he had dreamed of the young American republic and its free institutions, and in 1803 when the Trappists had finished their long flight to Russia and began trickling back to La

Val Sainte, he sent out one of his captains, Dom Urban Guillet, with a goodly group of monks to the United States.

It was this adventurous group, imbued with Dom Augustin's austere zeal, that came to Pennsylvania, then went on to Kentucky, and finally reached the Mississippi. During the winters of the four years that they carried on their monastic labors in their log-cabins at Cahokia in Illinois, Dom Urban Guillet and Father Joseph Dunand, his active lieutenant, would mount their steeds and trot carefully over the ice of the Mississippi to render missionary service to the scattered flocks in the St. Louis and Florissant districts of Missouri. The zealous community had hoped to obtain a grant of four thousand acres from the federal government at Washington to support the technical Indian school which they were organizing. Then suddenly they were called back to New York from Monks' Mound, and a few years later with the fall of Napoleon they returned to France.

However, they left there behind them in the Mississippi valley one solitary Trappist, the former prior, Joseph Dunand, whose missionary adventures were a little later to reach out to the Dubuque and Wisconsin districts.

There, in a nutshell, is the early and later Cistercian background of the Iowa Trappists. When Abbot Bruno Fitzpatrick and his companions signed the documents in the home of Bishop Loras they probably appended the letters "O.C.R." to their names, meaning Order of Cistercians of the Reform. Today they would sign themselves "O.C.S.O., which always mean "a monk, a Trappist, a contemplative," and these letters stand for Order of Cistercians of the Strict Observance.

Today, especially in the United States and Canada, there is a renewed intellectual interest displayed in the Cistercian history and program. Due to the shock of disillusionment in the materialistic minded world following World War I and II, and to various other causes, some obvious and some mysterious, (a minor one among them probably being the spectacular flash of the military conflagration at Monte Cassino within the last decade) there has been a growing urge in the hearts of good men who realize that true peace can be arrived at only through a perfect union of their wills with God. They see this in the quiet, contemplative orders — in the Trappist way of life. Merchants, students, farmers, and, of late, soldiers and sailors — both officers and men — coming back from the wars, have trudged up to the monastic gates to peer through them in search of spiritual security.

New Melleray Abbey is among those institutions which have thrown open their portals to them. And now the brown robed lay brothers, some picturesquely bearded, bringing in their sputtering tractors and their groaning army trucks from the rolling Iowa cornfields, the shaven choir brothers coming in from the orchards or poring over their Latin chant-books, and the tonsured white-robed priests working at their desks, all hear the abbey bell ringing in the clear air of the Mississippi valley and they converge on the high-arched chapel there to pay their devoirs to the Christ. New Melleray Abbey is their spiritual fortress. The monks are front-line soldiers of God. Their arms are the shield of silence, the sword of prayer, the sharp-pointed arrows of self-denial. Of these spiritually armed monks of the Dubuque Trappist institution do we herewith tell the sometimes sad, sometimes glad, but always glorious story. Arma, Monachum Cano — Arms and the Monk I sing!

III

THE MELLERAYS OF FRANCE
AND IRELAND

. . . .

The very name of the Iowa abbey, New Melleray, like the names New York and New Mexico, indicates that it has a bond or a relationship with a previous place of a similar name. Its connections as well as its roots go back far and deep, first, to old Melleray in France, and later to Mount Melleray in Ireland.

The ancient abbey of Melleray near Nantes on the northwest coast of France had been founded when the Cistercian Order was in the flower of its first development, and had been visited by St. Bernard of Clairvaux himself in 1142, eight years after its inception. Two of the founding brothers, spending the night in the forest, found in the hollow trunk of the tree under which they slept, a honeycomb, which supplied them with the food they desperately needed. This hollow tree marked the spot of the site of their new monastery, Meilleraie, which means honeycomb, and which in the long course of time has become Melleray.

The abbey flourished for hundreds of years, was reformed by the austere renovations emanating from La Trappe in the seventeenth

16

century and at the time of the French Revolution in 1791 was a strongly established monastery. Suppressed by the tyrants of the Directory in that year, it was soon raided and pillaged by the revolutionary soldiery. Some of the monks were imprisoned and others went into exile, a few reaching La Val Sainte in Switzerland with Dom Augustin de Lestrange, and the vacant and silent structure of Melleray lay stunned in mournful loveliness, a prey of the winds and storms of Brittany.[1]

Then, in the continued course of the dangerous and exciting years of the Revolution and later during Napoleon's meteoric ascendency, a couple of these monks along with a few others from La Trappe and other destroyed Cistercian monasteries of France, while refugees in England, established a Cistercian monastery there. That splendid old Catholic family of the Welds made a handsome offer of land to them in Dorset, and assisted them in erecting their new home near their own castle of Lullworth and a half mile from the sea coast. Their foundation grew: other French refugees and a number of zealous English converts entered the order as novices and soon became full-fledged Trappists, in this first Cistercian house in England since the monstrous destruction of the monasteries by Thomas Cromwell and Henry VIII.

Not long-lived was this abbey, known as St. Susan's, in the bigoted England of that day. Its progress and its conversions aroused prejudices and suspicions, and finally the British Prime Minister restricted the novitiate entirely to Frenchmen. He further demanded that as the members of the community had been tolerated in England only as French refugees they should return to France as soon as possible. This was complied with and in 1817 the dauntless abbot, Dom Antoine de Beauregard, — now that Napoleon was on St. Helena and the Bourbon monarch, Louis XVIII was on the throne — led his members, Frenchmen and Englishmen alike to the now hospitable shores of France. And here the Melleray thread of Iowa Trappist history once

[1] One of the links in the relationship of Dom Augustin de Lestrange of La Val Sainte with Iowa was the predilection of Bishop Loras for the Trappists because one of Lestrange's followers, Father Alexis, fleeing from Napoleon's wrath, had taken refuge with the Loras family at Lyons. As a further result of Father Alexis' influence, two of Loras' nephews, reared with him in the same household as they were almost the same age, became Trappists. Romuald and René Tallon, sons of Loras' eldest sister, entered the Bellefontaine Trappist abbey. René died there in 1830 and Romuald later became one of the Cistercian officials at the famous Staoueli Trappist monastery in Algeria, Africa, and he corresponded with Bishop Loras up to the time of the latter's death.

again is taken up, but before it is further unravelled, an interesting word must be said to American readers about Lullworth and the grand triple-centuried Lullworth Castle.

The Lullworth monastic house, whose ruined cloister walls still stand around the green sward of the brothers' cemetery, became through the exile of its sons the parent house of six distinct monasteries: two in France, one of which was the revived Melleray; one in Ireland, Mount Melleray; one in England, Mount St. Bernard; and two in the United States, Our Lady of Gethsemani, near Bardstown in Kentucky and Our Lady of New Melleray at Dubuque in Iowa.

Lullworth Castle is further related to the United States in that its chapel was the locale of the consecration of the first bishop of the young American republic in 1790 — Bishop John Carroll of Baltimore.

On the 17th of July, 1817, on board the beautiful government frigate, *La Revanche*, which had been appointed by the French king for their voyage, Abbot de Beauregard and his peaceful band of Cistercian monks sailed into the harbor of Nantes and landed on the soil of France. The only monasteries left standing in that country after the hurricane of the French Revolution had swept by were the buildings of Melleray and the Grand Chartreuse. Dom de Beauregard could have bought the Grand Chartreuse but disliked its cold and bleak situation in the lonely Alpine valley. He succeeded in purchasing Melleray from several parties and received as a gift from a pious lady a farm attached to it. Earlier in that same year Dom Augustin of La Val Sainte had hoped to buy this abbey for his Trappist monks.

Again did this ancient abbey of Melleray begin to flourish. The first person to present himself for admission into the novitiate was a sailor from the frigate, *La Revanche*. So impressed had he been by the courage and holy demeanor of the religious brotherhood which he had helped escort back from English exile that he had raised sufficient funds to secure his discharge from the naval service and had come directly to the abbey-gate of Melleray to solicit admission. Within a few years the numbers grew rapidly and the silent corridors, the church and the gardens were peopled with industrious monks. To facilitate the religious life and exercises of the two national groups at the abbey, — the one of Frenchmen, and the other of Irishmen and Englishmen — Dom Antoine made use on week-days of two Chapter Rooms, each under a different Father Master, where the brothers could accuse themselves in their own language; but on Sundays they met in common in one Chapter Room with the abbot who spoke both languages fluently. Much of the soil of their property was stony and sterile. Upon these fields they applied their skill learned from the improved methods of English farming, introducing new types of plows and the first threshing machine ever used in Brittany. The backward farmers of that part of France imitated these experiments with a great degree of success; and the high proficiency of farming on the rich Iowa soil which later was always to accompany the work of the Dubuque monks at New Melleray can be traced back to these skillful agricultural methods introduced at this time at old Melleray.

The gifted abbot, Dom Antoine de Beauregard, restored at Melleray the Rule of St. Benedict as it had originally been written. Eschewing some of the excessively strict regulations that had crept into the order by way of Dom Augustin, he preserved the correct austerity of the contemplative life as it had been practiced by Bernard of Clairvaux and St. Stephen Harding. Under his wise leadership the community grew from fifty-nine to one hundred and ninety-two members. Then came the 1830 revolution which put Louis Philippe, the Duke of Orleans, on the throne and brought trial and near-calamity to both La Grand Trappe, which had built itself up after Napoleon's downfall, and to Melleray, as well as to other houses of the Cistercian order. This revolutionary anti-clericalism had pursued Father Joseph Cretin at Ferney, where a mob had broken into the convent of Carmelite nuns and attempted to wreck his college; he had refused to pray for the "King of the French" after his Masses, and because of the government's persistent opposition he had been happy to come to Iowa with Bishop Mathias Loras.

But the attack of the revolutionary government on Melleray had been, if not so violent, much more formidable. Dom Antoine de Beauregard had correctly read the signs of the approaching storm as soon as the revolutionary change of government had taken place in Paris in July, 1830. As the Archbishop of Dublin in Ireland had recently solicited the establishment of a Trappist foundation in Ireland, and as Abbot Antoine had received offers of a handsome supply of funds from Irish persons "of both sexes" for this purpose, the abbot quickly made plans for such a venture. He immediately sent the prior of Melleray Abbey, Father Vincent Ryan, and another monk, Father Malachy, to Ireland to exploit this design.

As Dom Antoine expected, the storm finally broke, and in August of 1831 the French departmental prefect secured a governmental arrest by the power of which the religious community of Melleray was suppressed and dissolved. Dom Antoine had been a friend of the family of the overthrown king, Charles X, and so the new revolutionary government, making use of an old ordinance dating from Napoleon's time, was vindictively determined to abolish the community. Late in September, more than six hundred soldiers of horse, foot and gendarmerie surrounded the abbey and went through the formal motions of a siege. For the next seven or eight weeks an opera bouffe warfare was carried on by the military against the passive — and in many instances, highly amused — monks. Abbot Antoine was courteous, but firm in his resistance which he based on his rights as a free French citizen. But later when the troops with bayonets and bared sabers reinvested the abbey, the abbot and his French brothers put on civilian attire and discontinued the religious exercises until an appeal could be made to the courts.

However, as a large number of the Melleray Cistercians were Irishmen and Englishmen — British subjects — the English consul at Nantes entered into the fray on their behalf. They had been forcibly expelled from the monastery because they were foreigners, and ordered to depart from France. Confined to the St. James military prison at Nantes they were put on a bread and water diet and were refused permission to attend Sunday Mass. Mr. Newman, the English consul, protested in energetic terms, and pointed out that as the French government had, fifteen years before, conveyed the British Cistercians from England to France, it should now that it was expelling them from its shores be responsible for their return journey to their own country. The government agents immediately seized on this proposal as a safe avenue out of their embarrassment and arranged for a vessel in which the religious could sail.

Sixty-four of the British monks chose Ireland as their destination, and at the end of November a French sloop of war, the *Hebe*, departed with them from St. Nazaire for Cork, Ireland. Fifteen English Cistercian brothers remained at Nantes, and Mr. Newman arranged for their accommodations under his own protection. A number of them were soon to depart for England where they were to assist in the foundation of Mount St. Bernard's monastery, which was to be a filiate of Melleray Abbey and a granddaughter of Lullworth. In fact, one of the members of old St. Susan's, Lullworth, — Father Benedict Johnson — who had gone to Melleray in 1817, became superior and prior of Mount St. Bernard's. This was likewise the case of the first abbot, Bernard Palmer, who had been first at Lullworth and then at Melleray.

Melleray itself, after the shouting and the rude jostling of the new government's prefects and politicians had died down, was left in the quiet possession of Dom Antoine and the remnant of his religious. Crippled in its exercises for a few years, the old abbey soon again became crowded with novices and postulants. By the year 1848 it was full to overflowing with almost two hundred members. Then Louis Napoleon began to loom in the offing, another revolution was on the way, and Melleray sent a number of its sons to Kentucky in America, to establish the Gethsemani foundation just one year before the New Melleray monastery was opened at Dubuque in Iowa by other Cistercians who came from Melleray by way of Ireland.

Meanwhile, on the first of December, 1831, the French war-ship, *Hebe*, had arrived in the Cork harbor of Cobh in Ireland, and the sixty-four persecuted Trappists on deck were received with a tremendous welcome by the inhabitants, whose enthusiasm and uproarious joy struck the French sailors with great astonishment. The penniless exiles were embraced with warmth and generous hospitality. The prior of Melleray, Father Vincent Ryan, who with Father Malachy had been sent by the far-seeing Dom Antoine de Beauregard to Ireland about a year before, had after many hardships and disappointments at last secured for temporary quarters a house and about fifty acres of land at Rathmore just twelve miles from Killarney. Prior Vincent then began negotiations whereby he was to obtain for a mere nominal rent six hundred acres of rather barren mountainous land, near Cappoquin, in the county of Waterford, with the view of founding and establishing there an Irish Cistercian house. It was a Protestant gentleman, Sir Richard Keane, who made this favorable settlement with the prior.

Until this could be ready for occupancy, however, the brothers were compelled to live an intensely crowded life at Rathmore under the severest hardships. It was necessary that work should be rushed at their newly projected establishment to relieve them of their appalling distress. The brothers sent there — near Cappoquin — for this work, were soon assisted by a demonstration of charity and cooperation that has probably been seldom equalled in this selfish world. Priests and people from many miles around came in crowds to volunteer their labor with pick, spade and hammer. Father Walsh, the pastor of Cappoquin, arrived with two thousand able bodied parishioners, most of whom were provided with building tools, or with agricultural instruments for fencing and ditching the fields. One day, four hundred men leaving their village at four o'clock in the morning marched four abreast with spades on their shoulders, led by the music of their band. In most instances the groups were accompanied by wives and daughters to care for the feeding of the men and even occasionally to help with the labor, most of which was on the hard moorland and the stony mountainside. At least ten thousand persons gave of their labor at one time or another in this great Christian task.

The carpenters among the brothers with the masons from the neighborhood began working on a commodious dwelling house which stood near the site already selected for the projected monastery. The hitherto miserably lodged and half-famished monks now on their own land began to live with at least a minimum of decency. It was Prior Vincent himself who gave the foundation the name of Mount Melleray to commemorate the mother abbey from which he and his brothers had come. At this time, it is of interest to mention, the monks had not ventured to wear the religious habit because of fear of the English penal laws which could still be enforced against them.

Their poverty did not delay them in preparing for the erection of their stone monastery. The first stone of Mount Melleray monastery was laid by Sir Richard Keane, their Protestant friend, after it had been blessed by the Bishop of Waterford. Thus on the 20th of August, 1833, in the presence of a great crowd of 20,000 people, was formally reestablished the solid foundation of Cistercian life in Catholic Ireland nearly three hundred years after its expulsion by the bloody rapacity of Henry VIII.

Work on the building of what was to be the Abbey of Mount Melleray continued until it was inhabited by the community in 1838. Meanwhile, the indefatigably zealous prior, Father Vincent Ryan, was elected the first abbot of the new community. Great preparations were made for a public ceremony for the reception of the abbatial blessing, but at the last moment what was to have been a giant open demonstration of the Faith of the people of south Ireland was cruelly interdicted by the British penal laws, and the function was soberly performed in the private chapel of Bishop Abraham of Waterford.[2]

During these years the poverty of the community was extreme, and appeals had to be made several times to the faithful at large in Ireland as well as to those in England for assistance. The edifying lives of the hard-working brothers made these appeals effective. Among the patrons of Mount Melleray was the internationally renowned champion of civil and religious liberty, Ireland's own patriot and emancipator, Daniel O'Connell, who visited the abbey and gave what financial aid he could. The order grew steadily in numbers. In 1837, Brother Adrian McCarthy, a graduate of Trinity College, was both professed and ordained. In the following year among those admitted to the holy profession, were three more well qualified and highly educated young gentlemen, Brother Clement Smyth, Brother James Myles O'Gorman and Brother Xavier Melville. By 1840 there were over eighty members in the community; and this despite the fact that in the previous few years a number of the monks, especially the English members, had been allowed to transfer to Mount St. Bernard's Abbey in England.

In the immediately following years schools were inaugurated for the children of the neighborhood under the auspices of the Trappists, now that the penal laws were being gradually relaxed. An academy for young men was placed under the direction of Clement Smyth, now ordained, who was assisted in this endeavor by Brother Xavier Melville. The successful development of this academy led to the addition of a seminary department which was also placed under the superintendency of Father Clement.

In the community was Brother Macarius Keegan whose talents recommended him to Abbot Vincent as a collector of funds. Armed with letters from the Mount Melleray abbot and from the prior of Mount St. Bernard in England, he moved from 1838 on through English cities and counties, collecting with equal success from English noblemen, from liberal Protestant gentlemen and from the poor Irish

[2] In *The Red Book*, a collection of his social essays, published by Wm. Powell, in Dublin, in 1835 appears a curious section entitled "Form and Ceremony of the Consecration of the Very Rev. Father Vincent Ryan, Abbot of Mount Melleray Abbey, Which Will be Performed in the Church of the Holy Trinity in Waterford, on the 14th of May, 1835." However, the blessing was given on May 17th, 1835, in the Rt. Rev. Dr. Abraham's private chapel.

Catholic laborers. In 1845 Abbot Vincent sent him to America where he travelled in Canada and the United States, and, as it will soon be learned, took himself as far west as Dubuque in the state of Iowa.

The saintly Abbot Vincent died in December of 1845 beneath the graceful spire which crowns the noble pile of buildings so painfully and patiently erected through his efforts. Abbot Mary Joseph Ryan who was elected to succeed him, held the office less than two years; the members of the community having petitioned the Holy See to be united to the French Congregation of the order in France, the abbot resigned the abbatial dignity in October of 1847. His resignation was accepted by the Holy See, and a bull was sent from the Propaganda for the election of a new abbot as well as for uniting Mount Melleray Abbey to the Congregation of La Grande Trappe in France. Father Clement Smyth, whom Abbot Mary Joseph Ryan had appointed as prior and who also continued to serve as president of the seminary, acted as superior of the community until a new abbot would be elected.

The choice of the monks as they gathered in the Chapter Room on the 4th of April, 1848, fell on the young and outstanding Father Bartholomew Bruno Fitzpatrick, one of the future founders of New Melleray Abbey in Dubuque, who for the next five and forty years was to shape the path of progress and advancement of the American institution in a general way, and of Mount Melleray Abbey in Ireland in a most particular way. On the occasion of the solemn blessing of this third abbot of Mount Melleray on the 14th of the following September a Papal Brief was read aloud wherein the Abbey of Mount Melleray was declared exempt thenceforward from episcopal control and subject only to the authority of the General Chapter of the Order of Cistercians of the Strict Observance.

The canonical visitation — which is a formal visit for the purpose of inspection and examination of the religious and temporal affairs of a monastery — of Mount Melleray from that day on has been made by the abbots of La Grande Trappe and Melleray in France. One of the customs restored because of these visitations was the ancient one of the Cistercians of burying their dead without coffins, a custom which had long been departed from at Mount Melleray as a concession to popular prejudices.

This was one of the most trying periods in the history of Ireland. The terrible Irish Famine was on. It was the awful years from 1845 to 1849, during which Abbot Bruno Fitzpatrick was ushered into the office of superior, that pestilence, starvation and reckless English misrule united their forces to depopulate the land. The monks of Mount Melleray showed their heroic mettle by carrying on a herculean program of charity. Poor as their food was, they hastened to share all of it from their farm with the suffering masses. The records of those agonizing years will show that almost every day from four hundred to seven hundred destitute and distressed individuals obtained relief at the abbey. Meal and potatoes were all the food consisted of, but the gratitude of the starving crowds was the most celestial dessert the monks ever tasted — the monks, who only through unflinching self-denial and the exercise of the strictest economy of their own slender resources were able to give what they gave. This valorous band of Cistercians in 1848 numbered a hundred souls, just about the capacity of the house, under Dom Bruno's prudent and solicitous direction.

IV

AMERICA—TRAPPIST LAND
OF PROMISE

. . . .

The year 1847 was probably the most frightful in the long history
of Ireland. While fever slew its victims right and left by the hundreds, famine numbered its slain by the thousands. The poor, dis-
possessed by the stonyhearted and ever encroaching landlords, wan-
dered about the country in starving crowds. Prior Clement Smyth
wrote later of the profoundly shocking impressions made by the
mobs that he saw the monks feeding every day at Mount Melleray.
This constant drain of their limited resources reduced the monastery
to the very verge of destitution, and compelled Abbot Bruno Fitzpatrick in 1848, almost from the moment he took over the reins of
spiritual responsibility of the institution to look for some means of
amelioration for the members of his flock. How long the idea of
establishing a colony elsewhere — in America, for instance — had been
developing in his mind can only be conjectured. However, it is certain that the plan was not as sudden as it seemed at the time.

As early as 1841 Abbot Vincent Ryan had ventured with a few
companions on a journey to Sardinia, off the coast of Italy, in an
attempt at establishing an affiliate, but the affair was a disappoint-

ing one and was dropped. In 1845 he had sent Brother Macarius Keegan to America to collect funds, and the latter's reports must have caused some speculation at the abbey. In September of that same year Bishop Ignatius Reynolds of Charleston, South Carolina, visited Mount Melleray and offered Abbot Vincent ten thousand acres of land for a foundation; but the Sardinian experiment had made the abbot doubly cautious, and realizing that since the death of the illustrious Bishop John England this southern diocese was in a precarious condition, its Catholics few in number, poor in worldly goods and scattered over an immense territory, and that therefore his monks would again face a heart-breaking struggle for survival, he politely refused the offer. The first contact with Dubuque and Bishop Loras seems to have been made in 1846. The bishop had sent one hundred pounds to Abbot Ryan who in his reply on November 6th said: "I want a dictionary to teach me some new form of grateful thanks for the bounty of God through you . . . would to God it were in our power to feed every hungry soul in the land." Through its relations with Melleray Abbey in France the authorities at Mount Melleray doubtless knew of the French institution's intentions of seeking an establishment in the United States. What probably brought the matter of a colony for America to a head and to the special attention of the new abbot, Dom Bruno Fitzpatrick, was a letter from Father Francis Xavier Kaiser, superior of the Petit Clairvaux Monastery of Tracadie, Nova Scotia, in Canada, written early in 1848 and strongly appealing for some religious brethren for their convent, and even implying that the Canadian house would be turned over to the jurisdiction of Mount Melleray if new blood could be injected into it for its perpetuation. This Canadian foundation, by the way, was established in 1825 and was the first permanent Cistercian house in America.

Dom Fitzpatrick realized the necessity of making a radical decision: the crowded state of Mount Melleray, the waste and barren condition of its land when a fertile soil adapted to agricultural pursuits was an absolute requirement for a growing community, the threat of a disturbed political future for the country, all this was forcing his hand. This last element of the situation is sometimes forgotten today but at that time it seemed quite formidable; the Young Ireland party was growing noisy and fast departing from the fundamentals of a peace policy in dealing with the English government as laid down by the ageing Daniel O'Connell. The Fenian movement was just beginning to show its dangerous claws. In fact, during that very year of 1848 after the failure of one of their uprisings, the Fenian chiefs, Stephens, Dillon, and Doheny, spent a Sunday afternoon in the visitors gallery at Mount Melleray Abbey but left without making themselves known lest they might compromise the monks. And across the channel in France the revolutionary clouds of Louis Napolean were gathering on the horizon, already frightening the Trappist houses which had suffered so much from previous revolutions. Agricultural America with its freedom and religious toleration seemed the safest haven for a new Cistercian colony.

In the early summer of 1848, Brother Cyprian Slattery of Petit Clairvaux Monastery in Nova Scotia, who had been one of the monks of Melleray Abbey in France expelled by the troops in 1831, was in Europe representing his superior, Father Francis Xavier Kaiser, in an endeavor to secure brothers or novices for his American foundation. He was in Ireland, probably in June and July, and apparently as a result of his visit at Mount Melleray and his representations about the monastery in Nova Scotia, Dom Bruno decided to send one of his priests to investigate the proposition. So on the 25th of July, Father Bernard McCaffery, accompanied by a choir novice, Brother Anthony Keating, left Mount Melleray for Canada with instructions to visit Petit· Clairvaux with the possible view of adopting it as an affiliate, and otherwise, of seeking out an alternative site for an entirely new foundation. Brother Cyprian evidently returned to America with Father Bernard, also, because a little later the two of them were together in New York. Father Bernard, selected for this particular mission by the abbot because of his prudence and common sense, was at this time thirty-five years of age.

Shortly after the departure of these brothers, Dom Bruno decided that before he would go farther with a venture of such import both in its nature and in its consequences, he would put the project of a filiation in America to a vote of the entire community. Accordingly he announced that at the end of a week he would call on the members in public chapter to give their opinion relative to the undertaking. Eight days later the silvery voice of the great bell in the lofty tower of the abbey broke the calm pre-dawn silence as it called the brethren to assemble and give their views for or against this important project. Of the choir religious, twenty-four in number, there were only five who disapproved; of the lay brothers of whom seventy-four were present, only seven expressed their opposition. From this expression of the top-heavy majority of eighty-six to twelve the conclusion was readily drawn by Abbot Bruno that it was the will of God that he should continue with this venture.

Meanwhile Father Bernard McCaffery reached Trachadie in Nova Scotia and found that the little monastery of Petit Clairvaux was subject to no house of the Cistercian order but to the diocesan bishop. It may be, as it is alleged, that he found their climate too cold, their notions of perfection too austerely severe, and their superiors unwilling to resign to him and his abbot "their authority, their wills, their property, their all." It is more probable that the opposition to the jurisdiction of Father Bernard and Mount Melleray came from the extreme asceticism of the prior, Father Francis Xavier Kaiser. This monk, born near Freiburg in the German Black Forest, had been admitted in his youth to Val-Sainte in Switzerland, then under the direction of the celebrated Dom Augustin de Lestrange, and the austere views of that Reform which he inherited clashed strongly with those of Father Bernard.

It is doubtless true that Father Bernard McCaffery cherished the hope of a foundation in the United States rather than in Canada. So he cheerfully changed the direction of his voyage and went on to New York City. From what he had heard in Ireland he was led to entertain the most sanguine hopes of hospitable reception by the bishops of the United States, especially by the bishops of Irish birth and education. In this fond expectation he was to be rudely disappointed.

A few days after his arrival in New York, he called on the Right Reverend Dr. John Hughes, the bishop of that diocese, in order to pay his respects and to lay open to him the object of his mission. According to the monks' version, Bishop Hughes met Father Bernard with "all the insulting dignity of a Saxon lord and all the pomp and importance of an Irish tyrant peer," and the climax of the bishop's remarks was: "Your order, Sir, does no good either for yourselves or for anyone else." After hearing the bishop's denunciation of the Cistercians, the poor monk, naturally, was crushed and humiliated. Silently and respectfully he handed to Bishop Hughes the letter of approbation given him by his superior, Dom Bruno Fitzpatrick, and was again mortified before he left by the bishop's "contemptuous refusal of even deigning to open it."

In partial mitigation of this alleged attitude of the New York bishop
is the possibility that his ire had been aroused by what he considered an unauthorized publication in the New York press of Father
Bernard's plans and intentions. Whether the publication of this
article had occurred before or after the monk's call on the bishop
cannot be ascertained, but if it preceded his visit, the bishop's displeasure may be somewhat understandable.

In the early part of October the New York *Tribune* had carried
the following article which doubtless had been inspired by Father
Bernard and his friends among the priests of New York.

Extraordinary Ecclesiastical Intelligence; — Introduction of
the Cistercian Order into the United States.

Two members of the Cistercian Order, Rev. H. B. Mc-
Caffery and Brother Cyprian Slattery, have arrived in this
city from Mount Melleray in Ireland, authorized by their
superior to select a suitable place for founding a monastery
of their order, in some part of the United States. It has
long been the anxious wish of the Bishops, Priests and laity
of the United States to see an establishment of the Cistercian
Order founded in this country. The improvements made at
Mount Melleray in Ireland, notwithstanding the sterility of
the soil, the good effected by the brethren, by instructing
adults in their moral and religious duties, by educating gra-
tuitously the children of the vicinity, and particularly by
holding up to the world the example of piety, temperance
and industry, could not fail to excite a desire among our
clergy to have a similar establishment in the country. Many
applications were made to the late Abbot, Dr. Ryan, but owing to peculiar circumstances, without success. The time has
at length arrived when a house of the order can be founded
in this country. All that is required is a large farm of good
land, from 500 to 1,000 acres, in a healthy climate, and fit
for cultivation. Those who have such farms to dispose of
can write to the Rev. H. B. McCaffrey, in care of Rev. J.
Walsh, St. Paul's, Harlem, New York.

This article seems harmless enough, and probably caused the usual
ripple of interest among the readers, many of whom, without a doubt,
had already heard of the plans for the founding of the Gethsemani
Trappist monastery at Bardstown, Kentucky, during the previous few

months — a piece of news which had been widely published in the
secular as well as the Catholic press, including the New York *Freeman's Journal*. This latter journal was under the control of Bishop
Hughes and some of its articles came from his pen. In its issue of
October 14th, 1848, the *Freeman's Journal* reproduced the above news
item from the *Tribune,* and immediately beneath it published the following comment:

> We are requested by the Rt. Rev. Bishop to say that the
> above extraordinary announcement is, to him, and to the
> clergy of this diocese, a piece of unexpected information.
> It may be that some of the Bishops, Priests, and laity of the
> United States have desired an establishment of the Cister-
> cian Order, but they are not of the diocese of New York.
> In fact, the Bishops, Priests, and laity of this diocese would
> regard the Rev. Abbot of Mount Melleray as rendering
> a service to religion, if he would recall those members of
> his community, who have been collecting money in the
> United States and in the British Provinces during the last
> three or four years, and allow them to re-enter on that life
> of religious retirement which, by this time, they must have
> almost forgotten, and a return to which could not but be of
> advantage to themselves. It is proper to add for the in-
> formation of the faithful, that the Bishop of this diocese has
> not been consulted by either of the parties mentioned in the
> above notice, on the subject of which it treats; that he re-
> gards the proceedings as irregular, and advises the clergy
> and laity of the diocese to give it neither countenance or en-
> couragement.

Allowing for the provocation Bishop Hughes may have suffered because of Father Bernard's failure to call on him before the *Tribune*
article appeared — conceding that this was actually the fact — it is
certainly no overstatement of the truth to admit that his language
was unconsionably strong and bitter. Many of Abbot Bruno's brothers
had suffered arrest, contumely and exile for the Faith in France; all
of them were undergoing for years a war of famine and pestilence
in Ireland; they represented one of the holiest and most honored
orders in the Church; who but Bishop John Hughes, a good but
impulsive prelate, would state so boldly and baldly that they were
not welcome? Brother Macarius Keegan, who was the only one of

Mount Melleray's subjects of whom there is record as being a collector of funds for the order in America, was probably an unpolished
monk and a crude bargainer for alms and favors as his record shows,
and with him it is possible that the New York bishop had had an
acquaintance, but today, at least, it is difficult to understand how
this should have called for such an ignoble indictment of the venerable Abbot Bruno and his brothers.

That other Catholic newspapers at the time resented this attack on
the Cistercians is clear from the attempted rejoinder made by the
Freeman's Journal on the following November 11th:

> The *Orleanian,* of New Orleans, of the 26 ult., has a brief
> notice of the Cistercian Order, which winds up with an allu-
> sion to the remarks of the *Freeman's Journal* on that subject,
> a few weeks ago. Our Southern friend has not taken pains
> to understand the object of our remarks. The Bishop of New
> York has as high an opinion of the Order, and of the meri-
> torious objects which it proposes to accomplish, as any one
> can have, and his remarks were not directed against the or-
> der, but against the practice of certain members thereof, who
> have been, with or without permission of their superiors, en-
> gaged for some years past in collecting money in the Diocese
> of New York and elsewhere. The effect of this mode of
> life on these members of the Order is supposed to diminish
> their attachment to the retirement and quiet pursuits of a
> monastic life. It has also ceased in a great measure to edify
> the people among whom these collections are made.
>
> In the case alluded to by the *Orleanian,* an advertisement
> was published by a secular paper, without the knowledge or
> consent of the Bishop of this Diocese, which was calculated
> to mislead persons at a distance by leaving it to be inferred,
> as it naturally would be, that the Bishop either approved, or
> was not opposed to the vague and irregular project thus an-
> nounced and its consequences.

This rejoinder was, if anything, even more mischievous than the
first article. Bishop Hughes protested that he had the highest opinion of the Cistercian order, and then, possibly justified by certain
facts not known today, he published his accusations: the order al-
lows its members "with or without permission of their superiors" to
collect funds in America; the abbots and other superiors are remiss
in their duties because they allow the brothers to give up their at-

tachment to the quiet and retirement of monastic life; the brothers disedify the people; Father Bernard gave out the news of his mission to America without Bishop Hughes' consent; his action was calculated to mislead people.

This treatment of the Irish Trappists could not but rankle for a long time among the members of Mount Melleray, and it dismayed others. "It was truly impious as a certain holy Bishop in America, the Rt. Rev. Doctor Loras, publicly declared, when speaking of this uncalled for and unmerited censure" — so writes Prior Clement Smyth three years later of this affair.

Brother Anthony, the choir novice who had accompanied Father Bernard to America, had already returned to Ireland, and now Father Bernard with fond hopes blighted and all his optimistic prospects for an American colony blasted, prepared to do the same. His passage on a sailing vessel was secured, but on the very day before his scheduled departure he received a letter which caused a change in his plans and immediately restored the roseate dreams of a successful American filiation for Mount Melleray. The letter containing a promise of abundant lands freely given should they meet Father Bernard's intended purpose was from the Very Rev. Thomas Heyden, the vicar-general of the diocese of Pittsburgh in Pennsylvania and the pastor of Bedford in that state.

With well-grounded hopes and elated by the new prospects, the monk accompanied by Brother Cyprian Slattery of Petit Clairvaux, left New York immediately and arriving at Bedford was cordially received by Father Heyden. Impatiently he drove out to the intended abbey lands, called "Harmon's Bottoms," situated about eighteen miles from Bedford, at the foot of the Alleghany Mountains. The recoil from the painful disillusionment he had suffered in New York made Father Bernard now unduly sanguine and enthusiastic. "Hope told a flattering tale." At the end of the day, tired but happy, he sat down and wrote a most favorable account to the abbot of Mount Melleray: a thousand acres of beautiful land could be purchased for a thousand pounds, fee simple forever; the thousand pounds would be lent him without interest for the period of ten years by two or three generous and wealthy Catholics of Bedford; the soil was good, the springs salubrious, the climate was healthy; on the intended purchase were a grist-mill and a saw-mill in full operation; and there were farm-houses, barns and other improvements making the land desirable to any purchaser.

It was small wonder that the arrival of this auspiciously promising letter at Mount Melleray Abbey created excitement in the community. Dom Bruno, discouraged by the news from Nova Scotia and heartsick over the insolent rebuff at New York, summoned the brothers to the chapter hall and with buoyant feelings read Father Bernard's enchantingly descriptive letter. Now, all ardor and vigor, he would suffer no delay and immediately discussed plans to send a group of monks to Pennsylvania to commence operations forthwith.

At the very time that Father Bernard McCaffrey was spending his days at Bedford and "Harmon's Bottoms," Brother Macarius Keegan was receiving another offer of land as the site of a filiation for the Irish Trappists. Brother Macarius, at the request of the now deceased Abbot Vincent Ryan, had been travelling through Canada and the United States since 1845 seeking funds for his hard-pressed order at Mount Melleray. It is entirely possible that in his quest he had ventured beyond the Mississippi as early as 1845 after his arrival in America. One of Bishop Loras' vicar-generals, Father Terence J. Donaghue, mentioned that he had met a Trappist monk at Dubuque in Iowa who was on his way to southern Wisconsin in that year. He referred to him merely as Brother Malachy, possibly confusing that name with the odd one of Macarius; and Brother Macarius was the only Irish Cistercian who at that time could have been in the West. Probably because of his kindly reception by Father Donaghue he returned to Dubuque in November of 1848.

There he met and discussed with Bishop Loras and Father Joseph Cretin the matter of a location for the Trappist monks in Iowa. Brother Macarius was of the graceless type denounced by Bishop Hughest of New York with more than a modicum of justice; and his bargaining methods to secure for his order the best terms failed to impress Loras and Cretin very favorably. Nevertheless, the Iowa bishop definitely made him a generous offer at the time, and later from Kingston, Canada, the travelling monk wrote to Bishop Loras that he would present this offer to Abbot Bruno Fitzpatrick at Mount Melleray.

It was really this visit of the unpolished and unprepossessing Brother Macarius to Dubuque that swayed the tides of Fortune and Fate in favor of the ultimate establishment of Irish Cistercians on the fertile prairies of Iowa. For, — just a week later Bishop Loras announced to a congregation in his little stone cathedral his hopes of having his vast diocese blessed with their presence. Learned and zealous man that he was, it had been Dr. Loras' custom in Alabama and now in Iowa to give lecture series to mixed audiences of Protestants and Catholics on certain controversial subjects that unfortunately divided them. Just a few days after Brother Macarius' departure he commenced a winter series of talks and he devoted his first lecture to the subject, "On Religious Orders in the Church," and there, in his very opening sentences, he alluded to the plans that were budding in his mind.

"Beloved Christians," he addressed them, and we have today, one hundred and four years later, his neat and clearly written manuscript before us, "You have undoubtedly observed in reading the late newspapers, that a convent of the Religious called *Trappists* is to be established in Kentucky. Besides this, a venerable monk of the same order was last week in Dubuque, collecting some means to have another one founded in Kingston in Canada; &, owing to the generosity of many catholics & to the liberality of several protestants in the U. S., the work will be commenced next spring. This, our far West, may also be blessed before long, with an institution of the same kind! But, as it is certain that many persons in this very town, have been imbued, from their very infancy, with deep prejudices against *Religious* orders and convents, we cannot select a subject, for our 1rst lecture, more appropriate, &, we may say, more interesting, as it will give us a favorable opportunity of calling to your minds many historical facts connected with it, which will instruct you & enable you to pass a correct judgment on those holy, *religious orders* so very much slandered for 3 centuries.

"We shall address you, Beloved christians, more willingly, because we remember gratefully that, 2 years ago, you paid a great attention to our evening instructions."

The bishop then launched out on a profound but interesting discussion of monasticism, and one is truly amazed as one reads his clever and devastating refutation of the gross misrepresentations of the Protestant historians Mosheim and Hume and Bingham, and his masterful pulverization of the vulgar charges of Maria Monk and the other nauseously vile slanderers of his day. In his concluding summation he referred pointedly to his own connections with the Trappists:

"Now, Beloved Friends, who can be better judges of the real merit of *religious orders,* as they are now in the catholic church, those who have never put their foot in any of them, & who wrote abominable books against them, or those who, like ourselves, have seen many, both in Europe & in America, who have acted as chapelain in several of them; who have some of our own kindred members of them; who have spent some times in the most severe of them, we mean the cistercians or Trappists. Now, *in the presence of God!* we can assert that with very few exceptions, we have seen in them nothing but edifying, holy and truly religious. So that we are intimately convinced that *religious orders* are a blessing to a country, a source of good example, & of usefulness of every sort, both for this world & for the next. Amen."

When Bishop Loras mentioned that he had Trappist kinsmen he referred to his two nephews René and Romuald Tallon of the Cistercian abbey of Bellefontaine in France, where he had visited and made retreats. René Tallon had been regarded as one of the most saintly members of the abbey, and when in 1837 Bishop Loras had returned from Bellefontaine where he had made a pilgrimage to the grave of this illustrious kinsman, he was "deeply impressed with the spirit of sanctity breathed by that whole order" — so wrote his grandnephew, Louis de Cailly, — "and there and then resolved to introduce those saintly religious in the course of time to his diocese."

The soil in which Brother Macarius had so rather cavalierly planted his seed was the benevolent and more-than-half Trappist heart of Mathias Loras, the great French bishop of the Northwest.

V

THE ODYSSEY OF PRIOR CLEMENT

After pondering over Father Bernard's optimistic letter on the Pennsylvania lands, Dom Bruno decided that the proper person to execute a foundation in America for the Mount Melleray monks was none other than Father Clement Smyth, the prior of the abbey and the president of the seminary. Eminently successful in his educational and administrative endeavors, the prior also held the trust and affection of his superior. Somewhat dismayed at the assignment, the prior accepted the appointment with a rather reluctant obedience. He was happy though at the selection of his companion, Brother Ambrose Byrne, who was not only a skillful agriculturalist but a man of good sense and of a naturally quick and intelligent mind.

Fortunately for posterity, about a year later when Prior Clement was safely situated at the new Iowa monastery, he began to write down a personal narrative of the events in which he was involved from the time of his appointment to the American venture, continuing it on until the end of the year 1852. We can safely follow him in this chapter as he describes his adventures, but occasionally his observations and conclusions must be qualified by authoritative data obtained since his time from other sources. Father Clement was a keen student whose mind reflects for us today the reactions of a cultured immigrant to America in 1849. His narrative, however, includes many philosophical homilies on man and eternity; and when he rhapsodizes on the beauties of nature his eloquence too often slips into rhetorical verbosity.

Dom Bruno, under the influence of Father Bernard's magic letter, advanced the idea of sending ten or even twenty brothers along with Father Clement in order to get the monastic foundations going in Pennsylvania as soon as possible, and he pointed out that with two mills on the place, as described by Father Bernard, it would not be difficult for the monks to find work and support almost immediately. Prior Clement prevailed on the abbot, however, to wait until he could send him definite corroboration of the hoped-for paradise.

The two monks departed on January 20th, 1849, by way of Dublin, and then Liverpool. A good Presbyterian captain refused to violate the Sabbath by sailing on the Sunday scheduled and the next day the ship, a new iron "four master," promptly ran into a terrific storm. The two Cistercians paid thirty-six pounds for their second-class passage and were awed by the sight of the luxurious furnishings in the first-class salons. Twenty-five days of unusually stormy weather brought them to a New York whose thermometer ranged ten degrees below zero and whose streets were deeply covered with snow. They tarried here but two days as they were anxious to reach their Pennsylvania destination. They travelled to Philadelphia by the "evening Cars," arriving too late for a meal. They said their respective offices and performed other pious devotions at a little hotel, and at eight o'clock in the morning, after having contented themselves with only a dry crust of bread, they again took the "Cars." They rode to "Harrisburgh" and then to "Chambersburgh" without any refreshments along the way. At the latter place the owner of the stage hotel, an Englishman "well versed in Saxon trickery" arranged with the coach agent to detain the passengers stopping with him as long as possible. After three days the poor monks climbed into a crowded horse-drawn coach, paying the exorbitant price of twenty dollars for a forty mile trip, and never before in their lives did they perform so painful, so disagreeable and so dangerous a journey by land. As night came on and they dipped up and down over the rough terrain "the Coach lamps shed a lurid light around thousands of towering rocks, and lofty trees which enclosed some miles of their journey."

About two o'clock in the morning the coach noisily negotiated the passage of a perilous wooden bridge into Bedford, and later that day the prior and the brother found to their disappointment that the Very Reverend Thomas Heyden, who had originally invited Father Bernard to his district, was absent on missionary duties. So the next morning without him they proceeded to Harmon's Bottoms, twenty miles away.

The country was desolate looking, and the soil was rocky and slaty. Their first impressions of the Bottoms were of sharp disillusionment from what they had been led to expect. At a little after noon they approached the rough, tiny chapel where services were occasionally conducted. Prior Clement stopped in his tracks when he heard soft, sweet strains of harmony apparently issuing from the little hut, and so heavenly was the music that he seemed "to be transported to the valley of Rasselas." Father Clement was extremely susceptible to music. When he had left Liverpool on the four-master he was deeply impressed by the music on deck: "Here the violin with its sweet and delicate sounds, there the clarinet with its soft and agreeable melody, charmed the ear of the attentive listener, yet these appeared as dull and doleful sounds when contrasted with the rich and melting harmony of a few German voices, artfully blended and producing a sensation more agreeable and less fallacious than Siren melody could create or excite in the minds of their devoted victims." Here among the wild and barren foothills of the Alleghenies on this cold noon the prior was almost transported with delight as his ears drank in "such soft harmonious strains that Euterpe or Apollo himself might justly envy." Followed by Brother Ambrose he gently opened the door of the chapel and beheld near a blazing fireplace playing upon his accordion "with as much execution as he was master of" — Brother Macarius Keegan!

Soon Father Bernard and Brother Cyprian Slattery appeared upon the scene and astonishment was the sensation all around. It was too soon for letters to arrive from Mount Melleray with the news that Dom Bruno had despatched the two monks to investigate the proposed abbey lands. Further, Prior Clement had not seen Brother Macarius since 1845. Brother Macarius, it seemed, had left Dubuque in November of 1848, with New Orleans apparently as his destination. Already puzzled by this strange and enigmatic monk, Bishop

Loras was probably not too surprised to receive a letter from him from an entirely different direction — from Kingston, Canada, a month later. In this missive Brother Macarius stated that he was writing to the Abbot of Mount Melleray concerning "the offer made by your Lordship to our community," and he concluded the letter with a warning against "a person named Brother Cyprian Slattery who," he alleged, "was not authorized to collect for the Trappists." This was an unjust reflection on Brother Cyprian, a good and holy monk if ever there was one. A member of the order at Melleray in France, he had been expelled with the other British subjects in 1831 by the revolutionary agents. Instead of returning to Ireland with the majority, he later entered the monastery of La Grande Trappe from where he went to the Petit Clairvaux at Trachadie in Nova Scotia. At the moment of Brother Macarius' attack on him he was, as has been noticed, with Father Bernard at Bedford where he soon was to receive Brother Macarius on friendly terms being entirely unconscious of that monk's attitude toward him. A short time after this he was to go to the Gethsemani monastery in Kentucky to teach for a time before returning to Petit Clairvaux where he died a happy death on January 4th, 1860.

During his stay at Kingston, Ontario, Brother Macarius was impressed by the invitation of the Right Rev. P. Phelan, Coadjutor Bishop of Kingston, to the Irish Cistercians, and went so far as to buy some land in the name of Mount Melleray. Hearing from Father Bernard about the Pittsburgh vicar-general's offer of land at Bedford he immediately left for Pennsylvania, and on reaching Pittsburgh wrote Bishop Loras another long epistle on February 2nd. "I have strong hopes," he wrote, "of being able to make the necessary preparations for complying with the terms of your Lordship's very noble offer . . . I have ardent hopes of being able to obtain assistance from the Catholic nobility of England. I doubt not your Lordship's generous offer will be hailed with joy by the Monks of Mount Melleray . . . It is to be understood that the branch of the order established at Dubuque shall only be subject to the House of Mount Melleray in Ireland." From Pittsburgh Brother Macarius then went to join Father Bernard and Brother Cyprian at Bedford, and was accordingly with them when they received the unexpected but welcome visitors at Harmon's Bottoms.

Careful inspection of the Bottoms lands on the following day convinced the shrewd and prudent geologist, Brother Ambrose, that they could never be converted into good farms. The cheap loans that were originally held out as bait to Father Bernard were now forgotten or the terms changed. Neighboring land-owners refused the monks passage to get to the mills, or to permit the water to pass through, unless their lands would be purchased at exorbitant prices. Father Thomas Heyden's own brother-in-law, according to Prior Clement's account, made an unfair financial proposal to which the prior did not even give an answer. And when the very reverend vicar-general himself returned from his mission journey, his attitude was described by Father Clement as one of cold indifference toward the entire matter. This is probably a bit of exaggeration on the part of the prior's pen, still unacquainted with American ways and manners. Dr. Thomas Heyden had certainly been very hospitable to the monks before the prior's arrival. It may be added that he was a distinguished churchman of his day in the young United States: some years previous to the events recorded here he had been offered — and he declined — the bishopric of Natchez, Mississippi; that he was a man of learning and of letters can be gleaned from the biography he wrote on Father Demetrius Augustine Gallitzin, the apostle of western Pennsylvania, the first book ever published on that illustrious priest of princely Russian blood, and a copy of which Dr. Heyden inscribed and gave to Father Bernard during the weeks he entertained him as his guest.[1]

At any rate, the whole project of abbey lands in Pennsylvania proved to be a dismal failure. Well it was that Prior Clement had persuaded Dom Bruno not to send a large group of monks along with him. Meanwhile Brother Marcarius had informed the prior of the generous offer Bishop Loras of Dubuque — apparently the only American bishop who hitherto had shown a friendly attitude toward the Irish Trappists — had made to him the previous Novem-

[1] At the same time that Mathias Loras, Vicar-General of Mobile, was appointed Bishop of Dubuque (1837) "the Holy See named as the first Bishop of Natchez Rev. Thomas Heyden, then pastor of St. Paul's Church in Pittsburg. When Father Heyden became acquainted with this appointment, distress and perplexity seemed to disturb his soul. Should he make the sacrifice that would be entailed in leaving his comfortable home to become bishop of a diocese where there were no priests, no churches, and where nothing but problems and hardships would await him? It seems to have taken him a long time to decide. The Natchez congregation wrote him expressing delight at his appointment and urging him to accept. His personal friends wrote him — some of them advising him that he should not accept; others urged him that he should accept the office as being given him by the will of God." — *Cradle Days at St. Mary's at Natchez* (1941) by Bishop R. A. Gerow.

ber, and he also described in glowing terms the lands he had inspected in Ontario near Kingston. After a consultation among the five members, it was decided that Brother Ambrose, the agricultural authority, accompanied by Brother Macarius should proceed to Iowa to examine the Dubuque farm, while Father Clement would start for Kingston, Canada, to inspect the three hundred acres of land, already purchased by Brother Macarius for the Trappists, and then to await there the return of the two brothers from Iowa before making a final decision.

Father Bernard McCaffrey, sick and discouraged, accompanied Brother Cyprian Slattery to the Gethsemani monastery in Kentucky, where he was to remain the next six months. And so ended abruptly the dream of a new Cistercian abbey in Pennsylvania.

Two days after the brothers had departed Prior Clement left Bedford and wearily took himself back to Harrisburg, and back again to Philadelphia, somewhat depressed by the prospect of the long journey before him, one of almost a thousand miles through a strange land and in the midst of the rigors of a fierce winter, the like of which he had, of course, never experienced in Ireland. And then another peculiar blow confounded him. He had imagined that the Brothers Ambrose and Macarius were now well on their way to their destination west of the Mississippi, but on calling at the house of a mutual priest-friend of the Trappists in Philadelphia he was handed two letters that had just arrived from these two reverend gentlemen informing him that this was certainly not the case. Brother Macarius wrote that he had decided after all to return to Kingston, Canada, as that place held out, in his opinion, the most favorable future; Brother Ambrose stated in his letter that he had no choice but to accompany this companion, since he, Brother Ambrose, was penniless and Brother Macarius carried the purse, and that he thus could neither return to join the prior nor go on to Iowa alone.

A further peculiar fact is that Brother Macarius before he left Bedford sent a telegram to Bishop Mathias Loras, and whether this action was taken with Father Clement Smyth's knowledge cannot definitely be stated. The telegram sent on March 3, 1849 — and, by the way, one of the first ever to reach Dubuque — read: "Have you sent the money? If not, do not send it. Brother Ambrose and I leave immediately for Dubuque. We have the sanction of the Abbot and the consent of the Monks to build a great Abbey at your place if it answers. Answer immediately at Bedford." From the notation made by Bishop Loras on this telegram, still in the old Dubuque diocesan files, it appears that he answered this telegram. By what strange mental process Brother Macarius so suddenly changed his plan and went on to Kingston is difficult to understand.

Meanwhile Prior Clement resumed his journey toward the frozen north, battling through storms that became veritable blizzards after he left the city of New York to which place he had gone upon leaving Philadelphia. From Albany on to Lake Ontario all of his travels were by stage coach in rickety vehicles whose sides were usually half open to the fierce wintry blasts. After a week of this arctic torture he arrived at long last at Cape St. Vincent, a village on the American shore of Lake Ontario separated by about sixteen miles from the British side. Here he encountered what proved to be about the most perilous part of his entire journey. Most of the passengers and all the pilots were reluctant to venture out on this lake of ice which was now broken and open in some sections. Finally one old pilot was induced, with his horse and sled, to convey the prior and a couple of other passengers to the opposite shore. The horse broke through the ice once but floundered out immediately and was on his legs as active as ever. The long sheets of ice frequently bent as though they were highly elastic. Fortunately, the intelligent steed appeared so much accustomed to the ice that whenever he came to a crack he leaped over it with the greatest facility taking sleigh and passengers with him quite safely.

From out on the lake Prior Clement could see the city of Kingston standing clear on rising ground, and as he approached it, his eye was attracted by the Catholic cathedral, a large and beautiful Gothic structure. Sententiously he wrote: "Above the cathedral was the Royal flag of England, displaying in its crimsoned folds, as it proudly floated on the breeze, the Cross, the glorious emblem of man's redemption, waving defiance to the Orange firebrands who live just in the vicinity of the Church, and distilling around the triumphant song of victory in favour of Catholicity in Orange Kingston and silently reproaching the Saxon peer and the Saxon peasant for rejecting that glorious emblem which was the pride and the boast of their Catholic ancestors." The presence of that British flag waving from the Catholic tower was later explained to him as necessary "to awe Orange bigotry and to prevent Orange enthusiasts from daring to lay violent hands on the Church of God, where Irishmen had then met to adore the God of their forefathers and to hear an appropriate eulogy on the life and virtues of the great St. Patrick, the illustrious Patron and renowned Apostle of their dear Native land" — for this day of his arrival, as he a loyal and native son of Erin had almost forgotten, was the 17th of March, the feast of St. Patrick. But even then as he passed through the streets to call on the bishop, he was astonished to see so many of his countrymen neatly dressed, each wearing a green sash around his waist or a broad green baldric around his shoulder and across his breast, proudly displaying their national emblem, the "Shamrock so green." In answer to his inquiry for such a display "in a far distant land," he was told that "Irishmen both Catholic and Protestant (Orangemen excepted) together with the Scotch in Kingston and its vicinity, had assembled on that day, with banners and Music, to honour the great Patron of the green emerald Isle, forgetting all National antipathy, all Religious prejudices."

The prior was warmly received by Coadjutor Bishop Phelan of Kingston, and soon Brothers Ambrose and Macarius were among those who welcomed him. Hoping that now at last he could secure the proper location and the good land needed for a Trappist foundation, he accompanied Brother Macarius to see the farm he had purchased for the order. Brother Ambrose had already warned him that it was not suitable for the community, and the prior, after viewing the place, agreed with him. Only one hundred of the three hundred acres was good land, the site was inaccessible, there were no roads and no bridges in the wilderness of that day ten miles from Kingston, the streams that had to be crossed were deep and dangerous. And this was but the prelude to a series of similar disappointments. As week followed week the monks drove about the wild country inspecting various sites which always were painted in the beginning as most attractive locations for their new monastery, and which in each instance were found by the shrewd and judicious agricultural expert, Brother Ambrose, as entirely unsatisfactory for a promising Trappist foundation. Two of these prospective sites had the picturesque Indian names of Cananoque and Tiandanaga, but these intriguing appellations added not one white to their value. Finally, Brother Macarius Keegan, apparently resentful at the stubborn course of events and piqued because the farm he had selected and purchased had not been accepted, left Kingston for Mount Melleray Abbey with the implied declaration of never again returning to America.

It was also during this time that Prior Clement wrote to Abbot Bruno Fitzpatrick in Ireland requesting the use of certain new monies in addition to the liberal funds he had already received, an action which not only displeased the abbot but likewise suggested the ideas which led to the prior's subsequent replacement by another monk as superior of the American colony of Trappists. All this time the prior and Brother Ambrose were hospitably entertained at Kingston College by Father Angus Mac Donnel, the vicar-general, and the prior was frequently pressed into service in hearing the confessions of the prisoners in the Ontario Provincial Penitentiary. Father Mac Donnel, as a further token of his kindness, proposed another offer: he had succeeded with Bishop Phelan in getting for the monks four hundred acres of what he considered very good land, and in addition he donated a parcel of one hundred acres more which had been his own possession. This land was however quite a distance away — one hundred and twenty miles from Kingston, near a town called Alexandria. Brother Ambrose proceeded immediately to reconnoiter this new situation and wrote back that some of the land was good but other parts were swampy and indifferent, and requested the prior to come and satisfy himself on the matter. Prior Clement arrived at Alexandria and the two of them at first were pleased with the examination.

Unfortunately, however, the prior overevaluated the good points Brother Ambrose had indicated, and forgetting all about the many strictures he had also enumerated, he travelled back the long journey to Kingston, where hoping that this at last was to be the permanent site of the abbey lands, he purchased provisions and other necessaries for their new establishment. With much toil he managed to load on board a steamer on the St. Lawrence river about two thousand pounds of stocks and stores including a stove and other heavy articles, and on the evening of that day he debarked with his cargo at Cornwall about thirty miles from Alexandria. Here with extreme difficulty after two days of search he induced a waggoner to convey him and his load to Alexandria. On his arrival there what was his dismay to find Brother Ambrose so dissatisfied with the lands that he was compelled to tell the prior frankly that they would not support the expected community. This was about the most disappointing and most painful blow that Father Clement Smyth had so far sustained. He simply dared not undertake, as he put it, "to be responsible for the consequences of settling on the farm and of bringing a Community from Mount Melleray to what they would perhaps term Mount Misery." He was forced to sell all his purchases, bag and baggage, to the Catholic pastor of Alexandria, who had kindly kept the two monks at his own house as long as they remained in that locality.

Riding back on the St. Lawrence steamer to Kingston, on May 10th, the prior, discouraged at all he had gone through, unburdened himself to Brother Ambrose, and made the statement that "the only thing remaining to be done was to return back to Ireland, that all future attempts would prove like the past, perfect failures." This same sentiment he had previously written in his letters to Abbot Bruno Fitzpatrick and this fortified the abbot in his belief that Prior Clement lacked the fortitude necessary in a leader of the attempted American colony.

The only unexplored offer that still remained was that of Bishop Mathias Loras of Iowa, an offer that had been highly spoken of by Brother Macarius despite the fact that he had spurned it because of his preference for Canada as a Trappist foundation. So without further delay the prior sent Brother Ambrose to the far West with Dubuque as his destination. The weather was now mild and navigation had commenced on the Great Lakes thus affording a facility of travelling by water. Brother Ambrose Byrne left Kingston on May 14th, 1849. Prior Clement had debated seriously with himself as to whether he should accompany him. Despondent over the failures of Father Bernard's and Brother Macarius' projects, fearful that Brother Macarius' report on Iowa was as misleading as his descriptions of the Kingston lands, and believing that expenses could be saved by allowing Brother Ambrose to travel alone, he permitted himself to be persuaded, probably by Father Angus Mac Donnel and other friends, to remain at Kingston and to await further word there from the West. He acknowledged later however that although, as it turned out, he could not have accomplished more than Brother Ambrose did, the wiser and more dutiful course would have been to accompany him.

The prior, still residing at Kingston College, was in hopes of receiving a letter from Brother Ambrose at least in ten days. But week after week rolled by and the prior's heart sank daily as each post reaching the college brought no intelligence, cheering or otherwise, from Iowa. Brother Ambrose, it was learned later, had written directly to Mount Melleray, Ireland, and had neglected to send a single line to Father Clement who worried "whether he was dead or alive or on horse-back." Finally the prior decided to pay a visit to Boston where his nephew, a young physician, had a successful medical practice. At Boston he was not only aided financially by his nephew, but was offered by him a small farm for the community. Father Clement could not accept this until he heard further from the West, and so after six days he returned to Kingston in high hopes that at last there would be encouraging news from Brother Ambrose and Dubuque.

VI

DOM BRUNO LEADS THE CHARGE —

. . . .

The man most interested in the success of an American colony of Irish Trappists was beyond any doubt — and naturally so, too, because of his position as abbot of the community — Dom Bruno Fitzpatrick. Inheriting the mantle of Dom Vincent Ryan of Mount Melleray and, really, also that of Dom Antoine de Beauregard of Melleray, he was made of that stern but sparkling stuff that has always formed the sinews of the fighting and praying knights of the Faith. For a long year he had seen the dream-walls of his cherished Cistercian foundation beyond the Atlantic smashed one after another by every bitterly disappointing report and letter that came back across the sea. It was a challenge to his holy zeal: he determined to march into the breach himself and by his own energetic action to cut the Gordian knot of all American obstacles.

Brother Macarius had left Kingston bitterly desolated by the fact that his farm had been refused as the site for the new American abbey. As a cabin passenger in a mail steamer he arrived in Ireland three weeks later, about April 20, 1849. He was determined to present his arguments on the American situation to the abbot with all the eloquence and force at his command. The pleading of his cause was helped considerably by an unfortunately worded letter from Prior Clement which had reached Mount Melleray shortly before his return. In this letter the prior had given his views which were entirely contrary to those of Brother Macarius, and in summing up his discouraging experiences he had used language, one sentence of which, at least, offended the abbot acutely. "Had I known," he wrote, "the circumstances before I left Mount Melleray as well as I now do, I would not have been so easily dislodged as I was." The abbot read this letter in public chapter to the community, and then declared that Father Clement was not qualified for his important charge and was unfit to be superior of the new filiation. This natural-ly afforded Brother Macarius the opportunity he needed to stress more strongly his views in favor of the Canadian foundation.

The decision that Dom Bruno then arrived at was that an Ameri-can filiation was so important, and at this critical time so necessary for the brothers, that he himself should leave for the new world and make the negotiations and whatever decisions were now so impera-tively required. He was well aware by this time of the general im-port of Bishop Mathias Loras' generous proposal in Iowa and was favorably inclined toward it. His deep sense of justice as well as prudence, however, made him listen with patient consideration to the claims of Brother Macarius. Before completing preparations for his departure he appointed Father Francis Walsh, a pious and circumspect priest, as prior of Mount Melleray who was to remain at home until the abbot's return, and he also designated Father Walsh as the superior of the new monastery when it would be established. He then chose for his companions on his American expedition Father James Myles O'Gorman and the four brothers: Timothy Duggan, Joseph Nolan, Barnaby Grace, and, of course, the experienced travel-ler and business agent, Macarius. Of these, Brother Timothy was the oldest; born in 1793 he had been professed in the French abbey of Melleray before his exile to Ireland.

Another new difficulty suddenly faced the abbot, a difficulty that might have seriously threatened the formation of a foreign affiliate at that time. It will be recalled that Mount Melleray Abbey had recently been united to the Congregation of La Grande Trappe in France. The permisison to erect new Cistercian affiliates should have been approved by this Congregation, but the news of this new rule of permissions had reached Mount Melleray too late — at least, not till after all the preliminary labors had now already been performed in America. All this Dom Bruno carefully and patiently explained in a letter penned in French to the abbot of La Grande Trappe who was vicar-general of the Congregation, as he and his monks were waiting at Liverpool for the departure of their boat. "For that matter, I shall not excuse myself to the General Chapter;" wrote the humble Abbot Bruno Fitzpatrick. "I want to accept in advance all the penances you wish to impose upon me."

And then he cogently explained his necessarily quick departure: "Our unhappy Ireland is devouring its inhabitants, and everywhere you hear the cry: *Sauve qui peut!* . . . If you ask me why I am going myself to America, I will give you the reason in a few works. I have given 500 pounds sterling to Prior Clement to begin with, and there he is, losing courage, and instead of asking for brothers, he asks for more money. Famine is pressing in on us on all sides, and it is an enemy far more terrible than Louis Philippe. I cannot give him any money, but I want to send the brothers so as not to see them dying of starvation. The Bishop of Dubuque is willing indeed to give us 450 acres of land, but Prior Clement does not like the United States. There is a year almost lost and nothing as yet done for my first children. The diocesan bishop has blessed my project and it seems to me that I am doing the will of God. Certainly, I have already suffered a little . . . I am taking with me five brothers of whom one is a Priest. The forty or fifty brothers will not leave [for America] till after my return, it being then understood, of course, that you have no objections."

This letter was written on the 11th of May, the day before Dom Bruno and his little company of monks departed on the *Caledonia*, a mail steamer, for the city of Boston. This was coincidentally almost the same day that on the American continent Brother Ambrose was leaving Kingston for his voyage through the Great Lakes with Iowa as his destination. On the *Caledonia*, when it was learned by the monks that their vessel would stop at Halifax, Nova Scotia, to deliver the European mail, Brother Macarius urged that they should call on Bishop William Walsh of that city who had been very kind to him when he had made his collections for Mount Melleray in the Halifax diocese. That frank annalist of New Melleray at Dubuque,

Brother Kieran, from whose pungent writings one must frequently quote in this Iowa Trappist tale, made this remark: "It would be well for the Abbot had he left Brother Macarius at home, he would be spared many a sore pang by doing so, twice he was very near losing his life on that Brother's account." Brother Macarius dragged the abbot and brothers with him to pay their compliments to the bishop who received them warmly, but on their return to the wharf they were horrified to find that the *Caledonia* had sailed on to Boston without them, and carried in her hold all their baggage. As no other vessel was to sail southward for a week they were obliged to hire a carriage to take them to Digby, a distance of one hundred and twenty miles, and then proceed from there in a one-masted open boat across the Bay of Fundy, another seventy miles. A sudden squall struck the boat and the passengers were compelled to keep emptying the water thrown in upon them. Landing at Eastport in the state of Maine they secured a ship which took them to Boston harbor where they found the *Caledonia* as well as their baggage.

Father Clement Smyth was visiting his nephew in Boston at this very time, but Abbot Bruno and his party, unaware of this, started on their overland journey to Kingston under the persuasive guidance of Brother Macarius. They travelled by the "Eight O'Clock Cars" to Albany and continued on to Oswego on the shore of Lake Ontario, four hundred miles from Boston. Here a steamer took them the next hundred miles to the city of Kingston. The optimistic influence exerted on the party by Brother Macarius in favor of the farm he had bought at Kingston for the order induced them to bring along a beautiful cooking stove and other utensils. Hospitably received by Bishop Phelan, they were again made at home at Kingston College.

The very next day they set out to see the lands Bishop Phelan and Brother Macarius had chosen for the new monastery. It was the first week of June and the weather was hot and oppressive. On their arrival they found the heavily timbered lands full of swamps, but they decided to stay overnight in the little cabin that Brother Macarius had erected there. The heat and the swarms of mosquitoes made the night a most painful one, and in the morning the brothers were sufficiently alarmed by the sudden illness of Dom Bruno to send Brother Joseph on a furious gallop into Kingston to inform Bishop Phelan. The latter at once sent out his carriage to convey the abbot back to the college where he speedily recovered. All this, of course sounded the death-knell of any Kingston monastery foundation.

It was at this time that Father Clement returned from Boston, and arriving at the College of Kingston the news of the presence there of the abbot and his companions struck him, as he wrote later, like an electric shock. He was affectionately embraced by Dom Bruno and Father James and the brothers who accompanied them. The abbot spent a few days more in Kingston awaiting word from Brother Ambrose or expecting his possible return. He had sent a telegraphic letter to the brother in Dubuque but heard nothing in return. Brother Ambrose previously had written him a long letter about Iowa, but naturally had addressed it to Mount Melleray, Ireland. Brother Macarius, as soon as he arrived in Kingston with the abbot, had written or telegraphed Brother Ambrose at Dubuque, informing him of Dom Bruno's arrival, and urging him to return to Kingston immediately and to give up the Iowa project in favor of Bishop Phelan's offer in Canada. Whether this message was mentioned by Brother Macarius to the abbot is highly conjectural. At any rate, nothing daunted by this silence of Brother Ambrose, the abbot then decided to leave for the West himself and took with him as his only travelling companion, Brother Barnaby.[1] Before his departure, which took place on the 15th of June by steamboat for Toronto and the Lakes, he gave instructions that on the arrival of the first letter of invitation from Iowa the remaining monks were to follow after.

Such a letter arrived six days later. It was addressed to Abbot Bruno Fitzpatrick in the unmistakable handwriting of Brother Ambrose. Father Clement broke the seal and as he and his companions read its contents, they found them a most flattering and encouraging description of the proffered lands near Dubuque. A fairy land they were, wrote Brother Ambrose, in whom exaggeration was seldom a fault; rich and beautifully diversified were the lands with hill and dale, with enchanting wood and verdant, rolling prairie "through whose shady valleys a lovely Creek in a long, meandering course wended its way into the dark and slow-moving waters of the Mississippi." Small wonder it was that new hopes sprang up in the hitherto doubting minds of the brothers, and that their impatient desire to

---

[1] Brother Barnaby Grace's nephew, a Dominican, later became the second bishop of St. Paul, Minnesota, (1859-1884) — the Right Reverend Thomas Langdon Grace, O.P.

start on their western journey would suffer no delay. On Monday, the 23d of June, they left Kingston from Buffalo and the Lakes.

But not all departed; one remained — poor Brother Macarius. Wounded to the quick by the abbot's refusal to accept the site he had so assiduously schemed and labored for, he at this time parted company with the brothers and "walked no more with them," remaining in Kingston until his pious and penitential death only two years later. Of this strange monk one can most appropriately remark, "De mortuis nil nisi bonum," for of him Father Clement Smyth who knew him so intimately and recognized his failings as well as his virtues wrote while he was still living, as "a man as void of reason as he was of malice in his designs or of guile in his intentions." It was he who for years had so devotedly drawn the funds from the laps of the rich in such widely separated places of the globe as the British Isles and Canada and the United States and had turned them over to Mount Melleray Abbey when they were so desperately needed even for survival; and it should not be forgotten that it was Brother Macarius who had first arranged to meet with Bishop Loras and Father Cretin and induced them to make the original generous offer which has led to the existence of New Melleray Abbey of today.

The route taken by Abbot Bruno and Brother Barnaby was apparently much the quicker one. The second group tarried long enough to be awed by the majestic Niagara Falls and leaving Buffalo on the 27th of June went by steam ship through Lakes Erie, Huron and Michigan, just as Brother Ambrose had done before them, a passage usually lasting five days to Chicago. From Chicago the railroad took them forty miles as far as Elgin, from where the stage coach or the "mail stage" as some of the conveyances were called, carried them a fast two days' travel to Galena, Illinois. Steam boats constantly passed back and forth between Galena and Dubuque on the Iowa side, a few miles to the north.

At Chicago Father James and Father Clement had sent the two brothers, Timothy and Joseph, with the luggage to Davenport from where they later proceeded to Dubuque by steamboat on the Mississippi. Abbot Bruno and Brother Barnaby reached Dubuque almost a fortnight before the others, and proceeding to the episcopal mansion, were greeted with warmth and received with delight by the Iowa vicar-general, Father Joseph Cretin. It was there that the abbot listened with rapt attention when Brother Ambrose, notified of his arrival, hastened to meet him and informed him of the success of his efforts. A number of days later when Father James and Father Clement went from their steamboat to the City Hotel, they rested a day before presenting themselves at the bishop's house at twelve o'clock at noon on the 6th of July, and here the entire group shared in all the humble comforts of that hosiptable mansion.

Dubuque was a lusty young city of hardly more than three thousand inhabitants in 1849, but at that it was the second largest city of the state. Iowa had just been admitted as the twenty-ninth state of the Union two and a half years before. The monks in their black and demure civilian garb, arriving on the steamboats in the bustling Dubuque harbor, were a congruous part of the colorful and motley element that was pouring into Iowa at that time. The gold rush to California was on. Arriving daily into the port on their way to the various points in the West, were adventurers, homesteaders, farmers, ambitious new settlers of Iowa and hundreds of others merely passing through. Dom Bruno with his Irish and French background, and his companions with their training in European culture, had seen strange sights in this new world — at Boston and New York, at Kingston and at Chicago. This was a different spectacle at Dubuque where a mixture of Americans and Europeans, spurning the steamboats and stages and the new railroads, came with their own wagons and on foot overland and crossed from Illinois into the new state. During the early days of their arrival the monks saw long processions of emigrant wagons carried over to the Iowa shore by flatboats and ferries. The "long blue wagons" — the old Conestogas — were beginning to give way to vehicles of greater capacity. The wagons when landed on the Iowa side, were again yoked up to their steeds brought over on other boats — and these steeds were oxen, mild-eyed, soft-toed, and slow.

Some of the wagons had four or five yoke of oxen, while heavier wagons had eight or even ten yoke of oxen drawing them. Practically all of them were of the covered wagon type — they had canvas tops. Some were clean and brightly painted, but most of them were muddy and dirty. When the brothers, Timothy and Joseph, arrived from Davenport and struggled to carry off from their steamboat the luggage of the little community which had been confided to their care, they found themselves among the immigrants coming off the flatboats with their cattle and sheep and hogs and crates of chickens and geese, and barking dogs everywhere.

It was here that Dom Bruno and Father James and Father Clement stared with curiosity as they saw for the first time the stream of Mormons, many with packs on their backs and women pushing wheelbarrows and followed by their children, all on their way to Utah. They gazed at the native Americans from the poorer sections of the East mingling with European newcomers all seeking what they themselves were seeking – free land, Congress land, any land, in order to settle in the new state of Iowa. Bishop Loras doubtless explained these sights to the interested Trappists. He visioned the great West peopled with the Catholic immigrants flocking to America. He wished to draw them from the crowded slums of the Eastern cities where they were hewers of wood and drawers of water, and make them self-reliant and independent farmers of the generous Northwest where lands were cheap and natural resources unlimited. Unfortunately the narrow-visioned prelates of the Atlantic seaboard, Bishop John Hughes of New York prominent among them, frowned on his efforts among their peoples, and the fair promise of his colonization plans was considerably blighted. A stupendous opportunity was lost thereby for a great Catholic commonwealth in the West.

And Dom Bruno, gazing at this still semi-wild valley of the Upper Mississippi, would have been astonished had he known that thirty-two years before his arrival, another Trappist superior had tarried in these precincts, the first priest in history to carry on missionary work in this part of the valley. He was Prior Joseph Marie Dunand, one of Charles Dickens' "mad monks," formerly of Monks' Mound and St. Louis. Born in Lorraine, he had served as a grenadier in the Republican army of France during the Revolution. In 1791, horrified because his squad had been ordered to execute a priest, he deserted and fled to La Val Sainte in Switzerland where he became one of Dom Augustin de Lestrange's Cistercian followers. He was one of the group which had come to the United States in 1805, and when the remnants of this community returned to France later, he was permitted to remain in the vicinity of St. Louis as a missioner. In pursuance of his work he came up the Mississippi river, past the Dubuque Mines, as far as Prairie du Chien, in 1817. Welcomed by the military officials of Fort Crawford, he made Prairie du Chien his headquarters for a month. "I administered holy baptism to a great many, large and small," he wrote later in his diary, "among whom were many half-breeds and savages . . . Protestants came every day to the instructions; even the Jews were converted. The savages of different nations were exact in attendance of Mass; the savage women brought me their children in groups, some to be baptized, others that they might behold a Makita Courage, that is to say, a black robe." The parish records at St. Gabriel's Church, Prairie du Chien, show that from April 1, 1817, to May 3, 1817, Prior Dunand, called by the people "Pére Prieure," baptized 135 persons, Sioux, Winnebago, and Fox Indians from the Dubuque Mines.

From Prairie du Chien that Trappist prior made several missionary excursions inland, on some of which he doubtless entered the Iowa wilderness. To show in what a hopeless and savage condition this part of the Northwest was just three decades before the arrival of Dom Bruno and his monks at Dubuque, this one instance of several revolting scenes witnessed by the missioner is recounted here: "One day, when again going up the Mississippi, I arrived with my canoe and the men who accompanied me, near a house which the Indians had set afire. The father and mother whom they had scalped were lying dead before the door. Besides this, they had massacred seven children, most of them girls . . . With much confusion I viewed this burning house and the bloody corpses, when a sight, sadder still, at least more apt to excite pity, caught my eye. A poor old man, nearly sixty-five years of age, came before me having been scalped and left for dead by the savages. 'Father Joseph,' he said to me, 'save my soul! save my soul!' (speaking in the English language). We took all possible care of him but at the end of a few days he died."

Abbot Bruno knew nothing about the past history of this locality in which he found himself; but it was about the future that he had been apprehensive. This far excursion into the western wilds to establish a Trappist monastery was a daring thing, to put the matter mildly, and in this strange, new land how would it fare? Now, however, that he had met Bishop Loras and his vicar-general, he threw all fears aside; and as he listened to the story of Brother Ambrose, who had been the "precursor in the wilderness" for the community, his heart beat still more hopefully.

VII

—WHILE BROTHER AMBROSE HOLDS THE FORT

Brother Ambrose Byrne was a simple and pious Trappist lay brother. He was also a shrewd and experienced agriculturalist. And above all he was endowed with more than the usual amount of common sense, sane judgment and prudence. He gave his clear-cut opinions about the land-sites in Pennsylvania and in Canada and he refused to be swayed from his decisions. He made the long and lonely journey from Kingston to Iowa with a completely open mind. Brother Ambrose, it should be mentioned, had made his Trappist vows in old Melleray in France, and was one of those who suffered exile for the Faith in 1831.

The week of his arrival in Dubuque was not merely a red-letter one for the Church in Iowa, but one that could actually be marked on the calendar with initials of fire. For during that fateful week of May, 1849, a fire broke out at the mother-house of the Sisters of Charity of the B.V.M. a few miles southwest of the city whose location was actually contiguous to the lands which Bishop Mathias Loras was holding in escrow for the Trappist community. This convent, which when rebuilt was to be a close neighbor and generous friend of the Cistercian house for many years in the future, had its academy and chapel burned to the ground through the action of an irresponsible incendiary. Although the books and other effects of the students of the academy were saved, nearly all the personal apparel and household goods of the twenty-three Sisters who resided on the premises were lost in the buildings destroyed.

The smoke and confusion of this conflagration — quite a catastrophe at that time in sparsely-settled Iowa — tended to obscure completely the presence of the humble monk who had arrived as a guest at the bishop's house. After a couple of days the vicar-general, Father Cretin, who was directing the affairs of the young diocese during the absence of the bishop, became suddenly aware of the identity and purpose of his visitor and immediately demonstrated an acute interest in Brother Ambrose and his mission. Bishop Loras, who had been in Baltimore attending with the other bishops of the United States the Seventh Provincial Council, was at this moment, coincidentally enough, finishing a visit with other Trappists. On his return journey to Iowa he had stopped at the monastery of Our Lady of Gethsemani in Kentucky which had been founded just the year before by a colony of Cistercians from Melleray in France. Unaware, of course, of the Trappist guest in his own home, he discussed with his Kentucky friends the possibility of securing some religious order of men for his diocese. From Gethsemani he departed for Keokuk and Burlington in the southern part of his Iowa see.

Father Cretin, sufficiently confident in his own mind that the bishop's lands would prove highly satisfactory to this expert agriculturist of the Cistercians, arranged to have Brother Ambrose go alone and at his leisure carefully inspect the proffered sites. He further arranged to have him driven out to the "Twelve Mile House," where the proprietor of this tavern and hostelry, Mr. Lemuel Lytton, would act as his guide. The highway leading out to this inn was a splendid one; it was the famous Military Road constructed as a part of the government road from Dubuque to the northern boundary of Missouri. Mr. Lytton was a distinguished looking Protestant gentleman originally from New England and several of his children were in later years to enter the Catholic Church under the catechetical instructions of the Trappist priests. Mr. Lytton had saddle horses and he and Brother Ambrose rode about over the lands through the tall prairie grass. He informed the brother that there were other prairie lands yet unclaimed and lying close to the bishop's holdings which could be procured for the "congress price" of one dollar and a quarter. Pleased by this piece of news the brother was further gratified when he galloped over with Mr. Lytton to the fine timber lands only a few miles distant. The two men parted company that evening at the Twelve Mile House, and the happy Trappist brother the next day wrote a glowing account of all that had happened to Dom Bruno at Mount Melleray. As the abbot had already departed for America, the new prior, Father Francis Walsh, read the letter in public chapter to a breathlessly interested assemblage of monks.

Father Cretin was, of course, delighted with the highly favorable impressions made on his visitor. He admired the character of this Trappist brother and he wrote to this effect to Bishop Loras at Burlington: "A Trappist brother, Brother Ambrose, much more respectable than his predecessor [Brother Macarius], has been awaiting your return to make a decision on the subject of the offer you have made them." But the enthusiasm of both these gentlemen was rudely jolted by the arrival of a letter from Brother Macarius. The latter reported the news of his return to Canada in the company of Abbot Bruno, and requested Brother Ambrose to leave Iowa for Kingston, implying, one would certainly suspect, that the matter of the Cistercian foundation was swinging over now entirely in favor of Bishop Phelan's proffered site. While Brother Ambrose hesitated about his next move, Father Cretin made use of a shrewd and able ally in presenting his arguments. Father Terence J. Donaghoe, the chaplain and spiritual director of the Sisters of Charity who had so recently suffered the calamity of the fire, proved to be of invaluable assistance at this moment.

Since both this reverend gentleman and the Sisters under his charge were to have relations of generous charity and deep friendship with the New Melleray house and its members during the early years of its existence, a clarifying word of introduction should be recorded here. Father Donaghoe and Father Cretin had been old friends. Indeed they had been fellow students at St. Sulpice in France and had been ordained in the same class in Paris. When the then tiny community of the Sisters of Charity of the Blessed Virgin Mary, originating in Dublin, Ireland, had come to Philadelphia in 1833, Father Donaghoe had become their sponsor and adviser. The Sisters' superior was Mary Francis Clarke, a nun of illustrious and virtuous life, after whom Clarke College in Dubuque today is named. The community grew and prospered, and in 1843 at the cordial and insistent invitation of Bishop Loras, Father Donaghoe and the entire sisterhood moved to Dubuque, with the intention at that time of placing some of the Sisters on missions among the Indians of Iowa.

Two of the postulants had remained behind to care for the Philadelphia convent until it should be disposed of. Father Donaghoe had made a return trip to Philadelphia just at the time the great anti-Catholic agitation, the Know-Nothing movement, was breaking out in that city. On May 8th, 1844, St. Michael's Church and Father Donaghoe's house were both burned down; and in the afternoon a mob attacked the convent. Mrs. Mary Baker, a postulant and a convert, was in charge of the convent and with her were two young girls. During the disorders Mrs. Baker was struck down by a brick hurled by the mob, but she and the girls were finally saved by a group of resolute Irishmen who had come to their rescue. A few minutes later the convent was reduced to ashes. Father Donaghoe remained in the East for a year, instituting suit for the recovery of financial indemnities for the burning of the Sisters' convent and his church. Through his efforts the Sisters received about $6,400 from the city of Philadelphia as compensation for the destruction caused by the rioters, and, incidentally, most of this money had been used for the erection of the buildings which had burned down during the week of Brother Ambrose's arrival in Dubuque.

Now, in this month of June, 1849, Father Donaghoe used his eloquence on Brother Ambrose in behalf of Iowa and Bishop Loras, and what success he was having is related in this letter sent to the bishop at Burlington:

> Brother Ambrose from *Melleray* arrived here and expected to find you at home. He is one of the few to be met with for judgment and prudence, a priest came with him and remains at Kingston upper Canada. The Bishop endeavors to induce him to settle there — 20 monks or more are to come out — Br. Marcarius desires that Br. Ambrose should come on to Canada as the Abbot has arrived in Canada — Father Cretin opposes it until he hears from you — The good Father Cretin is all on fire to have the monks *now* — my opinion is still the same — furthermore I told *him* — the monk, that your approbation to settle in the Diocese was more than the largest offer made by the Bishops east or in Canada and that too if you had not been so kind — I have his whole Con-

fidence — I now wish you to write me a letter to hold him
here — it is all he wants to justify the call made on him by
Br. Marcarius from Canada who appears to be too much
influenced by his Canada friend — In one word — It will be
a blessing for your Diocese to have them settled within it.
Jerry and Doogan [farmers] would give up their lease I am
told — but *inter nos* I would undertake if I were allowed
freely by you and the Abbot — to make an establishment for
40 monks that would astonish ourselves — and all others —
Our ever Blessed Mother will aid us —

The means will not be wanting — If left to me I would go
out West with land warrants not to be had for $112 — but
in the first instance I would have you continue your grant
of the 500 acres and leave the rest to Providence.

In a postscript Father Donaghoe mentioned to Bishop Loras that
he had received a letter from him from "Latrappe, Kentucky," and
added: "Your heart shows that you love religious orders. God pro-
vides for them territory, 'Domini est terra,' and now is your time
to induce thereby a Catholic emigration. I am delighted I can aid
in the good work — write as this excellent monk is uneasy."

Thus, for some time Brother Ambrose despite assurances from
his friends at Dubuque continued to remain uneasy until suddenly
to his astonishment and immense relief, Dom Bruno and Brother
Barnaby arrived on the scene to be Father Cretin's guests. This
was about June 23rd, and so it was more than five months since the
brother had seen his abbot. As soon as the latter had heard Brother
Ambrose's gratifying report, a report that warmed the cockles of his
heart, he insisted on going with him the next day to study the location and view the rich but wild uncultivated prairies. Shrewd specu-
lators had naturally heard rumors of the possible monastic establishment and had seen the visits to the new lands in the vicinity of
the Twelve Mile House of Brother Ambrose, and now that the abbot
himself had appeared, there was grave fear that these land brokers
might buy up the leases. Immediate action was imperative; whether
it was by the advice of Father Cretin or by his own suggestion the
resolute Dom Bruno and Brother Ambrose immediately slipped down
the river to Burlington to get the final consent and full approval of
Bishop Loras to the foundation and lands. The result of this quick
and vigorous action may be seen in the following jubilant letter
of Father Terence Donaghoe to the Bishop:

Dubuque June 28th eve of St. Peter
and St. Paul — 1849

My dear Bishop

As soon as Brother Ambrose reached me with your important commisison I started for Dubuque determined to fill up the measure of your liberality. I scarcely breathed to mortal until I had 4 land warrants secured although they had raised 30 dollars each within 5 days — The Surveyor and Brother is now harnessing their buggy and I take these moments to write — we have a certified land plat which I obtained and I am now looking at the 16 forties within our grasp — alias 640 acres — alias one mile square — your 500 and 120 — Bt of Yount — or $250 of Br. Macarius money — total 1260 acres secured — Glory be to God —

I am now satisfied there is little land in 12 miles of Dubuque that is not entered — speculation was on the stretch but the Abbot going down to see you blinded them imagining that nothing would be done until he would return. We took advantage of it — I was sorry that I did not see him but now he will rejoice in the Lord.

Yours devotedly in Christ
T. J. Donaghoe

Here comes the buggy —

The figures given here by Father Donaghoe in his hastily scribbled letter to the bishop were only approximately correct in one or two instances. At this time Bishop Loras turned over 440 acres of land to the Trappist brothers as a gift. 480 acres were secured through three land warrants paid for by the order, and another 80 acre addition was bought by the monks from a local farmer, Jeremiah Healy. It was sometime later that Bishop Loras donated a 160 acre tract of timber land. The money of Brother Macarius referred to in the letter was a fund of the order left with the bishop when the brother had visited him in November of 1848 and was mentioned by him in his telegram to Loras sent in March of 1849 from Bedford. This sum was used now, naturally, by the monks in purchasing their new lands.

About the beginning of July Dom Bruno returned from southern Iowa with Bishop Loras and it was probably at this time that he decided to give the name "Our Lady of New Melleray" to the foundation he was establishing. On the new lands were two small frame

buildings acquired with the acreage, and in one of them, about fifteen
feet square, the monks immediately prepared for their housekeeping.
The account book of the order was commenced on Independence
Day, and it may be of interest here to quote from that book only
the entries of that particular day with the heading which reads:
"The following are the expenses incurred in the establishment of
New Melleray since its Commencement

"1849 . . .

July 4	To Purchase of 480 Acres of Prairie	
	by 3 Land Warrants at 145 $ per	435.00
	To Land office entrance &c of Do	6.50
	To Land office for plat of range	1.00
	To Jerry Healy for purchase of 80 acres	100.00
	To Deed and Record of the above	2.40
	To Kitchen Stove &c. $22 Tin Work	26.00
	To one table and eight chairs	9.50"

And a few days later was entered the purchase of "1 cow and
calf" from Cornelius Duggan for fourteen dollars.

Thus when Prior Clement Smyth and Father James Myles O'Gorman were welcomed on their arrival at the episcopal stone mansion
on July 6th they found that practically all arrangements for the new
monastery had been completed with despatch by the abbot and
Brother Ambrose — the bishop's hearty consent and cooperation secured, the sites selected, the lands bought and recorded, the housekeeping arrangements started. Father Clement was still titular prior,
nominally at least, and the abbot had not as yet designated a new
superior for the Dubuque monastery.

The small dwelling on the new lands served the little community
as an oratory, a refectory and a dormitory. Abbot Bruno, except
when he was the guest of Bishop Loras, resided with them, sharing
the wants and privations that were inseparable from such a pioneer
institution. He helped Brother Ambrose draw the plans for the
erection of a larger building, some sixty feet by twelve, in anticipation of the new group of monks which was soon to be sent for. For
this new and humble monastery the ceremony of laying the corner-
stone was as simple and direct as most of Dom Bruno's actions. The
latter pointed with his cane to where it should be located, and what
served as the corner-stone — an oak sill squared in the woods — was
laid on July 16th. Along with Brother Ambrose, the two brothers,
Joseph and Timothy, assisted by a hired carpenter performed the

labor on the building which was sufficiently completed for partial occupancy by the following November.

And then down went Dom Bruno with a serious illness that frightened everyone. Whether it was a recurrence of the sickness that attacked him at Kingston, whether it was an entirely new disease, or whether it was the dread cholera, — who could tell? The cholera was taking its toll of victims at the time, not only in Dubuque, but everywhere up and down the Mississippi. The Sisters of Charity were called into the city from their convent near the New Melleray monastery to nurse the numerous patients. Sister Mary Catherine Byrne was assigned to the abbot's case. He recovered and later wrote the Sisters' chaplain, Father Donaghoe: "Under God, Sister Mary Catherine saved my life; and my gratitude to her and to all the Sisters will be as lasting as my life."

Finally restored to health, he and Bishop Loras arranged for the signing of the last documents connected with the formal establishment of the Iowa Cistercian house, and the most significant is given here:

"We, the undersigned, on behalf of ourselves and of the actual and future Superior and Members of the Communities of Mount Melleray, Ireland, and of New Melleray, Dubuque, Iowa, do hereby promise that the 440 Acres of Land given by the Right Reverend Doctor Loras, Bishop of Dubuque, shall return to him, or to his Successor for the time being, in case that the Monks should ever leave the locality lately known by the name of St. Anne's, and now called New Melleray, they being allowed only the value of their improvements upon the land.

"We likewise engage, that within twelve months after the death of the Right Reverend Doctor Loras, 300 Masses shall be celebrated for the repose of his soul."

Dubuque, Iowa

6th August, 1849

Barth<u>w</u> Bruno Fitz Patrick
     Abbot of Mount Melleray, Ireland

Timothy Clement Smith
     Prior of New Melleray

James O'Gorman
     Priest of New Melleray."

On the reverse of this document is written in Bishop Loras' hand: "440 acres given to the Cistercian fathers. Aug. 6th, 1849. 300 Masses promised. 150 before his death, 150 after the same." And beneath this in a strange hand, apparently written after the bishop's death, are the words: "All said." In connection with Father Clement Smyth's signature two things are to be noted: first, the strange spelling in this instance of his own name, "Smith"; secondly, his title, that of Prior of New Melleray. And as prior he remained until shortly before Abbot Bruno was to leave America. The abbot then offered to continue him in that office, at least, presumably, until Father Francis Walsh, the prior of Mount Melleray in Ireland should arrive in Iowa. Father Clement thought it better, however, to resign the priorship, and this he did in a humble and respectful manner. Dom Bruno then appointed Father James Myles O'Gorman as the superior of the new monastery.

Toward the end of August the abbot left Dubuque to return to his abbey by way of France and La Trappe where he was to attend the meeting of the General Chapter of the Cistercian Congregation. Sometime before his departure, about August 18th, he wrote to Mount Melleray with instructions to Prior Francis Walsh to send on immediately to the new Iowa Trappist house fourteen members — three choir brothers and eleven lay brothers; and he named the particular brothers whom he selected for the colony. On one of his last Sundays in Dubuque, he preached an eloquent sermon in the Dubuque cathedral. Then, knowing that Bishop Loras was soon also to visit Europe to secure priests and financial help for his diocese, he pressed him cordially to be his honored guest and that of the community in Ireland.

At last the little community at Dubuque was actually established; the monastery of Our Lady of New Melleray was launched and under the superior, Father James, there now were two other priests, Father Clement and Father Bernard McCaffrey who had recently come on from the Gethsemani monastery in Kentucky, and the four brothers, Ambrose, Joseph, Timothy and Barnaby. They were the nucleus of the great hoped-for abbey of the future, and they were compelled for the time-being to lead a life of rough and pioneer hardihood. The new superior was foremost in every humiliating employment and imparted a new stimulus to the minds and wills of his brethren. They all suffered somewhat from the burning heat of a summer sun with which they had hitherto been unacquainted.

Brothers Joseph and Timothy were actively engaged in building the new frame monastery; Brothers Ambrose and Barnaby were indefatigable in their labors in the fields; and the three priests when they were not helping either on the structure or with the farm work, were honorably employed as cooks in the kitchen. They received food and generous help from St. Joseph's convent nearby; lacking an oven, their bread was baked for them by the Sisters of Charity during that year of 1849 as well as during the greater part of the next two years. *Quam dilecta tabernacula tua, Domine virtutum.*

VIII

TRAPPIST TRAGEDY AND TRIUMPH ON THE MISSISSIPPI

.   .   .   .

I n the early fall of 1849 the two principal founders of the Iowa Cistercian monastery left Dubuque for Europe. The Irish abbot went to France; the French bishop went to Ireland.

Dom Bruno had not until now been able to attend the General Chapter of the Congregation of La Trappe, and on arriving in France he hastened to spend nearly a fortnight at the Abbaye Maison Dieu of Notre Dame de la Grande Trappe. The General Chapter, it should be explained, is a legislative and judicial body made up of the abbots and other titular superiors of the entire Cistercian Order. When called upon at the sessions to address the Chapter Abbot Bruno informed it of "the settlement he had just founded in the State of Iowa (United States)." So reads the report of the sessions of 1849. "He has already installed there six religious; thirty-four others are only waiting his return [to Mount Melleray] in order to go to complete the community. The General Chapter gives its approbation to it. This will be the monastery of Our Lady of La Trappe of New Melleray."

Bishop Loras arrived in Ireland while Dom Bruno was still in France. He visited Mount Melleray Abbey on October 7th and re-

mained there for part of a day. He was led by the prior to the
chapter room where he spoke piously and feelingly to the community and gave it his blessing. Learning that sixteen monks had
departed for the Dubuque foundation some three weeks earlier he
left the abbey highly pleased, and proceeded to the College of May-
nooth in search of priests for his missions and then went on to Dublin. It was while he was visiting here that he had the good fortune
to encounter Dom Bruno who had just returned from La Grande
Trappe. The abbot was proud to take him about and introduce
him to the dignitaries. He had seen this polished and suave missionary bishop on Mississippi steamboats and in Iowa ox-carts. Of
this visit in Ireland he wrote enthusiastically a few weeks later: "I
had the truly great pleasure of meeting Doctor Loras at dinner in
Dublin. We had Dean Meyler to meet him, all who saw him, Seculars as well as Regulars, were delighted with him; his manners were
admired more even than those of Dr. Murray, the Archbishop, of
whom Queen Victoria said that he was the most elegant courtier
she had met with."

On reaching England on his way to France, Loras wrote a remarkable letter which was published in the *London Tablet* and in
which he described the scenes of starvation and suffering he had
witnessed in Ireland. Roused to profound indignation at the sight
of the princely dwellings and parks of the rich English landlords
amidst the miserable poverty of the helpless Catholic tenants, he
severely pilloried the English government: "One is at a loss to
understand how this state of things can be tolerated in this age of
light and philanthropy . . . One could hardly believe that Ireland
and England were both under the same laws and protected by the
same government; and more than that, the poor Irish are either incarcerated or transported whenever they attempt to better their
miserable condition."

It was to help his impoverished monks to escape from such conditions that Abbot Bruno was now sending them to America. Knowing that when the sixteen monks who had departed before his return
would reach Dubuque there would be difficulties to face, he immediately sent a bank order on London for one hundred and fifty
pounds to Father James, the superior at New Melleray, and a month
later he sent one hundred more. In late November he wrote to
Father Terence Donaghoe at Dubuque: "I love New Melleray as
much as Mount Melleray. Cheer up the Brothers, dear Father, in

case they require to be encouraged, though I hope and believe that they know too well the History of the Cistercian Foundation to need any comfort from creatures . . . If necessary, I will mount an ass, and beg through the world, like St. Stephen of Citeaux, rather than leave my debts unpaid.

"I expect to have fifty Brothers in New Melleray before the first of April. I fear nothing, for we have God with us."

It was well that he feared nothing; but when the news of the disaster now to be described reached Mount Melleray it flung him and the entire community into the deepest mourning.

Prior Francis Walsh after receiving the abbot's letter written on August 18th in Dubuque instructing him to send the three choir and eleven lay brothers immediately to America, added two more lay brothers to those named by Dom Bruno, and on September 10th, two days after the receipt of the letter, these sixteen left for Liverpool. They were accompanied by a priest, Father Patrick Mohan, who had labored for twenty years in the diocesan clergy, and at the age of forty-six — four years previous to this time — had received the habit of a Trappist monk. With him were the two choir brothers, Brothers Benedict, a doctor of medicine, and son of John McNevin, an officer of the Royal Navy, and Brother Mary Bernard Murphy. The lay brothers were: Victor, Patrick, Ignatius, Michael, Peter II, Stephen, Francis, Mark, Kieran, Athanasius, Philip Neri, Edmund and John Evangelist. Among these brothers almost every trade had a representative. Most of the monks were in their twenties and thirties and were strong and hardy men; the oldest one by far was Brother Victor, who had been born in 1777, entered Melleray Abbey in France when he was forty-five, and was now in his seventy-third year.

At Liverpool the group waited a week in order to secure passage on a sailing vessel for New Orleans, which was much cheaper than by steamer, and because from New Orleans they could more easily transport all their luggage by boat up the Mississippi to Dubuque. At last they found such sailing passage on the *Carnatic*, and as Brother Kieran pointedly put it in his account, "Father Francis paying our passage fare just two pounds five shillings per head for 16 steerage passengers, it was in all 36 pounds, or what Fr. Clement and Br. Ambrose paid for their fare on a steamer."

Father Francis, the prior, bade them farewell on the 18th of September, and exactly seven weeks later on November 6th the two hundred and seventy-six passengers, most of whom were Irish folk, were landed in New Orleans. The very next day they were transferred to a four hundred foot steamboat, among whose three hundred odd passengers the Irish brothers found Germans, English and Americans. The steamboat, the *Constitution* under Captain George Washington Cable, started north immediately for St. Louis, twelve hundred miles distant. "The scenery on both sides of the Father of Waters as the Mississippi is called," wrote Brother Kieran, "was grand in the extreme, the beautiful villas, the sugar plantations and refining houses with the poor slaves as busy as bees packing the sugar casks, but above all the orchards of oranges with their yellow fruits waving in the odoriferous tropical breezes of Southern Louisiana. We were shown the residence of Zachary Taylor who was then President of the United States."

The ocean sailing vessel, before it had reached New Orleans, had run short of food, and what provisions had then been served to the steerage passengers were so tainted and decayed that the brothers were in a weakened condition when they boarded the "Constitution." This steamboat had carried cholera patients previously that year and there was little doubt later but that infection was in that ship. There was delay in arriving on the steamboat, the berths were already filled, and the monks were placed in an open part of the vessel with nothing to protect them from the sudden transition from the heat of the day to the intense cold of the nights along that part of the Mississippi in November.

A little over two days after leaving New Orleans, the boat stopped for a while at Vicksburg, Mississippi, and Brother John Evangelist and two other brothers bought bread in the city. Shortly after their return to the *Constitution* Brother John Evangelist was seized with the cholera, and after a vehement struggle, died the next morning. His was the first death of a long list of passengers who succumbed on this voyage. He was buried that evening at Walnut Point, Warren County, in the state of Mississippi. Two of the brothers who helped to bury him were the next victims, dying the next day, Sunday, the 11th of November — Brother Patrick and Brother Stephen. They were buried in the same grave at Miller's Woodyard in Bolivar County, Mississippi, and with them was placed the body of a little Catholic child from Coblentz, Germany.

Father Patrick prepared these brothers and the others who were to follow them in their journey into Eternity by hearing their confessions and shriving them, but none could be anointed as he had no holy oils. He had them buried in their Trappist habits and a cross set up at each of their graves. Meanwhile panic had broken out on the crowded steamboat. Father Patrick and his monks worked heroically among the stricken passengers. Captain Cable, observing the disease ravaging the brothers and remarking their valiant service among the other sick on board, manifested a special interest in them and sought as best he could to ameliorate their condition.

Brother Edmund was the next to pass away, dying on Monday, and was buried that evening at Ash Grove, Obion County, Tennessee, north of Memphis. While the monks were reading the litany for the dying, there was one brother — so writes Brother Kieran who witnessed all the tragedies — "who will not be named — well, the boat though 400 feet in length was hardly long enough for him to keep away from his dying companions. Yet it is a matter of thanksgiving that cowardice in this crisis was exceptional."

Brother Ignatius died the next morning, on Tuesday, and was buried at Donaldsville, New Madrid County, in the state of Missouri. Near him were buried a negro and a white Protestant woman. The last of the cholera victims was old Brother Victor. Being aware of the death of the other five brothers he was heard to utter a little before he died: "Oh my, oh my, will any of us live to reach Dubuque?" He passed away on the evening of the 13th after the longest struggle of all and was buried a few miles below Cape Girardeau in Missouri.

On reaching St. Louis three letters were immediately despatched to Mount Melleray recounting the consternation of the horror-stricken remnants of the lonely little colony of monks in a strange land over the disaster that had befallen them. All of them spoke of the extraordinary solicitude of Captain George Washington Cable toward them. The edifying manner in which the brothers ended their career and the charity which the surviving brothers had manifested toward them had so impressed this veteran Mississippi steamboat captain that he confided to Father Patrick before leaving him at St. Louis his determination to embrace the Catholic Faith. Mention here must be made of the valiant work of Father Patrick. In his letter to Mount Melleray he had cited Brother Mary Bernard for his fearless ministrations to the sick and dying, and this brother, gratified by the commandation, wrote to Abbot Bruno: "Father Patrick has particularized me and others in his letter, and I think it only

my duty to do so to him but words fail me. I cannot tell you with
what humility, courage and charity that good old man has conducted himself not only on this trying occasion, but since we left
home. May God bless him and have mercy on us."

The monks had passed the spot where just four hundred years
before the first Christian explorer of the valley had also been buried
in the Mississippi and from the days of De Soto to their own there
had been numerous martyrs of charity and martyrs of blood for
Christ along the mighty river. But just the year before a much
larger group of Cistercians, forty-three in number, mostly French
with a few Spaniards, coming from Melleray on their way to the
Ohio river and what was to be Gethsemani, had followed the identical
passage from New Orleans without a death, without an illness, without a single untoward occurrence. As for the Irish Trappists, however, it seemed as though the hand of a tragic destiny was continuing to shape the course of their history.

It was a cold and murky day, the 14th of December, when the
sad news of the catastrophe reached Mount Melleray, and a mantle
of melancholy settled over all the Cappoquin countryside as the bell
in the abbey tower tolled out the terrible message. Each mournful,
musical chime was a throb of anguish in the soul of Dom Bruno,
as he lamented the plight of his dear sons and his cherished foundation in America. "What can I say," he wrote a little later, "but Blessed
forever be the Name of the Lord! Alas for the Dead, the early
Dead, the untimely Dead, — alas, alas for the living — but I should
not write this for the Dead are safe and the living are resigned.
May the Holy Will of God be blessed and praised forever." A
high mass was sung for each of the deceased brothers, every priest
of the community offered up three masses for each unfortunate monk,
and all the lay members assembled to recite the usual prayers for
the dead as if they had passed away at the abbey itself.

Back in America, especially in the West, the newspapers carried
the accounts of the tragedy, and the somewhat matter-of-fact description of it as the account appeared in the *Missouri Republican*
of St. Louis on November 16, 1849, bears quoting:

> The Cholera. — The steamer *Constitution*, Captain Cable,
> arrived at this port yesterday morning, about 5 o'clock, from
> New Orleans. She left that port on the 7th, having on board
> about 300 emigrant passengers, fresh from the holds of filthy
> ships, and with all the seeds of disease about them. They

were composed of Irish, German, and English people; and as is usually the case, there was no appearance of disease until the boat had left Vicksburg. Between that time and her reaching this port, there were about thirty cases of sickness, and seventeen deaths, including three children. Of this number about a dozen died of cholera, or of cholera in a modified form, the patient surviving the attack two or three days.

Among the passengers were sixteen Monks, from Milrey Monastery, county of Waterford, Ireland. They were destined for Dubuque, or some point in that vicinity. Of this number, six died on the *Constitution*. The clerk had a register of all their names, but he was unable to distinguish the living from the dead, and did not furnish us with a list of the names.

At St. Louis less than sixty passengers of all those taken on board at New Orleans were brought into port, as the others had fled in crowds from the plague at each stop. At St. Louis there was a delay of three days for the monks as the north-bound boats feared being caught in the ice on the upper Mississippi. At last one old stern-wheeler was found willing to run the risk, and Brother Mary Bernard, the housekeeper, paid the agent seventy dollars as cabin passage fare for the ten Trappists who had escaped from the cholera. Eight days later, exactly eleven weeks after leaving Mount Melleray, the little group landed in the Dubuque harbor at night, and were met by Brother Ambrose who through long days had faithfully awaited their arrival. He was shocked and astounded at the terrible news of their losses on the river, and explained that neither the superior, Father James Myles O'Gorman, nor any of the brothers had heard a word of the disaster since no mail had arrived ahead of the steamboat. He led them to the City Hotel for their first night in Iowa, and there they were welcomed by Mr. Dennis Mahoney, a prominent man of his day who later became a leading Iowa legislator and newspaper editor. Their firm friend during many years, he became an object of their solicitude, when during his stormy career he was imprisoned by order of President Lincoln because of his Southern sympathies in the Civil War.

The country about Dubuque with its hills and prairies covered with snow seemed rugged and desolate to the new arrivals. The next day two yoke of oxen hauled their luggage out to the New

Melleray monastery, while Brother Ambrose crowded Father Patrick and all the brothers into a horse-drawn conveyance. In the confusion their bedding and bed-clothes had been left behind, and they spent their first night's lodging in New Melleray in a heap of straw in the new shed where the sheeting kept out the snow and let in the freezing breeze. With their accession the Trappist community now numbered seventeen members, of whom four were priests: Father James, the superior, Father Bernard, Father Clement and Father Patrick; two were choir religious: Brother Benedict, the medical doctor, and Brother Mary Bernard, the housekeeper, or bursar; of the eleven lay brothers, seven were tradesmen — Brothers Joseph and Peter were carpenters, Brother Michael was a tailor, Brother Francis a shoemaker, Brother Athanasius a tailor, Brother Mark a mason, and Brother Philip Neri a blacksmith; the remaining four brothers, Ambrose, Timothy, Barnaby and Kieran, devoted their time to the farm and gardens of the monastery lands. Among the unfortunate brethren lost on the Mississippi had been several of the most skilled artisans in the order. All these seventeen brothers and fathers now composing the gallant little community were diligently employed during the winter and spring as the voice of Cistercian obedience dictated, entirely indifferent whether it was at their ordinary trade or in other labor less agreeable to their wishes. The accommodations in the new frame monastery building were still primitive; the frost had come early; the food was coarse. The kind Sisters of St. Joseph's convent nearby made and mended the brothers' stockings, baked their bread for them and often nursed them during their illnesses in this first, strange winter in Iowa.

Meanwhile in Ireland at Mount Melleray Dom Bruno continued in his determination and preparations of sending a second and larger contingent of his Cistercian brothers to New Melleray at Dubuque. The spirits of the members of his abbey as far as the contemplated voyage to America was concerned were by no means depressed by the tragedies of the previous November. A letter from Father James that reached them about the beginning of the year of 1850 had encouraged them: "I hope that the afflicting news will not damp the courage of those destined for this country. I would tomorrow take the same route (indeed there is no other at present by which luggage can be conveniently brought) but I would be more particular as to the character of the vessel and as to the berths I secured."

Prior Francis Walsh had, it will be recalled, been previously chosen to be the superior of the New Melleray institution, and selected to go with him were the four choir religious, Brothers Jules, Francis, John Baptist and Liguorio; the lay brothers, thirteen in number: Edward, Philemon, Peter I, Hilarion, Matthew, Lawrence, Robert, Mary Augustin, Romuald, Clement, Nicholas, and Andrew, and lastly Brother Malachy Rochford from the English house of Mount St. Bernard, who joined the Irish group at Liverpool, England, just before they sailed; the four novices: Gregory, Joseph, Anselm and Vincent; and two postulants, of whose names we have no record. Of these, the majority again were young or middle-aged men. Two of them, Brothers Edward and Philemon, had been members of the French community of Melleray, back in the 1820s; the choir brother, Francis, who was an architect and had helped in the erection of Mount Melleray Abbey, was the oldest of the group — sixty-three years of age. Several were specialists in their trades; Hilarion was a cabinetmaker, Clement was a millwright, while Brother Peter Mannix, also known as Peter I, was a cook. Jules, a choir brother, was a Frenchman, who at thirty was professed at Mount Melleray and was a great benefactor of the community; to the former abbot, Dom Vincent, he had given over two thousand pounds towards the erection of the abbey.[1]

On the day of their departure from Mount Melleray, the 17th of January, 1850, Abbot Bruno assembled these eager Cistercian colonists in the abbey church at the sound of the eight o'clock bells. There, with stole and crozier, he knelt at the foot of the altar and recited with them the litanies of the Blessed Virgin Mary and the prayers for travellers; then ascending to the altar he gave them his solemn benediction. After he had accompanied them on foot to the gates of the abbey lodge, and given them a God-speed as they left for Liverpool, he wrote to Father James, the superior at Dubuque, enclosing a bank order: "I consider a short note with £50 better than a long letter with no money . . . I calculate that the Brothers will have a tedious passage for we have had a dreadful storm here. Such a storm we had not in Ireland since the hurricane in 1839.

[1] Before becoming a Cistercian monk, Brother Jules' name was Henri Maurif. Born in Angers, France, in 1808, he was the son of M. Maurif and Jeanne Olivier, members of the French aristocracy (according to some plausible accounts, of the French nobility). Some of his wealth may also have gone toward the erection of the secular church at New Melleray.

May the Lord preserve our dear Brothers!" At Liverpool the Trappist band waited for a week in order to secure passage on a sailing freighter, the *Amelia,* which was to carry no other passengers but themselves. Dom Bruno had arranged that they should take on board this vessel while it was anchored in the Mersey river plentiful and good food so that there should be no repetition of suffering because of foul provisions. They had their own quarters and Brother Peter was to continue serving the twenty-three of them as their cook. From the start to their final destination their voyage was in strong contrast to that of the brothers in the previous autumn.

They had a splendid crew of sailors on the *Amelia* which was a vessel of only six hundred and thirty tons. Brother Clement, the young millwright, in one of the many letters sent by these brothers and that fortunately are still in existence today, wrote to Abbot Bruno: "There are 17 Seamen, and it is strange they are from 11 different countries and also speaking different languages, viz: Irish, English, Scotch, Polish, Italians, Russians, Portuguese, Germans, Swedes, Danes, Americans. A more moral crew I believe there is not at present on the Atlantic; they are in general a model for us; every attention is paid to our wants, and indeed we assist them in pulling the ropes, so we agree very well; to crown our happiness we are alone, nearly as comfortable as if we were at home." However, for the first two or three weeks of their passage they ran into extremely stormy weather, and the severe pitching of the ship caused the monks a considerable amount of suffering. Brother Hilarion broke his collar bone; Brother Anselm badly sprained his leg; Brother Jules, the Frenchman, was sick for three weeks and several others were sick for rather long spells during the first half of the voyage. A young Scotch sailor, only eighteen years of age, fell overboard one midnight and was drowned; Brother Francis, the elderly achitect, took very ill and never recovered. A droll side-light on their trials is gained from this excerpt from the letter of one of the novices, Brother Gregory: "We continued in this awful state until the day on which the Prior got 2 great falls, but not hurt . . . this was not all, for there was nothing but tumbling and tossing, and when at dinner they and their dinner wd be dashed across the table. The Prior seeing this confusion, said to them, Brethren try to bear your cross as well as you can, for the Lord knows it is a cross, and a great cross to be falling and breaking our bones, I wish we were in Dubuque!"

"Poor Peter, the Cook," as he signed himself, put a somewhat humorous note in his perplexities: "I tell you that I had not ½ an hour sickness since I left Liverpool, yet I had to drink deep of that bitter cup of which Adam's Children, each in his turn partake more or less . . . I will tell you, the Amelia was not advertised for passengers, hence, the place fitted up for cooking our food, reminded me of Fr. Augustin's turf box. It was about 6 feet in height, 5 feet long, by 3½ broad, in this box I had to work 9 long weeks without one day's respite. The cooking utensils made the matter worse, a ½ stone pot, a kettle, pan and saucepan; neither of these would fit well on the miserable grate. When the ship wd heave all was tossed up and down, and I had to follow them in all directions to pick them up, and at my return the kettle etc were upset, the fire nearly out, and the poor brothers, waiting for something to eat, and my face black from the smoke. Many of the brothers said that I could not nor wd not stand it, but thanks to God and to the glorious Queen of Heaven I did stand it, even to the surprise of the hardy tars."

Only one member of the group, the novice Brother Joseph, failed to show the resoluteness and patience which distinguished all the other Trappist monks. Unwilling and disobedient, he finally threw all docility to the winds and openly defied Prior Francis on several occasions and spoke abusively to many of the brethren. When the prior was finally compelled to inform him that he could never profess him, he replied that he intended to depart as soon as he reached New Orleans.

Meanwhile the illness of Brother Francis became worse and developed into acute pleurisy. When it became apparent that he was to die, even the sailors joined in with the brothers in their prayers. Prior Francis imparted to him the last rites, and at four o'clock on the afternoon of Ash Wednesday he expired as the community was reciting the litanies. Captain Jordan and the crew were all sympathy and kindness, and arranged to have the monks to hold their wake during the night. In the morning the captain ordered the sails to be hauled up so that the ship rested quietly on the slightly swelling sea. While the members of the crew stood uncovered, the short service was enacted on the open deck at half after eight. The monks chanted the *Miserere* and Father Francis, reciting what he could of the Trappist funeral ritual, crossed the hands of the lifeless monastic architect on his breast, those hands which had helped so cleverly to draw the plans and so faithfully to lay the stones of stately Mount Melleray abbey. The corpse was sprinkled with holy water and then as the musical groanings of the gently moving ship and the winds and the wash of the sea blended into a Requiem symphony, the procession of the brethren escorted the weighted body to the rail where the sailors allowed Brother Francis' remains to slide silently into the waters of the mid-Atlantic.

The weather and the climate had been changing and from here on the conditions of the voyage were ideal. As it grew hotter the brethren spent most of their time, even during their prayers and religious exercises, on deck; every morning at four they bathed in a barrel-tub placed in front of their quarters. They saw porpoises and flying fish and whales. When favorable winds shot their splashing vessel through the lovely Carribean they watched interestedly as flocks of birds from distant verdant tropical shores flew far out over the waters, and with joyful spirits they approached the Mississippi delta below New Orleans.

They passed the bar in a dead calm and had proceeded with the help of a tug some twenty miles up the river when a fierce hurricane of rain and wind suddenly broke upon them, a storm forcibly described by Prior Francis: "The sun was going down when a squall rushed upon us, like hell opened, pitching the ship on beam ends. The Captain screamed to the Pilot to save the sails by lowering them as the storm was sweeping them away like cobwebs; the Pilot shouted: 'To hell with your sails, but save the ship. To sea! To sea! up with your helm, and keep her to the wind.' Oh, how we prayed — how we trembled, how we repented, and flew to Mary, and not in vain: We are safe." Back out in the gulf they waited until the storm had declined. How harrowing and terrific this last storm must have been is further emphasized by this excerpt from Brother Clement's letter: "Oh, it was frightful, the fore top sheet was torn away, the lightning and thunder, the agitation of the sailors with very little cursing for the first time. The Prior assembled us all to prayer, many of us gave the Sailors great assistance and we were wet to the skin. O to see the waves rolling! when prayers were finished, there was an abatement visible . . . A steamer towed us back in. There are 105 miles from the bar to N. Orleans. Palm Sunday. We are on the great river, O what a splendid sight! the plantations, the niggers out of their huts: 4 o'clock this morning, we are 60 miles from N. Orleans, we expect to be in today!"

Arrived safely in the bustling southern city on Palm Sunday, March 24, the monks attended the mass that was celebrated by Prior Francis in the newly erected St. Theresa's Church and all of them received Holy Communion. The convent of the Sisters of Charity and the large orphanage conducted by them were connected with the church and through these the brothers were led on a hospitable tour of inspection. After the mass it was Prior Francis' sad duty to dismiss the obstreperous novice, Brother Joseph. The latter, now quite contrite over his rash behavior, begged the pardon of the brothers whom he had offended and remained some time with them assisting them with their heavy baggage; then bidding them farewell he left with the announced intention of becoming a sailor.

It was here at St. Theresa's church that the Cistercian group visited with one of the most distinguished world figures of their day — Father Theobald Mathew. This noble Irish gentleman of international fame, universally known as the Apostle of Temperance, had reached New Orleans only a few days ahead of the Trappists and was now engaged in giving the pledge of total abstinence to some 16,000 persons in the city. He was still on what amounted to a triumphal tour of the United States, and only three months before had received in Washington one of the greatest honors that the American republic could bestow. In our present day the nation still resounds with the acclaim given by the United States congress to that illustrious national hero and pro-consul, General Douglas MacArthur, after his return from Japan and Korea in 1951. The accolade tendered to Father Mathew, the humble foreign friar, was of the same glorious measure, and only once before in American history had a similar honor been given and that was to the Marquis de Lafayette, the friend of George Washington, who had brought his name and his sword to the cause of American freedom. A short three months before this visit with the Dubuque Trappists, the immortal Henry Clay rising up in the hall of congress spoke of this honor to the Irish Capuchin as "but a merited tribute of respect to a man who has achieved a great social revolution — a revolution in which no blood has been shed; a revolution which has involved no desolation, which has caused no bitter tears of widows and orphans to flow; a revolution which has been achieved without violence, and a greater one, perhaps, than has ever been accomplished by any benefactor of mankind." And on the same occasion, that distinguished statesman, Lewis Cass, paid him this eloquent tribute:

"You grant a seat here to the successful warrior returning from the conquest of war" — referring to Lafayette, and prophetically also to the redoubtable Douglas MacArthur today; "let us not refuse it to a better warrior — to one who comes from the conquests of peace, from victories achieved without the loss of blood or life, and whose trophies are equally dear to the patriot and the Christian."

This was the priest who wrung the hands of his Cistercian countrymen, and inquired after his dear friend, Abbot Bruno, and asked to be remembered to him; he knew of Dubuque and Bishop Loras, who had written him and begged to have him lecture in Iowa on the cause of temperance which was also sacred to the heart of the immigrant French bishop.[2] Realizing the close circumstances in which the brothers found themselves at the moment he pressed a loan upon them which according to Father Francis amounted to fifty pounds.

A slightly distorted version of this meeting as well as of the amount of the loan appears in *Father Mathew: A Biography* from the pen of John Francis Maguire, a member of the British parliament, and published in 1864:

> While on his visit to New Orleans, a number of the brethren of a religious order in Ireland landed in that city. They were on their way to one of the Western States, there to establish a convent and a colony. The money necessary for their purpose was to have been remitted to them in New Orleans; but days passed, and no remittance arrived. The poor men were in great distress of mind, being naturally alarmed at their helpless condition, when they fortunately thought of applying to Father Mathew for advice and assistance. The assistance was readily granted by one who could feel for their position of embarrassment; and in a day or two after, the brothers were on their journey up the Mississippi, with a sum of more than 200£ in their possession, advanced to them by Father Mathew. The

---

[2] Louis de Cailly, the grand-nephew of Bishop Loras, wrote in his *Memoirs of Bishop Loras and of Members of his Family*: "I cannot remember whether Father Mathew, in his visit to the West, lectured in Dubuque; but it was in 1849 that he stopped at several river towns on the Mississippi . . .

"This was after Father Mathew's royal and triumphant reception in New York, in Faneuil Hall, Boston, and Philadelphia. He was given a grand dinner by President Zachary Taylor, and honored with a seat in the House of Representatives and in the Senate, all wishing to pay homage to him who had been the means, under divine guidance, of reclaiming six millions of fellow-men from the demon of drink."

money was faithfully returned, but not sooner than a year
after.

The account book of New Melleray, however, clearly shows that
the loan was repaid only a little more than four months later, namely on August 6th, 1850, and the amount which Prior Francis had
received from Father Mathew is distinctly stated as "$250.00" or
fifty pounds.

After three days in New Orleans, during which not only the
brothers' luggage but also those provisions that still remained fresh
were removed from the ocean sailing vessel, the *Amelia,* to the
handsome Mississippi steamboat, the *Sultana,* the Trappists started
on their voyage to St. Louis and this time as cabin passengers. The
passage was described by Brother Peter as "a first rate run up the
river Mississippi." And what was the surprise and universal happiness of the brothers when they learned that the owner and captain of the splendid *Sultana* was none other than Captain George
Washington Cable of whose profound kindness to the unfortunate
monks on the cholera-stricken *Constitution* they had all heard!
Again did the captain assume the role of brotherly adviser; he looked
after the comfort of everyone; he related in detail to them the story
of the tragic trip; he called attention to the steamer *Consitution*
itself when they passed it, now laden with cattle; he pointed out
for them the spots where the brothers were buried. On Good Fri-
day they passed the general locality of the grave of the first monk
who had died, Brother John Evangelist, but no cross could be seen
and nothing could be identified. And so it was with the other graves;
the river had overflowed its banks and washed away the crosses
and all distinguishable marks. Only the cross above the grave of
Brother Edmund which was passed on Easter Sunday morning could
still be seen. In the ensuing years since 1850 the mighty stream
has completed its task of absolute obliteration. The bed of the
Mississippi has in some places along its southern passage shifted
entirely. Even the geographical names of some of the spots where
the Trappist brothers were interred have vanished from human
memory as well as records. A search during recent years carried on
most accommodatingly by army engineers and Mississippi river pilots
at the request of the monks of New Melleray Abbey has proved
all but fruitless "'gainst the tooth of time and razure of oblivion."

At St. Louis, after Prior Francis had been hospitably received by
Archbishop Peter Richard Kenrick and his clergy, he and his gal-

lant band made the final lap of their voyage to Dubuque as cabin
passengers on the *Excelsior,* arriving at their destination of New Melleray monastery on April 12th, 1850. At their departure from him
in St. Louis Captain Cable had sent his warm and affectionate compliments to all the Trappists at the monastery, and when these gentlemen learned of his second meeting with the brothers conjecture
was rife on the subject of his conversion, which step he had told
Father Patrick the previous November he was seriously contemplat-
ing after witnessing the heroic and edifying death of the monks.
Father Terence Donaghoe, the Sisters' chaplain, claimed that he had
been informed that Captain Cable was baptized.

This rumor, however, was unfounded at the time, and so the
matter rested in doubt for a century. A few years ago a search was
made of the baptismal registers of various churches in the cities
along the Mississippi. At long last the record was uncovered: in
St. Francis Xavier Church in St. Louis on September 30th, 1855,
Captain George Washington Cable received conditional baptism as
a "Convert from Methodist Sect" from the hands of the celebrated
Dutch Jesuit, Father Arnold Damen, one of the most successful con-
vert-makers of America and after whom today Damen avenue in
Chicago is named.

IX

THE RULE OF PRIOR FRANCIS

. . . .

When the colony of Cistercians walked down the gangplank from the steamboat *Excelsior* at nine in the morning of April 12th, 1850, it found that the inhabitants of both New Melleray monastery and the city of Dubuque had been apprised of their coming arrival. A large concourse of people, most of them Catholics, had come down to the harbor to welcome the monks, and among them were Brother Ambrose with the horses and carriage of the monastery, and Brother Barnaby and a neighboring farmer, Tom Casey, with their yokes of oxen and wagons for the luggage. On pulling in to the monastery grounds, there was an enthusiastic and affectionate reception, touchingly described by Brother Hillarion in his letter to the abbot: "Blessed be God, we are all well, yes my dear Rev. Father, we all arrived strong and healthy, and we found our dear Brethren equally in good health, exulting with joy and aroused from a state of fearful apprehension for us; uncertain and even doubtful of our being alive. They all ran out to meet us: and we flung ourselves mutually into each others arms . . . The Sisters of the Ten Commandments [sic!] [1] are very kind, their goodness to us

[1] He meant, of course, the Sisters of Charity of the B.V.M.

is astonishing, you would scarcely believe me were I to tell you, but God will reward them." The new prior, with charitable indulgence, granted a general permission for mutual conversation for two or three days on the news of home, on the subject of absent friends and departed brethren, and on their joys and fears and hopes; and then the Trappist lips were sealed again to be opened only by obedience or duty or unavoidable necessity.

The superior, Father James Myles O'Gorman, now relinquished the reins of monastic government to this new prior, Father Francis Walsh, and in the capacity of subprior, served as his lieutenant. Improvements and expansion were soon under way; Brother Joseph, the carpenter, supervised the enlargement of the house by putting in a basement-refectory its full length and breadth; while Brother Mark built a new kitchen and bake-house, underground, near the refectory. Oxen and cows had already been bought and new ones were added. One of the brothers developed his skill with bees and their honey. Horses and wagons were purchased, and also tools and farm implements. The old account books reveal hundreds of interesting entries: an alarm clock — expensive little machines in those days — was bought for eight dollars; two dollars were paid "To a boy who travelled 18 miles bringing home our strayed oxen." The "Dutch" and the "Yankee" neighbors as well as the Irish were hired on frequent occasions to help the brothers break the prairie lands and plow up the soil. Expenses were many and expenses were heavy.

And then Prior Francis and the community began to encounter their calamities,—difficulties indeed severe enough to be called calamities and only slightly short of being disasters. In the year of 1850 no less than fifty acres of fall wheat were entirely destroyed by severe frosts; the potato crop was a partial failure as the blight appeared on the fifth of August and destroyed all future vegetation in a crop which had earlier been most luxuriant and promising. Hopefully the monks entered the year of 1851 but again the fall wheat was extremely bad after the spring wheat had only been fair; the potato crop was a complete failure as the blight appeared about the third of July, even before some of the plants were in blossom. The failure of the crops for two successive years, together with large expenses inseparable from all new establishments, involved the community deeply in debt.

Dom Bruno, ever solicitous for the new American affiliate, had hitherto strained his resources to the limit to give it financial aid, but now found himself with internal difficulties at Mount Melleray Abbey as well as with demands for help from other directions, and was unable to come to the immediate rescue. Prior Francis borrowed heavily from Father Donaghoe, and not so heavily from other clerical friends such as Father Cretin. The debts becoming more menacingly burdensome he sold one hundred and twenty acres of the foundation's valuable land and thus reduced considerably the weight of the obligations.

Bishop Loras, whose wide missionary diocese was constantly draining the personal fortune he had inherited in France, thought he had a solution for New Melleray's difficulties. In the hope of securing permission to use the Cistercian priests as missionary pastors for some of his scattered congregations, and thereby also helping them to secure parish incomes for their needy monastery, he petitioned the General Chapter of the Congregation of La Trappe in 1850 for this favor. However, the capitular Fathers all answered negatively. They could not well do otherwise without violating their constitution which makes the Trappists cenobites, — that is, contemplative monks of the strict order, — and not missionaries. Nevertheless, the General Chapter authorized preaching in the interior of the monastery to the strangers who might visit there, and this decision, the Chapter pointed out, applied to both American houses, New Melleray and Gethsemani.

Still other difficulties constantly embarrassed the charitable but easygoing Prior Francis. The novices he had brought from Ireland refused to remain at New Melleray. They pretended to be scandalized by an alleged spirit of laxity; one of them was horrified because on the voyage from Liverpool to New Orleans the prior had occasionally permitted the brethren to be served with porter and even with cognac; they could save their souls more certainly by separating from the monastic life. So they were permitted to depart whither they would, and one of them, Brother Gregory, a tailor, remained in the city of Dubuque where he edified everyone by his business thrift as well as by the moral and pious demeanor of his life. As the distressing months rolled on, three of the lay brothers also shook the dust of the Iowa foundation from their feet, one of them drifting back to Mount Melleray in Ireland. Another one of these three, Brother Matthew, went to Gethsemani Abbey in Kentucky, but after a short while, displeased by the French customs and French language of that house, he returned to the Dubuque institution and when he was refused readmission he continued to live and work in the vicinity, apparently loving the monastic atmosphere even though he could not participate in the monastic life.

In the succeeding years of the history of the Iowa Trappists, there were to be other members departing from the order, something to be anticipated in the ordinary course of human events. Very recently a book has appeared, "I Leap Over the (Convent) Wall," in which the niece of the Honorable Stanley Baldwin, who a decade or two ago was the prime minister of Great Britain, describes why she left the convent; and this gentle English lady continues today to be a devout and sincere member of the Catholic Church. Cistercians, for good reasons, just as members of other orders, may have their vows annulled or abrogated, and return to a life in the world, particularly if thereby they can find a surer path to eternal salvation. But these defections at this time in the struggling existence of the New Melleray foundation proved naturally to be hard blows to the heroically striving community.

The very life and existence of the New Melleray priory for the almost three years' rule of Father Francis became nothing else but a struggle for survival. The labors of the field now seemed to engage all the energies and most of the time both of the superior and the community. In the harvest season the brothers generally returned from the field, after the burning heat and fatigue of the day, at eight o'clock. After a meager supper — bread with a mixture of milk and water — and after the recitation of compline and the rosary they retired to rest about nine o'clock and arose in the morning at half after three or sometimes four. No wonder that from the excessive fatigue of the body the poor soul itself became prostrate. Spiritual reading was omitted, meditation sometimes neglected, and silence often violated. In short, severe manual labor was substituted for duties of a higher order and more sacred character, and naturally in such a state of confused elements there was little room for peace or order or regularity. Yet, though suffering much in mind and body, these heroic, pioneer Iowa Trappists clung with a dying grasp to the wreck of religious discipline.

It was to be expected, of course, that in the commencement of every religious establishment there would be confusions and difficulties, and at New Melleray particularly, during these trying years where the brethren had to place all their hopes of subsistence, next to God, in the labor of their own hands, there were certainly many justifying circumstances to prevent the strict observance of every regular exercise, at least for a time. They had in this new and strange western world no wealthy patrons to minister to their wants, no incomes, no revenues, no hopes in a charitable appeal to the skeptical American public of the 1850's. This public, this melange of native and foreign elements, and even a considerable part of the Catholic segment of this public, was not as yet sufficiently spiritualized to see the utility of religious institutions devoted to the silence and solitude of the cloister nor to appreciate those blessings which pious solitaries obtain for the world by their prayers and their saintly habits of life.

However, in desperation, Prior Francis Walsh decided to take a gamble on public charity. One of his lay brothers, Brother Malachy, who had come from the English abbey of Mount St. Bernard, and had formerly been an able collector of funds, was sent to New England on a vague prospect of securing assistance. But all hopes for success were quickly dashed by a hostile opposition from the Eastern prelates, and especially from Bishop John Bernard Fitzpatrick of Boston who refused to grant him permission to collect in his diocese. Brother Malachy then left for England to reenter Mount St. Bernard's Abbey there.

The rather cold indifference which the otherwise very charitable Prior Francis showed toward menacing misfortunes without or irritating infractions within caused certain members of the community to communicate the particulars of the situation to Dom Bruno of Mount Melleray. The alarmed abbot immediately wrote the Iowa monastery requesting the choir religious to send him privately their opinions and at the same time to declare whom they considered best adapted to promote the interests of their community as superior. These opinions, which constituted the only criterion whereby the abbot could form a fair judgment in a matter of such vital importance, were duly sent with the utmost secrecy but apparently were of such divided counsel that Dom Bruno determined to continue for the time being the priorship of Father Francis.

The latter carried on in his course quite unperturbed by events. America — the Iowa country part of it, at least — was naturally still strange to him and to the members of this new colony. He wrote to a friend in Ireland: "We are yet in a very wilderness. There is hardly a soul to be seen in the whole country but ourselves and an odd wagon moving along towards California as our place lies on the principal route to that attractive land." The neighboring farmers, whether native Americans or immigrants, had settled on the new Iowa land only a few short years before the arrival of the monks. A frank picture emerges from the pithy description of Brother Kieran, the early New Melleray annalist: "Here may be laid aside for a time the Bishop business" (he had been discussing episcopal affairs with piquant raciness) "and say something of our near neighbors when we first settled here. Preference must be given to the few Irish Catholics, then delineate the smart Yankees around here at that period. A few of the Irish Catholics are still living here . . . Mostly all of them were then living in log huts through the timber. Two or three families who kept on prairie in pits or what was known as dug-outs. Not a frame house was to be seen turn what way you may . . . But we had other neighbors, the 'Yankees.' To begin with, the best man of them was Lemuel Lytton who kept the 12 mile house. He was an honorable, honest specimen of a true American. He was also a real friend of ours from the commencement. We had others — a lot of Indiana Hoosiers; a glance at their names will tell what sort of beings they were, poor, as was possible for them to be, a lazy famished gang of wretched creatures with no religion but the 'dollar'; no home but the dug-out and at all times ready to sell out, put themselves and effects into an ox-wagon and so move 'west' . . . And they did sell out, their lands now belong to good Irish Catholics."

Late in the month of October, 1851, Archbishop Purcell of Cincinnati and Bishop O'Connor of Pittsburgh passed through Dubuque on their way to St. Louis. They had previously been in Chicago, and not finding the bishop of that diocese at home they decided, as the archbishop put it "to take a peep at Galena & Dubuque." From this latter city they drove out to the grounds of Mount St. Bernard's Seminary where they found "Monseigneur Loras among the grain stacks — his useful recreation or change of labour, after teaching class to his quartette of theological students or saying his prayers. He has lost the sight of one eye." Just a few miles distant lay the monastery grounds, and Archbishop Purcell remarked in this letter from which we are quoting and which was written two weeks after these events described here from the Mississippi river steamboat, the *Isabel* "nearing Cape Girardeau" to Archbishop Blanc of New Orleans: "Loras' Trappists have to send their Prior out to beg to enable them to live. Their potato-crop failed this season and they are moreover in debt."

It was true as Archbishop Purcell stated that Prior Francis was out begging, and this fact was entirely due to the archbishop's visit to Dubuque. When Prior Francis learned that the two prelates had gone to St. Louis after their visit to Bishop Loras he conceived this as a most favorable opportunity of going to that quite Catholic city and calling on them while they were being received in the home of Archbishop Kenrick of St. Louis, and of requesting all three bishops for permission to solicit funds in their dioceses. Having no money he borrowed fifty dollars from Tom Casey, a neighboring farmer, and left immediately for the South on October 29th, and arrived in St. Louis the early part of November. He waited on the dignitaries at the archbishop's house and laid open to them the object of his visit. After much hesitation the archbishops of St. Louis and Cincinnati gave a very reluctant consent but refused to afford anything like cooperation on their part and held out no encouragement whatsoever as to the friendly dispositions of their people toward an object of charity so unpopular and so circumscribed as this seemed to them to be. The bishop of Pittsburgh had no hesitation in giving a prompt refusal; he could not tolerate an appeal for charity to be made in his diocese where his own churches were generally involved in debt.

Although he realized that these cold and reluctant permissions did not augur well for the success of his humiliating mission, the prior began his painful task of begging in the city of St. Louis. He received only a few dollars given by several Catholic laymen but as most of his applications proved fruitless he decided to give up the quest. He further concluded that as fortune had thus frowned on his search in the Catholic city of St. Louis he would have no success in Cincinnati which apparently was less friendly to a monastic cause, and that he should therefore quietly retreat northwards to his Dubuque house.

He obtained passage on the steamboat *Archer* which left St. Louis on the evening of November 26th, and like all the other passengers he retired to the lower deck for rest as this steamer, used also as a freighter, had no cabins. At about two o'clock in the morning he

was suddenly aroused by a terrific crash, and throwing on his cloak
and seizing his watch and wallet, he rushed about trying to peer
through a dense mass of steam. To his horror he discovered that
his steamboat had been rammed in the darkness by another huge
boat and was rapidly sinking. He either leaped or fell from the
broken railing of the *Archer* to the deck of the strange steamboat
and thus had an almost miraculous escape from death. Nearly all
the other persons on the lower deck — according to some accounts
thirty-four, according to one thirty in number of whom ten were
deck hands or firemen engaged on the boat — perished in the sinking wreckage and the churning waters. Only three were saved by
having tumbled on the deck of the ramming steamboat, a young lad,
a maiden lady and the Trappist prior. The *Galena Daily Advertiser*
of November 29th, 1851, carried the following notice of the catastrophe:

Steamboat Collision!

Steamer Archer Cut in Two — 30 Lives Lost!

St. Louis, Nov. 27.

As the steamer *Archer* was ascending and the *Die Vernon*
was descending the Mississippi, at 2 o'clock this morning
when about 5 miles below the mouth of the Illinois river,
they came into collision. The *Archer* was cut in two and
sank in 15 feet of water. All the passengers on the lower
deck were drowned.

The St. Louis *Intelligencer* of the same date enumerated the names
of those who lost their lives and closed its news story with this
sentence: "The boy Smeyers, Miss Dick and another person were
taken up by the yawl of the *Die Vernon*." This other person was, of
course, Prior Francis and one wonders why his name was ignored
or suppressed; probably it was not known by the reporter who had
no access to the ship's books since they were all lost. The *Die Vernon*
cruised about in the darkness for two hours and unable to find any
other survivors continued its trip southward and took Father Francis
back to St. Louis. When the story reached the New Melleray monastery it was reported that the prior was the only one to be saved
and that he had been injured. This latter part of the statement was
true, for in his leap or fall to the deck of the *Die Vernon* he had
severely hurt his foot. He was cared for by the Sisters of Charity
in St. Louis, and after he had recovered he travelled further south

to St. Mary's Seminary at the Barrens, where he remained during the winter and failed to return to his Dubuque house until the beginning of the following April, 1852.

Fortunately, the patient monks at New Melleray were not without a few friends during this period who stepped forward to extend a hand of financial aid just when it was most needed. There was Bishop Loras, of course, who still from time to time sent out a bank check of fifty or a hundred dollars at most opportune moments. But one person who came on the scene providentially and happily was a recently arrived priest in northern Iowa. Father Thomas Hore, an elderly gentleman, originally from County Wexford, Ireland, had for thirty years labored as a missionary in eastern Virginia. Returning to his native haunts in 1850 he gathered a large number of needy friends and neighbors and brought them with him to America. They landed at New Orleans where most of them remained as they were poor and in search of immediate employment. Others came with him as far as Arkansas and a few as far as St. Louis. About a dozen families accompanied him to northern Iowa where in Allamakee County three miles inland from the Mississippi river he established a settlement naming it Wexford after his birthplace, and built a log church calling it St. George's. He bought "congress land" and helped his settlers establish farms and homes. This was in the early spring of 1851, and hardly had he completed the foundations of his settlement when he appeared at New Melleray. Impressed by the monks and their work, this generous gentleman immediately loaned them five hundred dollars. This was but the first of the favors he was to show them, and as will be seen, as time went on his benevolence to the Trappists increased.

Here an interesting glance may be thrown at the Catholic Directory of 1852 and its chastely prosaic reference to the Dubuque Trappist house. *The Metropolitan Catholic Almanac and Laity's Directory* for both 1851 and 1852, under the heading of the Diocese of Dubuque carried the following:

"An extensive and valuable piece of land, including rich prairies well watered and good timber, with valuable improvements on it, has been generously given by the right reverend Bishop, to a branch of the Cistercian Order, called the Trappists, who came lately from Mount Melleray in Ireland. They have purchased, at Congress price, much of the neighboring land, and they have built a chapel, where many persons come to Mass on Sunday, and a school house where they teach every day. They keep their rules well and give great edification to the people. Their number is forty, including five priests, viz: Very Rev. Francis Walsh, Prior, James O'Gorman, Superior; Bernard McCaffrey, Clement Smyth, Patrick Mohan. The name of the Monastery, which is situated twelve miles from Dubuque, is: Our Lady of the New Melleray."

The notice speaks of a non-monastic chapel, and a school conducted by the monks. The founding of the monastery in 1849 had immediately attracted to the surrounding district a large immigration, notably Irish. For a short time these pioneers attended Mass in the monastery, but soon a small church was built, partly of stone, and from that time on the pious services of the white cowled Cistercian fathers were employed by the farmers for their parish. Relates Brother Kieran, the inimitable annalist: "Father Bernard, Father Francis and Father Patrick attended the secular church alternately. Father James also went to it occasionally being the best preacher of them all, yes, and of all in the Diocese. Yet Father Bernard was considered from the commencement the Parish Priest." The school, of which these same fathers constituted the teaching staff, was conducted in a room which on week-days was partitioned off at one end of the church. It was for boys only. Some of the lads had to walk four or five miles to attend their classes, but in the winters most of them were hauled to school in lumber wagons drawn by oxen. After five or six years when the public district schools were organized, the boys' school was discontinued.

A critical affair, which was eventualizing during these months and years, and which had its origin in Mount Melleray Abbey, led Dom Bruno to realize the lack of firmness and possibly the lack of other necessary qualities, in the character of Prior Francis, and compelled him finally to remove the prior from his office of superior of the Iowa Trappist monastery. As was mentioned previously, internal difficulties at Mount Melleray had prevented the abbot from giving more direct aid and attention to his American affiliate. As the Father Immediate of the Dubuque foundation, it was incumbent upon him to manifest this aid and attention. A "Father Immediate" of a house is the abbot of the monastery that founded it, and he possesses certain supervisory powers over it and usually visits it each year to make certain that the Rule is being observed.

The critical affair of which we speak was probably the most painful experience in the entire abbatial career of Dom Bruno, who, as his life showed, was a brilliant and learned monk of great virtue and commanding intellect. In his community was a choir religious, Father Palladius Cosgrove, who had been among those who suffered for the Faith by being expelled from the French abbey of Melleray in 1831 by the revolutionary government. He was a man of deep piety and marked ability; indeed, he had been prior of Mount Melleray Abbey from 1834 to 1846. Yet, along with his virtues, a severe streak of obstinacy began to manifest itself towards the abbot, ten years his junior, and for fear that others whom he influenced might be made rebellious in their spiritual life, he was permitted to visit the Primate, the Archbishop of Armagh, and lay his complaints before him. Leaving Dublin for America, he proceeded immediately to Iowa to the New Melleray monastery. Prior Francis had previously been instructed not to admit Father Palladius to the Dubuque house, but hesitated and vacillated. The abbot thereupon wrote Bishop Loras in his usual energetic way, asking him to take over in the matter. "I, therefore, pray your Lordship to exercise your authority, and as it is possible that doubts may be raised regarding the extent of your Lordship's jurisdiction, I hereby declare, that it is my will and my positive command that Mr. Cosgrove should not be allowed to enter the Monastery of New Melleray. It may appear strange, that I should presume to convey through your Lordship a command intended exclusively for the Prior of New Melleray; but the fact is, the Prior will not, as far as I can judge, take upon himself the distressing task unless supported by an authority superior to his own."

This letter was received by Bishop Loras while Prior Francis was still sojourning with the Vincentian fathers in southern Missouri after his steamboat accident. Loras took the matter under advisement and decided to follow a prudent course. He learned from Father Palladius, now deeply penitential and humbly amenable to his authority, that it was at the suggestion of the Archbishop of Armagh that he came to the Iowa monastery, and of this matter the bishop duly apprised Abbot Bruno. The continuing correspondence revealed the magnanimous soul of Dom Bruno; he and Loras, as all their letters disclose had a strong affection and high regard for each other, and he finally left the decision entirely in the hands of the bishop of Dubuque. In fact, he had always been willing to allow

Father Palladius to enter Gethsemani Abbey in Kentucky, if he so wished. Apparently, at Bishop Loras' suggestion Father Palladius had written the abbot a sincerely contrite letter of apology. Dom Bruno's last word on the matter was written to the bishop from Mt. St. Bernard's Abbey in England while he was on a tour of visitation there in May of 1852:

"I met the Primate in Dublin. His Grace's words were: Father Cosgrove has done precisely the thing which alone I commanded him not to do; he has gone to New Melleray! . . . Is it the will of God that he should remain at New Melleray? This question is so difficult that I must pray your Lordship to decide it . . . I pray your Lordship to bear in mind, that, in words as plain and strong as words could be, I commanded the Prior to exclude from his Monastery the unfortunate Monks, who had rebelled against my authority . . . If your Lordship decide that Father Palladius should join the Community, I shall not offer any further opposition; but I beg to suggest that he should not be allowed to renew his vows until (later). . . . Kentucky in my opinion is the only proper place for him. Indeed, my wish is, that he should go to Gethsemani at once . . . I consent to his saying Mass in both Monasteries, though I prefer, that he should wait until his arrival at the French House in the event of your Lordship's deciding that he should go there . . . I sincerely regret the necessity I am under of thus tresspassing upon your Lordship's precious time. I hope, that never again shall I be obliged to write upon so painful a subject."

With the decision so magnanimously passed over to him by the abbot, the bishop chose discretion as the better part, and permitted Father Palladius to remain at New Melleray. His judgment was vindicated; Father Palladius became one of the most zealous monks in the monastery and in due time was appointed Father Master of the lay brothers, and died a holy death a few years later — in 1864.

Conditions being what they were, the New Melleray brothers began more and more to turn to Bishop Loras as their counsellor and patron. Dom Bruno was still unable to make a visitation of his American filiate, partly because of lack of funds and time but principally because the Primate of Ireland was unwilling to permit him to absent himself for so long a period from his abbey. So the abbot of Mount Melleray wrote to the abbot of Gethsemani in Kentucky, Dom Mary Eutropius Proust, requesting him to make the visitation of the Dubuque house. Gethsemani, the year before, although its members were still living in log houses, had been elevated to the dignity of an abbey, the first Trappist abbey in the United States. When the news reached New Melleray that Dom Eutropius had refused — for pressing reasons, no doubt, — the monks, at least some of the choir religious and lay brothers, wrote to Bishop Loras privately beseeching him to hold a regular visitation and insisting that his presence was much needed as he himself would clearly perceive on examination. This may not have been strictly according to the Cistercian constitution, but be that as it may, the Right Rev. Dr. Mathias Loras visited the priory in the summer of 1852, assembled the brethren in Chapter, explained the nature and object of his visit and proceeded to hear whatsoever the monks might have to communicate to him. He sometime later reported the results to the abbot of Mount Melleray Abbey and awaited his instructions as to further proceedings.

Dom Bruno up to this point had conscientiously given Prior Francis every kindly consideration possible but now realized that drastic action had to be taken. In a missive written to him from Dubuque on the 22nd of August, he had read again the prior's complaints that "the Brethren are literally in rags, and worse, full of vermin" and "the Brethren are in extreme distress for the want of money." Such letters coupled with the communication sent him by Loras as the result of his visitation grieved and mortified him, and on October 22nd, he wrote to the bishop: "It seems to me that after three years of toil and anxiety, Father Francis should be relieved from the burdens of office . . . If Your Lordship coincide in opinion with me, your own great prudence and charity will suggest the best means to be adopted, so as to spare the feelings of Father Francis. If on the contrary, Your Lordship considers my proposal rash and dangerous, the document can remain in your possession to be used at any further time, according to Your Lordship's discretion."

"The document" of which Dom Bruno spoke and which was enclosed in his letter to Loras was the formal appointment of Father Clement Smyth to be prior of the New Melleray monastery and presupposed the resignation of that office of Father Francis Walsh. The bishop weighed the matter carefully and prayerfully for well over a fortnight and then made his decision. He found Father Francis very willing to lay down his burden which for him had really been a most unhappy one, and he accepted his resignation on December 6th, 1852. On the same day Father Clement accepted his reappointment as prior and thus became the fourth superior in three and a half years of life of the infant Iowa institution. A providential appointment it was, as will soon be seen, for the faltering and wobbling career of New Melleray had brought it to a perilous crisis; now both its spiritual and material foundations were to be speedily and sturdily strengthened, and halcyon days were at last ahead — for a few years at least.

X

TRAPPISTS BECOME AMERICANS BUT NOT ABBOTS

. . . .

T he document appointing Father Smyth as prior differs little from
all such formal records. Its smooth and sonorous Latin phrases seem
to come gently, rolling along through the decades and centuries from
the old turreted cloisters of Citeaux and Clairvaux. It meticulously
enunciates the powers and prerogatives, the censures and penances,
connected with monastic life from the days of St. Bernard down to
modern times with few changes; it appeals to all subjects for obedience
and acknowledgement of legitimate authority. Its perusal gives
one an intelligent insight into the fundamentals of conventual discipline. As it is a document that can well be read with easy effort
and to great advantage even by one who is only slightly interested
in monastic history, this hundred year old scroll is given here in its
English translation:

> Brother Bruno, Abbot of Our Lady of Mount Melleray,
> of the Order of Citeaux, diocese of Waterford and Lismore;
> Father Immediate of the Monastery of New Melleray like-
> wise of the Order of Citeaux, diocese of Dubuque:

To our well-beloved and Christ's venerable priest, Clement Smyth, monk likewise of Mount Melleray, and professed specially therefor, the spirit of counsel and fortitude!

The above named monastery of New Melleray being without a Prior and we having the right to name the superior, since the worthy Father Francis, formerly Prior of that monastery, has resigned, it belongs to our office in zeal for the salvation of souls and for the divine worship's furtherance, when we had consulted the General Chapter as to your merits and your good character, zeal, knowledge and ability to administer affairs (this has come to our knowledge from others too,) we decide that you should be named and installed Prior of the above mentioned monastery (New Melleray), according to the tenor of these presents, by our authority as Father Immediate. This gives you all such power in spirituals and temporals as ought to belong to you, according to the Constitution of our Order, i.e., as to all persons therein, the power to teach, rule, correct, absolve and bind, even by the ecclesiastical censures, customary in our Order to punish those rebellious or stubborn, to appoint or designate a subprior, confessors and all officers, to examine, approve or disapprove all books of accounts, finally, of performing all things which priors in our Order by law and approved custom, usually perform.

So we command each and all persons of the monastery, New Melleray, our subjects and living at present, even by virtue of obedience and salvation, and under the censures of the Order — to acknowledge you true and lawful superior and to respect you as such and obey you even as ourselves, until we order otherwise: to make this worthy of confidence we subscribe these present letters and affix our seal, with the added subscription of our secretary too, today October 22, the year of our salvation 1852.

Brother Bruno,

Abbot, Our Lady of Mount Melleray

By order of my Rev. Lord Abbot,

Brother Placid, Secretary.

Almost from the start God blessed the efforts of Prior Clement as superior of the Iowa foundation, and whatever one may mean by

Fortune smiled indulgently upon him. Through the four and a half years of his benign but careful rule the Trappist house prospered, the fields annually yielded their crops without failure, the herds of cattle and sheep increased. The spiritual life of the institution rose to a high level. The brothers had confidence in Prior Clement and entertained respectful affection for him — such is the influence of some personalities on others.

Father Clement was a vigilant superior especially in the field of the financial affairs of the monastery. He had a horror of being in debt. "He kept a close watch on our housekeeper," remarked Brother Kieran, "which if another Superior who came after him had done, things would be different here today from what they are." Shortly before Prior Clement's reappointment, Brother Ambrose, the agriculturist, was sent to Kingston, Canada, to dispose of some of the properties there which after the death of Brother Macarius were left in the name of the Iowa Trappists. In this business journey of a little over a month, he succeeded in selling the various items — one of them a large church bell — and the sum he brought back with him was applied to the monastery debt. This left still between eleven and twelve hundred dollars in obligations but the entire deficit was wiped out by Father Clement in a little more than a year. The prior was ably assisted in these matters by Father James who continued as subprior of the house.

The courage and mettle of Prior Clement were shown in his spirited reply to Bishop Loras who in one of the earlier Lenten seasons of the prior's tenure had expressed some criticism of the monks for partaking of a full breakfast in Lent: "Theologians agree that Collation may be taken in the morning, justa cum causa. If ever a just cause existed it must be where men have of necessity to endure severe manual labour and cannot partake of one good substantial meal. There is no community in the world that has to undergo such severe labour as ours and has such very wretched food. Our meal or dinner is turnip-water with milk, potatoes and bread. Does the Church of God, that most tender Mother, consider this a good or substantial meal? Do our Rules and Constitutions oblige us to such meagre and unsubstantial food? No. Both our Rules and Constitutions have been dictated by the Spirit of God, which is ever a Spirit of Charity and prudence, equally remote from both extremes, either of ordinary indulgence or too much severity.

"Our Constitutions allow us for meals, besides soup, bread and potatoes, a portion of cheese, rice or beans, beer, cider, or wine as table drink, baked apples, peaches, grapes, etc., as a 'dessert,' and a third portion of legumes. We have not even any one of these. Our portion is poverty in the extreme without any present hopes of relief or remedy. We are observing a rule of life which no legislator ever yet dreamed of framing for a Community of men whose sole and only hopes of subsistence depend on their own individual exertions and on their constant attention to severe manual labor."

And then the monk declared to the bishop: "It would be my greatest wish to conform both to the spirit and letter of Church discipline regarding the hour for dinner and Collation, but when such comes in direct opposition to the Rule of our Order I shall not be the first to introduce such an innovation. I am not one to act according to caprice or fancy. I am determined to walk straight forward and to be guided in all essentials as the General Chapter may decide or the Abbot of Mount Melleray may sanction."

A glimpse of the prior's temper is obtained, when on a later occasion he again addressed Bishop Loras, from his use of Celtic invective: "On yesterday I was pained to learn from a certain layman that some angel of discord, some agent of hell, told you that I blessed clay or earth for the burial of Mrs. Logan. This, beloved Bishop, is as gross and foul a calumny as ever yet emanated from the lips of man. I do most solemnly declare to you, on the word of a Priest and a Religious, that I neither blessed clay for her funeral nor gave permission to any priest to do so. This I trust will be sufficient to refute such vile slander. If you be so kind as to give me the name of that whispering fiend, I shall compel him to go to you and retract his hellish calumny."[1]

---

[1] What this letter referred to may be gleaned from the enlightening paragraph by Brother Kieran in his Annals: "At this period there was no burying ground for seculars at or near our monastery. Bishop Loras desired that all the Catholics who died in this neighborhood should be interred in the Catholic cemetery he established on the hill west of the cathedral in Dubuque. One of our near neighbors, John McLaughlin died. His funeral proceeded on to Father Bernard's little church to bury him near it. They were met by Fr. Clement who told them in a menacing manner that he would not permit the interment on any part of the Monastery lands. There was much excitement. Finally they turned into the prairie where our cattle-yard is now; the land belonged to John Quinn. There they made a grave and buried John McLaughlin, about 150 yards from the church. Mrs. Logan was buried before this near the church. So the Bishop had to yield, and at last consented to a burying place at the monastery. The first body laid to rest in the new burying ground was that of Patrick McCarthy in August 1854."

A singular piece of good fortune for the monks through the striking benevolence of Father Thomas Hore of Wexford, Iowa, came their way in September of 1853. This priest had developed his farm and erected a commodious two-story house about one hundred rods distant from the chapel of St. George which he had erected earlier for his people. He stocked his farm with a herd of cattle and with some horses and sheep of the best breeds in the West. He made overtures to the Dubuque Trappists about its disposal and finally invited Prior Smyth for a visit on the occasion of which he made a present by actual deed of sale of his entire tract to the Cistercian monks of New Melleray. When Father Clement returned to Dubuque by the steamboat *West Newton* and went to the monastery he immediately wrote a happy note to Father Donaghoe at St. Joseph's Convent in which he related: "I secured all at Father Hore's by a new deed signed and stamped with the seal of the Notary for Allamakee County. He was most happy to see me and was more anxious to secure his property for us than I was to have it placed beyond the power of his heirs to recover it after his death. Deo *gratias!* On my return the Bishop expressed his great satisfaction at having the property secured for religion." However, Father Hore continued to remain in possession of his Wexford holdings for the time being, not being quite prepared as yet to retire to Ireland.

The establishment of a Trappist house in what was still regarded as a wilderness west of the Mississippi was no longer merely a news item of interest in Catholic and secular circles by now; it had also aroused hopes in the minds of the struggling bishops of the contiguous new dioceses for securing pastors and missionaries in their vineyards. The first bishop to have these hopes dashed was, as we have seen, Mathias Loras of Dubuque, whose request had been refused by the General Chapter of La Grande Trappe. In 1852 Bishop Martin Henni of Milwaukee arrived one day on the grounds of New Melleray monastery accompanied by that missionary *par excellence* whose dramatic exploits and spiritual conquests among savages and whites in Michigan, Wisconsin, Iowa and Illinois fill one of the most thrilling pages in the missionary annals of all Christian history from St. Paul the Apostle to the latest Chinese martyr, — the Italian Dominican, Samuel Charles Mazzuchelli. But the appeal of the Wisconsin bishop abetted as it was by the arguments of the illustrious missioner proved as fruitless as that of Bishop Loras.

However, the effort of Joseph Cretin, who had now become the first bishop of St. Paul, turned out to be a more lasting and a more stubborn attempt. As *Abbé* Cretin and vicar-general of the Iowa diocese he had done considerable missionary work among the Indians, especially among the Winnebagoes, and with this tribe he had remarkable success. No sooner had Bishop Cretin entered upon the work of his newly constituted diocese than the federal government moved the Winnebagoes *en masse* from Iowa to Minnesota. The bishop immediately began his exertions to secure missionary priests for them as well as for the Sioux and Chippewa tribes. He applied to the Jesuits, to the Oblates of Marseilles in France and to the Marists, but all in vain. When he learned that the government would gladly give him financial aid if he would take over the schools among these tribes he doubled his efforts and directed his attention to the Trappist monks at New Melleray. Not only their friend had he always been but also a sincere admirer of them and their work. He had one missionary, Canon de Vivaldi, among the Winnebagoes already but he also wanted an agricultural school conducted by the Trappists for the Indians, as he considered these monks ideal for such work.

Apparently he had received some affirmative assurances from Father Francis Walsh on this proposal for in September of 1852 he informed Governor Alexander Ramsey of the Minnesota Territory that the Trappists intended to assume the responsibility of a mission and school, and the governor had indicated his satisfaction in the matter. A yearly sum of six thousand dollars was to be paid for conducting the school and for the clothing and daily rations of the Indians. Cretin carried on much correspondence with Washington on the matter of educating the Indians and also wrote to Archbishop Hughes of New York. On January 15, 1853, he wrote to the archbishop's secretary, Father James Roosevelt Bayley, the distinguished convert and nephew of the saintly Mother Seton, who was later to become Archbishop of Baltimore:

> As these Indians wish more to be instructed in the cultivation of their lands than in reading, I intend to establish among them a branch of the Trappists who succeed so well everywhere in founding fine farms. The French Government could not find better teachers of agriculture for the young Arabians of Algiers.

Evidently anticipating the objection made to Bishop Loras on this score by the General Chapter Bishop Cretin asserted:

Some priors and abbots will object that the life of a missionary is incompatible with the life of a Trappist. But I will write to Rome on that subject.

The Cistercian order will acquire a great name among even the Protestants in this country if they can be induced to devote themselves to the conversion and temporal salvation of so many poor beings who otherwise inevitably will starve. They want Missionaries who give them the example of cultivating and farming for these forlorn people. When the Trappists of this country will be known to embrace such a Mission they will find plenty of applicants to join their order. If the Government truly intends to civilize these Indians a little money given to these Religious would do more than forts and soldiers to maintain these Tribes in Peace and live in settled places.

But Cretin, too, was disappointed in his quest of Trappists for missioners, apparently meeting a final refusal from Prior Clement Smyth, and on March 10, 1853, he wrote sadly and rather bitterly to Loras:

The Trappists would have acquired more of a reputation and of glory in their monastery in devoting four or five of their subjects to the savage missions. I still cannot understand the reason of their refusal. I have at last at my disposal since the 1st of January $6500 for this mission on the part of the government. This sum, well managed by the monks, would have been very useful. They would receive more novices. I am going to address the Trappist house of Kentucky. The savages have more need to know how to cultivate the soil than of learning how to read; and the Trappists are the only religious body remarkable for their success and ability in such work. The community in Dubuque, having a branch of their order in this diocese, would easily be able to erect their monastery into an abbey.

The attempt to secure the monks of Gethsemani Abbey referred to above — if such an attempt was made — manifestly failed also. It is strange that the bishops did not understand the true object of cenobitic life, and this fact makes more comprehensible the lack of knowledge on the part of the general public, including Catholics, about the prayerful and contemplative work of those holy solitaries who follow the strict Rule of St. Benedict.

Due to the now prosperous condition of New Melleray Prior Clement was able to buy land not merely equal in extent to what had been sold by Prior Francis but many hundreds of acres more. He also purchased a sand-pit for a term of twenty-one years. "It was Father Clement," boasted Brother Kieran, "that made the farm reach up to be one thousand eight hundred and forty acres of land, or ten and a half miles walk all around it." Yet the prior was quite modest about it all. "Well," he explained to Father Donaghoe to whose St. Joseph's Convent he and Father James were often called to conduct retreats, preach to the nuns and give instructions to the novices and postulants, "thanks to a merciful God, it is really a moral miracle how we have been blessed the last two years."

Bishop Loras in his 1854 report to the Propagation of the Faith Society in Lyons from whom he received much aid for his missionary diocese and to whom at the urging of his friend, Abbot Bruno Fitzpatrick, he made a strong appeal in behalf of New Melleray, painted a glowing picture of the Iowa Trappist foundation:

> May I speak now of our monastery of Cenobites, of our venerable disciples of St. Bernard, of our holy Trappists. In 1848 (sic) I gave them a piece of ground of 450 acres, 40 of which were cultivated, and a small farm. They were at first a little number. I went over to Ireland, visited their primitive monastery and obtained from their Abbé a new colony of these admirable monks. Today they have erected a vast building, bought new lands, which are cultivated by 40 Trappists, 12 of them saying divine office night and day, and 6 of them are priests. This was a strange spectacle for our Protestants; some of them criticized them in an impious manner, but the holiness, the penitence and the spirituality of these good monks shut their mouths, and the Catholics can enjoy in peace the good fortune of possessing among them a living picture of the religious and Christian perfection.

Encouraged by these reports from New Melleray Dom Bruno decided that there was no pressing need for him to make a visitation to his American affiliate at this time. Instead, he required all the choir religious to write to him confidentially, this action supplying the place of a visit. The operations of Prior Clement during the next couple of years continued to show his wisdom and progressiveness, as for instance, his insistence that the various members of the community secure their papers of American citizenship, and his prudent course of obtaining legal incorporation of the institution and its properties. This line of action he also urged on Father Donaghoe in regard to the Sisters and their St. Joseph Convent property. Said Brother Kieran of him succinctly: "He governed well and wisely, be his counselors whom they may."

It was only in growth of numbers of members that the Iowa monastery showed no distinctive success. When Prior Clement left its cloistered halls in 1857 there were forty-seven monks including choir religious, lay brothers and novices. It was true that postulants had entered but postulants had also left. Even some novices lost heart and departed. One year Father Rensen, a Dubuque diocesan priest, was received; three years later in the same month a sub-deacon from the Benedictine Abbey near Pittsburgh and a secular priest, Father Hamilton, the nephew of the bishop of Louisville, sought membership. But there were annual defections: some lost their health, others lost their courage; some were given dispensations and others requested to be sent back home to Ireland's Mount Melleray. Yet the great silent majority remained firm, hearty and happy.

And now must be recounted an episode which really should be referred to as an epic tragi-comedy and should be given the horrendous title of "The Battle of the Bishops versus the Abbot." It was of epic stature indeed for it involved all the archbishops of the United States, and many of the bishops, it had touched on part of France, it hovered about Rome and was finally settled — no, it was not even settled, it was "deferred" — by a commission of grave and wise, old Italian cardinals. The poor, struggling Dubuque priory was the cause of it all and the abbot whose word plunged this great fraction of the world's Catholic hierarchy into the controversy was Dom Bruno Fitzpatrick himself.

It will be recalled that Bishop Cretin of St. Paul had stated that if the Iowa Cistercian community had opened up an affiliate in his Minnesota diocese it would more easily have become an abbey, and it is apparent that he knew of some such movement being contemplated. Among the Trappists, the abbey has the supreme rank among the three kinds of monastic houses — the foundation, the priory and the abbey. When a monastery is granted this honor its members elect as their superior the abbot whose duties and privileges lift him to prominence among Church dignitaries. Naturally Dom Bruno wanted this very laudable distinction for his beloved Iowa affiliate, and having doubtlessly noticed how quickly the Gethsemani Abbey of Kentucky had been erected, he addressed an application for this dignity to the General Chapter of La Grande Trappe. The capitular fathers in one of their later sessions of 1851 granted this petition, stating that Dom Bruno of Ireland "Father Immediate of New Melleray recently founded in America asks permission to write to Rome to ask the erection into an Abbey of his Daughter-House, already sufficiently well established in order to obtain this favor . . . The Chapter permits it."

Sanguine Christian optimist that he was, Abbot Bruno could not believe that the malignant fates which had already apportioned so many bitter shocks and blows to the American colony would continue the series of disappointments; so he hopefully wrote to Dr. D. Bernard Smith, vice-president of the Irish College in Rome, in October of 1851 commissioning him to push the matter along, and Dr. Smith sent back the answer of Cardinal Fransoni, the Prefect of Propaganda, that the consent of Dr. Loras, the local bishop, was required in writing. Dom Bruno then turned to Loras who immediately wrote the Cardinal — on November 30th — urging the erection of the abbey, and seven months later, in August of 1852, having received no answer, he repeated his petition with vehemence.

And here is where the amazing series of events started. The delay in answering Bishop Loras' request was due to the fact that the cardinals were puzzled: they discovered while comparing this request with that of the only other Trappist house in the United States, Gethsemani in Kentucky, that this was now qualified as an abbey and that the superior in the capacity of an abbot had even been admitted to the "Synod" of Baltimore, but that there was nothing in the records of the Sacred Congregation of the Propaganda, granting approval to Gethsemani for the erection of an abbey.[2] Thereupon,

---

[2] This privilege was granted directly by the Holy Father. On July 21, 1850, Father Eutropius of Gethsemani received a *Rescript* issued by Alesandro Barnabo, Secretary of the Sacred Congregation of Propaganda, announcing that Pope Pius IX, "after reading the petition from Dom Hercelin [Abbot of the monastery of La Grande Trappe, Vicar-General of the Cistercians of the Strict Observance] and the letter of recommendation from Bishop Chabrat," had granted the Trappist petition for abbatial status.

on September 6, 1852, they wrote to Dom Thomas Mossi, the President General of the Cistercians, requesting information on Gethsemani Abbey as well as on "the rights and privileges and distinctions" granted Cistercian abbots according to the observance of La Trappe. Dom Thomas in his reply seemed equally puzzled and somewhat embarrassed: he knew something about the Trappist abbeys in France who had relations with the Father President General who resided in Rome, but unfortunately he knew little or nothing about Gethsemani in America. He could, however, supply information on abbatial distinctions, and among other things he stressed the fact that the cross and staff of a Trappist abbot are of wood, with at most some gold ornamentation; this practice of using wood is well followed "although experience shows its non-observance in the monasteries has its beginning in the violation of the vow of poverty." He added also that the abbot's every day distinguishing mark is the use of a ring with a small jewel.

So the cardinals were back again where they started. But happily for them, or so they thought at the moment, it was learned that two American bishops were in Rome at this time, and to them, of course, would they direct their inquiries about the Dubuque Trappists and particularly about the privileges that should be granted to Trappist abbots. These two prelates were Bishop John MacGill of Richmond, Virginia, and Bishop Bernard O'Reilly of Hartford, Connecticut. Remembering the views of the then Bishop, but later Archbishop, Hughes of New York and other Atlantic seaboard prelates a few years before this time, it will prove no surprise to anyone to discover these two eastern Bishops repeating the same indictments and complaints against the Cistercian monks in America. Bishop MacGill admitted that he knew nothing about the New Melleray priory in Iowa but he had "some knowledge" of the Gethsemani abbey in Kentucky. "Such an austere community is not altogether suitable in our country and already various monks have left the monastery and wander here and there seeking to sustain life in various ways and some have returned to France." He granted, however, that monasteries "as focal points of religion and prayer are of the greatest utility in every region," but as to the New Melleray community if the monks are few and "the hope of new ones is very slight, and if as happened once in the province of Kentucky" — referring to Charles Dickens' "Mad monks" who had gone from Kentucky to Monks' Mound in Illinois — "when they tried in vain to erect a Trappist monastery, then this one also in a few years must perish, and so without doubt it will be better not to create an abbot there."

Both bishops evidenced in their replies strong episcopal suspicion of encroachments by abbots on their prelatial privileges. The bishop of Richmond maintained that the poverty of American bishops did not permit them to enjoy many distinctions and "therefore *insignia,* which in the eyes of the faithful indicate and illustrate episcopal dignity," should be reserved for them.

Bishop O'Reilly of Hartford intensified, if anything, the views of his colleague. "As far as the use of the mitre is concerned," he wrote, "and the pectoral cross and the pontificals in general, it seems to me that in our country it would not be a good thing for the abbots to enjoy the use of these things. The faithful in our country are accustomed to see only Bishops with a mitre and other pontificals and it is evident to me that since reverence toward the episcopal character is not very great, it will be much decreased by the extension of the use of pontificals to Abbots." And pointing out that episcopal embarrassment might increase with the growth of the number of abbeys and abbots in the United States, he concluded: "Since you can give most ample power to an abbot to govern his religious without the right to pontificals, it seems to me better to reserve to Bishops alone in our country all such insignia."

The wise old cardinals must have shaken their respective white-haired or bald heads in doubt. Certainly, they were not convinced. They observed firstly, that as far as Trappist abbots and their privileges are concerned they are very different from those of bishops, and secondly, that just as in the case of the abbot of Gethsemani who was already in possession of such honors, these are restricted to the abbey church. Furthermore, there were other angles to the matter and they asked among themselves: "Will such concessions in favor of the Cistercian monks of the more strict observance established in the diocese of Dubuque incite the non-Trappists to ask for them, and especially, for instance, Father Wimmer and his venerable Benedictine monks in the monastery of St. Vincent of the diocese of Pittsburgh, the elevation of which to an abbey remains suspended?"

Prudent and cautious, they therefore instructed the Prefect of the Propaganda, Cardinal Fransoni, to write to Archbishop Peter Richard Kenrick of St. Louis and request him to sound out all the archbishops of the United States and all the suffragan bishops of the St. Louis province on the matter. The cardinals made the point of inquiry very succinct with their statement: "There would not be any difficulty certainly if through abbatial rank of this kind there were question merely of securing the greater stability of the foundation; but having in mind the circumstances of that Territory, doubt arises whether it is proper to grant those privileges that are customary for Abbots." This letter of inquiry was sent out from Rome in the beginning of January, 1853.

Naturally, it took Archbishop Peter Richard Kenrick a long time to obtain the views of so many churchmen and he sent the consensus of their replies to the Roman Progaganda six months after his receipt of the Roman letter. All had answered except one, Archbishop John Hughes of New York. All had combined in their opinions against Abbot Bruno's petition except one, and he was Archbishop Peter Richard Kenrick's own brother, Francis P. Kenrick, archbishop of Baltimore. The latter favored the elevation of the Iowa priory to an abbey provided no territorial jurisdiction would be given to the abbot. The opposition maintained that it was hardly expeditious to raise New Melleray monastery to higher rank because it was a new foundation and because of the poverty of the monks. Archbishop Peter Richard Kenrick of St. Louis went so far, indeed, as to claim that "should the Sacred Congregation agree" the bishops should have a right to vote in the election of an abbot!

And so what Dom Bruno probably imagined at the outset was a simple request, a request which Bishop Loras firmly supported, became suddenly a momentous ecclesiastical problem. Today in our nation we have abbeys and abbeys, and abbots and abbots, and we wonder what all the discussion was about. But the wise old cardinals took it all in their stride; they gave neither affirmation nor negation. Among the minutes of the meetings of the Sacred Congregation of the Propagation of the Faith for the year 1853 we find a long summary of the discussions on the matter with this final paragraph:

25. At a general meeting of the S. C. Propaganda de Fide held on June 20, 1853, there were present the Most Reverend and Most Eminent Lords

Brignole, Patrizi, Fransoni, Barberini, Altieri, Fornari, Recanati, Marini.

To the proposed doubts on the new position of ecclesiastical matters of the federated States of North America the most Eminent Fathers by the undersigned Relator replied

To 25. [Should the Monastery of New Melleray be raised to the rank of an Abbey?]

Deferred.

ITA EST. SO IT IS.

Rev. Card. Fornari, Relator.

XI

TWO TRAPPIST BISHOPS

. . . .

It is, of course, an unusual thing for a monk to be chosen a bishop, and especially a Trappist monk; for two Trappist monks to be chosen bishops — and within two years time and from the same monastery — is something that never occurred before or since this event at the Iowa foundation in the long annals of the Church in both hemispheres. Only once before from the time of the great Abbot de Rancé of La Grande Trappe had a Trappist monk been elevated to the episcopacy. What adds strikingly to the singular quality of this affair is the fact that the monastery and the community from which they were chosen were so humble and poverty-stricken in the estimation of contemporary Church authorities that they were refused abbatial status.

Just when Mathias Loras, bishop of the Dubuque diocese whose limits at this time were coextensive with the state of Iowa, first began to think of requesting from Rome a coadjutor, and when, casting about in his own mind, his attention become fixed upon Prior Clement Smyth, cannot be definitely established; whatever signs our sources reveal show that it must have been during the year of 1853. Born and reared during the hectic days of revolutionary and Napoleonic France, spending years of active missionary labors in the pioneer districts of Alabama and Florida among whites and negroes, and in his later life continuing his rugged and energetic career amongst frontiersmen and red aborigines in the far-flung see of the Northwest, it is small wonder that now in the sixty-first year of his life, his health and vitality were beginning to ebb. He wore glasses in his later years to save his fast weakening eyesight, his hearing had become impaired, and he was becoming subject to ever lengthening spells of illness.

During his close and intimate relations with the brethren of the New Melleray priory he had naturally been able to study the character and administrative ability of Father Clement. The illustrious Archbishop John Ireland of St. Paul, who took an intense interest in the early history of the Church of the Northwest, wrote this version of the selection: "It was a most remarkable incident — Bishop Loras, a Frenchman, and his priests, nearly all Frenchmen" (as a matter of truth, however, less than a third of the priests of the Dubuque diocese at this time were French) "debating as to who should be named his coadjutor and successor. The bishop had cast his eyes toward a French priest, the pastor of the Cathedral of St. Louis, Father Paris, not, we can well believe, because he was a native of France, but because he was, as we know, a holy and learned priest. But the clergy of the Diocese of Dubuque suggested that a bishop of another nationality might, all circumstances considered, be more useful in the Lord's vineyard. Bishop Loras readily consented to the wishes of his clergy, and the name of Rev. Clement Smyth was forwarded to Rome for the approval of the Holy Father." It is difficult, however, to find any evidence to corroborate this statement of Archbishop Ireland. On the other hand in March of 1853 Bishop Cretin in writing to Loras and revealing that he had been addressed by him on the matter of a coadjutor who would be a monk, said: "I have always thought that a coadjutor would bother you more than he would help you unless he would remain in his monastery and go out only to fulfill the missions which you might be able to confide in him." In November, 1855, Bishop Loras went to St. Louis to attend the First Provincial Council which was held in the old cathedral of St. Louis, and he had Prior Clement Smyth accompany him. Among the recommendations of this council was one creating a coadjutorship for Dubuque, and following his return home, Loras during the following month of December sent his choice of Prior Smyth along with his recommendations to Archbishop Kenrick of St. Louis who forwarded them to Rome. Shortly afterwards the bishop received the congratulations of his confidant, Bishop Cretin: "It would indeed be difficult to find a man more disinterested, more zealous, more capable. I think that his nomination at Rome will meet with no difficulty whatsoever."

Naturally and of necessity Bishop Loras had consulted his friend Dom Bruno of Mount Melleray on this step, and the latter had brought the request before the General Chapter of La Grande Trappe. The capitular fathers immediately frowned on it. Said their minutes of the second session of 1856: "The Reverend Father Clement, Titular Prior of New Melleray in the United States of America, is on the point of being promoted to the coadjutorship of Dubuque, no doubt with future succession: his Father Immediate, the R. Father Bruno, Abbot of Ireland, asks the opinion of the General Chapter. The unanimous opinion of the General Chapter is that the R. Father Clement decline both the honor and the charge which it is wished to bestow upon him. And on this subject the Chapter quotes the Definition contained in the 36th chapter of the *Nomasticon:* 'Neither an Abbot nor a Monk of our Order if he be chosen to the Episcopate may ever yield without the assent of his Abbot and of the Cistercian Chapter unless he shall be constrained by the Holy Father, the Pope.'"

And thus the matter hung in abeyance for a long time; Rome would have to speak. In all probability Bishop Loras was little perturbed by this refusal of the Cistercian chapter, for he had seen a similar obstacle overcome before. In 1848 the Jesuit, Father Van de Velde, had been instructed by his superiors to decline the nomination to the episcopal see of Chicago unless compelled by an express command of His Holiness. The consent of Rome had nevertheless been obtained in this case, as Loras well knew, since he had been one of the co-consecrators of Bishop Van de Velde.

It had been decided at the Cistercian General Chapter meetings of the previous year that the two American Trappist houses of New Melleray and Gethsemani should receive a formal visitation every second year, and that the two Abbots of Melleray in France and Mount Melleray in Ireland should alternately fulfill this duty. So in 1856 Dom Bruno came to the United States and Iowa on his second voyage and he did this more willingly because he hoped that Loras' importunate request of Rome would soon be granted and he wished to be present at the prior's consecration. He arrived in Dubuque on March 19th, the feast of St. Joseph. The sagacious abbot, keeping his own counsel, simply told Prior Clement that he "feared" the truth of the rumors now going about concerning his appointment to the Dubuque coadjutorship. But the prior confided to Father Donaghoe: "I have not the slightest apprehension that Rome could sanction such a choice, even if I were the person most strongly recommended, which I do not believe has been the case." Toward the end of June, the bishop who apparently had received some misleading news from Rome, wrote Father Clement that his prayer was heard, that a coadjutor had been appointed and that the prior was the chosen one, and demanded to know how long Father Clement had been in possession of the Bulls of Consecration. The prior indignantly denied having any sort of papal bulls and professed utter ignorance of the entire matter.

As should have been expected Rome was deliberate and slow as usual, and as month followed month Dom Bruno remained in America. While at New Melleray he was immensely pleased with what he beheld at the monastery. There was harmony, piety and concord among the brethren. There were neither debts nor doubts of future progress in the little community. The fertile fields continued to yield; the monastery possessed several teams of mules and horses and ten yoke of working oxen. The energetic abbot, seeing the pressing need of a suitable monastery church, consulted with the prior, selected a proper site himself, and then set the wheels of construction agoing. That very summer a large frame church eighty feet in length and twenty-two feet in width was built, and cloister-stalls and benches both for the choir religious and lay brothers were installed. Still not to be repressed Dom Bruno later supervised the erection of a number of smaller buildings — work-shops, a bakery, washhouse, tailor's room, carpenter's shop, and library room.

The new year of 1857 began to swing into its course and not until the middle of April did the documents arrive from Rome nominating Prior Clement Smyth coadjutor to the bishop of Dubuque with the title of an "Episcopus in partibus infidelium," a "bishop in the land of the unbelievers;" the bulls had been signed in Rome on February 17th by Cardinal Barnabo and named him titular bishop of Thanasis.

There was joy in Dubuque and among the silent, smiling monks in the halls of New Melleray to whom the news had been imparted. Bishop Loras had his coachman drive him out to the monastery in his carriage, and the following week the prior-bishop-elect wrote to Father Donaghoe at St. Joseph's Convent: "The good Bishop spent last Wednesday night here with us & appeared in all his glory. Never did I see him in such apparent good spirits before. We have arranged to meet, all of us in Dubuque on Monday next & on the day following to take the boat for St. Louis."

On the following Tuesday Prior Clement left for St. Louis accompanied by Bishop Loras, Abbot Bruno Fitzpatrick and Father Terence Donaghoe, the vicar-general. Before the departure of this group Dom Bruno had appointed Father James Myles O'Gorman to the priorship of New Melleray — the office which he had relinquished to Father Francis Walsh in 1850.

On Sunday, May 3rd, 1857, Archbishop Peter Richard Kenrick consecrated Father Smyth a bishop of the Catholic Church in the Cathedral of St. Louis and the Co-consecrators were Bishop Henni of Milwaukee and Bishop O'Regan of Chicago. An interesting glimpse of the occasion is obtained from the secular press of that day, *The Missouri Republican* of St. Louis:

Episcopal Consecration

Imposing Ceremonies

Yesterday was a gala day at the Cathedral when the ceremonies consequent upon a double consecration were performed. The parties most interested were the Rt. Rev. James Duggan, Bishop of Antigone to be coadjutor to the Archbishop of St. Louis, with right of succession to the archbishopric, if he survives the present Archbishop, and the Rt. Rev. Clement Smyth, Bishop of Appanasia [sic] to be coadjutor to the Bishop of Dubuque, also with the right of succession.

The ceremonies are of the most inspiring of the Roman Catholic Religion. The high officers of the church officiating were the Most Rev. Archbishop of this city, who was the consecrator, and the Rt. Rev. Dr. Spalding, Bishop of Louisville, who preached the sermon. We understand that all the Bishops of the Province of St. Louis were present.

Not all the bishops were present, however. Besides the prelates mentioned in the preceding paragraphs there were in the sanctuary that day Bishop John B. Miege, S.J., of the Indian Territory, Bishop Henry Juncker of Alton, and the Right Reverend Abbot, Dom Eutropius of Gethsemani Abbey, Kentucky.

From this time on Bishop Clement Smyth, although always entertaining a deep affection for his old monastery and the community over which he had so happily presided, and ever manifesting a great interest in their welfare, had only occasional relations of direct import with the New Melleray house. In fact, as bishop, he was never so intimately connected with the story of the Iowa Trappists as had been Bishop Mathias Loras during his incumbency of the Iowa see. Bishop Smyth was immediately plunged into diocesan labors, his first great task being the completion of the new Dubuque cathedral. And it is of note to mention that in 1858 after the resignation of Bishop O'Regan this first Trappist bishop in American history became Administrator for a time of the rapidly swelling diocese of Chicago. To Bishop Smyth's eternal credit was his firm and courageous handling of the case of the infamous schistmatic, Father Charles Chiniquy, whom he excommunicated and forced out of the Chicago diocese.

Prior James, having for so long a time cooperated as subprior with Father Clement, found it easy to follow closely in his footsteps as superior. "Good, generous, kind-hearted and withall so extraordinarily talented," exclaimed Brother Kieran in his annals, "Father James kept a vigilant watch especially over the movements of our housekeeper who even at this period manifested a tendency to run risks which eventually resulted most disastrously for our community. This state of things did not surely occur during the administration of Father James; it was reserved for his successors to accomplish so doleful an event." Dom Bruno continued being edified and pleased as he saw the fabric of his monastic affiliate being ever more carefully fashioned under the new prior's guidance, and was preparing to return to Europe with a heart brimming with gratitude to Providence, when still another source of gratification was disclosed to him and delayed his departure for a time. Father Thomas Hore who had some years previously deeded his farm and buildings in Allamakee County to the New Melleray community but had remained in possession of them, now visited the monastery and plac-

FOUNDERS
OF
OUR LADY
OF
NEW MELLERAY
ABBEY

MATHIAS LORAS
1792-1858
First Bishop of Dubuque

BRUNO FITZPATRICK
1813-1893
Lord Abbot of Mount Melleray

CLEMENT SMYTH
Second Bishop of Dubuque
Formerly
Prior of New Melleray

JAMES MYLES O'GORMAN
First Bishop of Omaha
Formerly
Prior of New Melleray

ing the deed in the hands of Dom Bruno and Prior James, announced that as he had received permission to retire from the active ministry and was returning to his native Ireland, he was relinquishing *Holy Valley* (referring to La Val Sainte of Dom Augustin Lestrange) to the monks. The abbot, with the concurrence of Prior James, sent Father Francis Walsh and six lay brothers to the Wexford farm to manage it for the community and to discover whether it might eventually become an affiliate of the Dubuque house; Father Francis was to act as pastor of the little Wexford parish and of the neighboring missions. Thereupon Dom Bruno, unable to delay any longer, left immediately for France to attend the meetings of the General Chapter at La Grande Trappe.

The acquisition of this property by the Trappist brothers was remarked upon in several Catholic papers and to one of them an ebullient enthusiast from Wexford wrote in June of 1857:

> This new branch of the Melleray Monastery will give an impetus to the Catholicity of Allamakee County. There will be priests in abundance: and such priests, eloquent, learned and holy men. Agriculture, too, will flourish where the monks are, for they are scientific and laborious farmers as the excellent cultivation of their fields near Dubuque abundantly proves. Their less enterprising neighbors will be directed and encouraged by their experience and success, and Allamakee County will become the Catholic garden-spot of Iowa. It will suit Catholics better than any other class of people, and few others will remain, if we judge from experience in the vicinity of Dubuque. The cowl and habit seems to frighten sectarians as much as a scarecrow does birds in a cornfield.

And the bishops in Dubuque when making their report to the Propagation of the Faith Society in France at the end of 1857 stated that there were now "2 convents of Trappists" in Iowa.

Alas, too soon did the colors fade from this roseate picture. The hilly land of the Holy Valley was hardly suited to the intensive cultivation sought by the monks and there appeared no secure future for a permanent Trappist foundation there. "Somehow the project fell through," related Brother Kieran, "and all were back again in less than one year and six months." The housekeeper, Brother Mary Bernard, was sent to Wexford to dispose of the land to the neigh-

boring farmers for the benefit of the monastery but Father Francis
Walsh remained for a time as missionary pastor. So attracted was
Father Walsh, the former prior, by this pastoral work that he sought
and was granted permission to enter the diocesan priesthood after
having been duly dispensed from his religious obligations by the
Pope, and withdrawing from the Cistercian order he devoted the
remainder of his life to pastoral and chaplaincy duties in the Dubuque diocese, serving, among other stations, for a number of years
as shepherd of the growing St. Patrick's congregation in Dubuque.

Meanwhile a startling event had been taking place in the abbey
of La Grande Trappe in France. Thither had gone Dom Bruno
after his prolonged sojourn in the United States. So impressed had
he been by the progress, both spiritual and material, of the Iowa
Trappist house, and so depressed had he become by conditions in
Ireland, both political and economic, that he began formulating a
daring, a radical plan of action in his mind. Already in December
of 1853 he had sounded out Prior Clement Smyth on the propriety
of the Dubuque foundation buying the farm at Mount Melleray and
thus allowing the Irish monks with these funds to transfer their entire community to Iowa. And now in the fall of 1857, addressing the
abbots assembled in General Chapter, he described with complete
detail all he had seen in America and in Iowa particularly on his
long journey, and then outlined the project he had long been medi-
tating of moving his abbacy and community to New Melleray. After
the discussions, the minutes of this interesting capitular session read
simply: "Things remain as they were: the project of the translation
of the Abbey is abandoned."

Although at the Iowa priory during this time "affairs went smoothly on," as Brother Kieran records, "yes, and very prosperous also —
difficulties and debt seemed as though such things were never to
exist," there were in 1858 two sad events to be noted. One was
the death of Brother Stanislaus Mullany, the first brother to die at
the monastery and whose name heads the list of those who lie in
sleep in the peaceful monastery cemetery. He was a young man
of only twenty-seven years of age and had been received into the
Dubuque Trappist house three years before. The community had
grown under Prior James to the number of sixty and just before
Brother Stanislaus' death, Brother Kieran had recorded: "We were
now living nine years and three months here" (in Iowa) "and dur-

ing that time no member of our community died in this monastery, though many were aged men." The other sad event was that of the death of Mathias Loras, first bishop of Iowa, the patron of New Melleray monastery and the friend of Dom Bruno Fitzpatrick, whose French accented voice had first called the Irish Trappists to the trans-Mississippi West. After his funeral which had been attended by government officials, civic leaders, church dignitaries and four thousand mournful followers he was buried in the crypt of the new cathedral which he and Bishop Clement Smyth had just completed.

A joyful event, however, of the same year was the first ordination to the priesthood of a member of the Dubuque Cistercian brotherhood. On August 21st, 1858, in the newly erected monastery church Brother John Baptist Hogan who had arrived in Iowa with the second Trappist colony in April of 1850 and was now forty-two years of age, was anointed with the sacerdotal oils by the kindly hands of his former prior, Bishop Clement Smyth.

When the new year of 1859 was ushered in the reports that Prior James was soon to be elevated to a bishopric had already obtained wide circulation. Archbishop P. Richard Kenrick of St. Louis had been impressed by his piety, his practical talents and his other eminent qualifications — so it was stated. The recent episcopal appointment of Clement Smyth was still fresh in the minds of the monks and of the public and possibly for that reason there was much less comment made or surprise manifested about Father James O'Gorman's nomination. Although Abbot Bruno was also aware of the coming elevation of his Trappist prior he could not, he felt, return so soon to America again. As it developed Prior James had already been nominated at Rome on January 18th, 1859, as Titular Bishop of Raphanae and Vicar Apostolic of Nebraska. Prior James confirmed the nomination by accepting the bulls which reached him on April 15th. He left New Melleray on May 2nd and was consecrated in the St. Louis cathedral on May 8th, 1859, a Sunday, by Archbishop Peter Richard Kenrick, the co-consecrators being Bishops Miege and Juncker. His fellow Trappist, Bishop Clement Smyth, who had accompanied him to St. Louis delivered the sermon on the occasion.

The Vicariate of Nebraska embraced what are now the states of Nebraska, Wyoming, Montana and the western parts of the Dakotas. There were probably not more than seven thousand Catho-

lics in that vast region, including the Indians, and particularly the
Black Feet tribe among whom the Jesuit missioners were then gain-
ing many converts. Arrived in Omaha the new bishop wrote to
Father Donaghoe: "How different has been my egression from
Melleray, and Bishop Smyth's. He had only to go thirteen miles
when he found everything he could rationally desire; I have travelled
as many hundreds of miles and have not found a home." He did,
however, find a remarkable old friend, Father Jeremiah Trecy, a
former Iowan. This priest who had served Bishop Loras well in
his efforts to secure immigrants for the West, had held the pastorate
of Garryowen, a few miles south of New Melleray, and had be-
friended the monks in their early years of destitution. Three or
four years previous to this meeting with Bishop O'Gorman he had
led a colony of farmers, some of them from the monastery district
and the others from Garryowen, to Nebraska where he was engaged
at this time in founding a city and a farm settlement. He immediately induced the willing bishop to accompany him on a long, "parch-
ing drive of 150 miles" through the Omaha and Pawnee Indian reser-
vations and almost smack into an Indian insurrection before they
reached the St. Patrick's settlement. Here the bishop found that
Father Trecy's city existed only on paper, — "but it was a beautiful
city," added the bishop, "and every saint of the calendar has on it a
street dedicated to him or her."

This extraordinary character left his settlement two years later
for Washington, D. C., and then for Alabama, where in the beginning of the Civil War he served as chaplain with the national guard
of that rebel state and later served with the northern troops in
Tennessee in the army of General Rosecrans — the only instance in
the history of that great conflict (and probably of any great conflict) where the same clergyman served as chaplain with both an-
tagonists.

As the extreme western part of Iowa was so far from Dubuque
and was just across the Missouri river from Omaha, Nebraska, Bishop
Smyth induced Bishop O'Gorman almost from the start to attend
to the Catholics in this region granting him full faculties and jurisdiction, and this sharing of the episcopal care of Iowa by the two
former priors of the New Melleray monastery continued until the
death of Bishop Smyth in 1865.

XII

ANOTHER CRISIS AND A FEW LETTERS THEREON

. . . .

Upon the departure of James Myles O'Gorman, nominated to the bishopric of the Nebraska Vicariate, Dom Bruno appointed Father Bernard McCaffrey as the superior of the Dubuque monastery, but not with the powers of a Titular Prior. Father Bernard, it will be recalled, had been the emissary sent by the abbot of Mount Melleray back in 1848 to find the site of an American Trappist foundation; he had favored settling at Bedford, Pennsylvania, at the invitation of Dr. Thomas Heyden; and after a six months' stay at Gethsemani monastery he had come to Dubuque in 1849. Since then most of his duties had been those of the acting pastor of the Trappists' secular church, and having been quite successful in this task and being now forty-five years of age, he was judged to be sufficiently capable and mature to take over the office of superior until Dom Bruno should select a prior.

The abbot certainly showed no haste in choosing a new prior. During his recent fourteen months' stay in America he had seen how smoothly monastic affairs had been running at New Melleray, and when he had made his formal visitation of the monastery on that occasion he had written a flattering report on the visitation card;

this is the document containing the impressions and advisory suggestions of the abbot or other official person who makes the formal inspection of the community and which is usually read to all the monks assembled in chapter. Herein he had stated his hope that on his next visitation, believing that Father James would then still be the prior, there would be a new guest house with a reception room, if not completed, at least commenced; and then after a fervent plea to the brothers to continue their pious and austere living, he made an exhortation so eloquent that it bears quoting: "But if on the other hand, there be in this monastery, even one, whether Choir or Lay brother, whose conscience tells him, in a deep and thundering voice, that he is not the charitable, obedient, silent Monk whom we have described, we could not but feel sad. And yet our sadness would be mingled with joy; for to that Brother, if such there be in the Community, we would say in the spirit of the most tender paternal charity, 'Lose not courage, dear Brother. This is the day of your visitation; now is the time to begin a new life, a life of prayer, of silence, of obedience, and more than all and above all, a life of perfect, fraternal Charity.'

"We have already communicated, and we shall continue most unreservedly to communicate to the very Reverend Father Prior, our views, our hopes and our wishes concerning the spiritual and temporal well being of this Community. The Brethren may rest satisfied that we shall make known to him every remark of importance, every useful suggestion that we have heard in private since our arrival in this monastery."

In concluding, after asking for prayers for Pope Pius IX, he also pleaded: "Pray in a most special manner for the Right Reverend Dr. Smyth, your late Superior and now the Bishop of this important Diocese . . . Pray that in him may be revived the ancient glories of the venerable Order of Citeaux, which in former ages gave illustrious Popes and Princes and Prelates to the Church of God."

When the General Chapter abbots met in France in the fall of 1858, their minutes recorded the receipt of a letter from Prior James O'Gorman explaining his inability to attend the sessions that year, and which then recounted certain difficulties which had sprung up between him and his Father Immediate, Dom Bruno. And these difficulties explain further why the abbot of Mount Melleray chose to remain in Ireland in 1859 instead of attending Prior James' episcopal consecration, although he had gladly come two years previously when Prior Clement was elevated. It was unfortunate, however, that he had not come because beyond any doubt he would have noticed the idiosyncrasies which Father Bernard, the superior he had selected, was already displaying. This priest, a good theologian, a clever controversialist and a profound classical scholar was nevertheless a pronounced eccentric.

While Father-Master of novices, and even as superior, he would read on Sundays to the monks the revelations and meditations of Anne Catherine Emmerich, the stigmatic and ecstatic German nun, and at the secular church while seated in a chair before the altar he would continue reading these revelations until the congregation fell asleep. The rich hills about Dubuque made lead-mining a profitable industry, and Father Bernard allowed himself to be imposed upon in these operations by a Dutch sailor who came to the monastery as a postulant, and posed as a chemical expert. Their prospecting led to large monetary losses. But this was as nothing compared to the jobbing in cattle and the land speculating business, a traffic of which he and Brother Mary Bernard, the housekeeper, were the chief organizers at this time, and which, increasing during the succeeding years, finally ended most disastrously for the community. Slightly inflated with his honors as superior he wrote Bishop O'Gorman at Omaha, proposing the erection of a Trappist filiation in Nebraska should the bishop be good enough to secure a few sections of land for him. Knowing that the former prior was anxious for news of the monastery he mentioned among other items: "Our community is increasing. We received 4 postulant priests & 2 laymen for the choir & 6 lay novices since you left. 12 in 3 months! I take everyone that comes. If they stand, well & good. If they go, there is the door for them." And influenced probably by his love of the "revelation" he recited to the amazed bishop: "All here are well & in peace, profound peace, nothing but peace. When vested with the dignity [of superior], I planted a cherub with a two-edged sword at the gate, & behind him a seraph with a four-edged sword, cutting east, west, north and south at every blow. And fearing that would not do, I erected a battery tremendously high, and on it I placed (what think you? not a cannon, nor a mortar, nor a howitzer nor even a blunder-buss, but, as Irish Pat would say) a Blundergun to shoot the D—l a mile off. So no D—l has entered here since, nor can he as long as the Blundergun is kept ready

for action. Indeed there is now but one heart & one soul at New
Melleray. Not the shadow of anything but profound peace. *Esto
perpetuo.*"

Father Bernard's term of office ran almost a year and a half, "without doing anything very remarkable," Brother Kieran hastened to
explain, "excepting this buying and selling of pigs and cattle," when
on October 2nd, 1860, Abbot Bruno arrived and introduced to the
community the thirty-six year old Titular Prior Ignatius Foley whom
he had brought with him from Mount Melleray. With them and
also from Ireland were Father Emmanuel French, Brother Patrick
Corbett, a choir monk and cantor, and Brother Michael Keegan, a
lay brother. Dom Bruno used this occasion for a formal visitation.
The year before — in 1859 — Dom Eutrope of Gethsemani Abbey in
Kentucky had made the visitation of New Melleray. Unfortunately,
his visitation card is unavailable, but that of Abbot Bruno in 1860
is before us and throws light on some hitherto shadowy corners of
the monastery scene. Apparently he had been immediately apprised of the business dealings of Father Bernard and Brother Mary
Bernard, and in the very beginning of his remarks he alludes to the
matter: "All circumstances being taken into account, we feel justified in advising the Superior to tolerate, for a limited time, a certain
kind of traffic, which, as might be expected, has produced feelings
of uneasiness in the minds of some members of the Community."
And although he spoke of the "consoling fact" that from the private
interviews with the monks he had learned that "charity, peace and
happiness are enthroned in this Monastery," he paid no flattering
compliments in this report but flung out his verbal castigations where
he hoped they would do the most good.

"Is it or is it not the fact, that the Spirit of the world is encroaching gradually upon the hearts that should be full of the Spirit of
God; that loud shouting is heard in the fields; that *money* and *money*
engages habitually and unnecessarily the attention of men, who have
solemnly renounced all to follow Christ, who are bound by their
vow of poverty, and who, after a few years, perhaps much sooner,
will find themselves in the presence of that terrible judge, Who has
said: 'No one can serve two Masters. No one can serve God and
mammon?' "

So much for the traffic and business; and then he thundered at
other abuses: "Is it or is it not the fact, that Newspapers are purchased and introduced into the Monastery, without the permission

of the Superior, and read even on Sundays; that, notwithstanding the shortness of life, and the value of time, and the absorbing duties of the Monastic State, some few members of this Community make Politics a study, and a favorite topic of conversation?"

Concluding, he urges with holy vigor: "If these abuses, or any of them, do really exist, we cry out against them, and with all the weight of our authority, and in the name of Our Holy Order, and in the name of the Holy See, which has united us in one body under one head, and in the name of the Adorable Trinity, we command their correction, and we forbid their reintroduction into this Community."

Even the practicing Catholics seldom see the interior of a monastery, and few of the millions in the United States today have been inside a Trappist cloister. They read and hear of the austere piety of these monks and accept it as natural that these cenobites should live a life of the Rule. They forget that it is a supernatural life of grace. The visitation card of a visitating abbot lets us peer not only within the monastic halls, but beneath the corporal surface that surrounds the soul of a monk. These words of Dom Bruno were addressed to sixty brawny Christian men, muscular, intelligent, witty, all human, accustomed to severe labor in the fields and long hours of prayer and meditation in the New Melleray monastery church; they received his words with a welcome humility, a soldiery submission to the great Rule of St. Benedict. And who would not be edified when he continues reading the little personal notes that accompany the visiting card and show the intense and tender humanness of the tiny favors sought and the peccadilloes hinted at:

"Father Patrick begs permission to lie down in the Couch for less than an hour, after the Distribution of Work."

(Father Patrick was now in his sixty-second year.)

"Brother Daniel wishes to go to Tracadie [monastery]. He must wait until spring; in the meantime I can consult the Vicar General, and Rome also, if necessary.

"Brother Jerome begs to be allowed to have a lock and key for the Woodroom.

"Brother Mary Joseph, it is said by a competent judge, would make a good Farmer, that is an Under-housekeeper. The office is held at present by Brother Barnaby. *A very grave question.*

"Father John Baptist wants a Stove in the Library, s. v. p.

"Father Emmanuel might begin to teach Singing.

"Brother Mary Augustin sings at Salve & Benediction: he is not in his place in the Stalls. He takes Potatoes for *himself*.

"Brother Paul gave money for Masses.

"Is it right to leave Brother Peter, the Cook, in charge of the Fowl?

"Could Brother Athanasius manage to prevent so many from assembling in the Wardrobe?

"Can Father Robert be bound to observe stricter silence?"

These are taken verbatim from the 1860 card of the Iowa Trappist monastery. In this more modern day, against our casually accepted background of Hollywood adulteries and other vices, of Communist enslavements, of political and commercial corruption, these monkish peccadilloes seem like scintillating virtues and Abbot Bruno's catigations sound like vile slanders of the Gallahads of the cross.

But — let us dip our pen in the ink of dispassionate history and recount the almost humorous affair of the new Titular Prior, Father Ignatius Foley. The latter, a pious and highly cultured gentleman from the collegiate halls of Mount Melleray seminary, was a bit of a monastic snob and it could have been predicted that the course of his career would be a rough one among the hardy and witty sons of St. Bernard at the still frontier-like Cistercian institution at Dubuque. Because of Father Bernard's peculiar administration, it was suggested by the abbot to Father Ignatius that he might attempt some sort of a "reform" of the community. As for Abbot Bruno himself, his visit in Iowa lasted little more than a month when he departed for Louisville and Gethsemani Abbey in Kentucky where he conducted the visitation. As Abbot Eutropius of Gethsemani, the proto-abbot of America, had resigned some months previously Dom Bruno presided at the election of the new abbot, Dom Benedict Berger, and then returned to Europe.

Prior Ignatius found the United States inhospitable, American life strange and the pioneer Iowa conditions hard. Winter set in soon after his arrival, and it was a severe winter, far fiercer than anything he had ever faced in Ireland. He already hoped that he would never have to live through a second such terrible season. And his disgust was brought to a climax when the spring brought heat and towards the end of May and the beginning of June of that year of 1861 the thermometer sky-rocketed to above ninety degrees in the shade. There was something wrong with the country and he even declared that the spring flowers of Iowa had no fragrance and the birds had no music. He was most discouraged by his inability to understand the manners and activities of some of the Iowa monks; and Brother Kieran explained: "It was the noise and perpetual bustle, even on Sundays, of those bought pigs and cattle and Brother Mary Bernard, or better known as Brother Murphy, shouting louder than any or all of his bought stock put together. Then to see so many of the brothers going at all hours both of day and night scouring the country far and near for Brother Murphy's purchase" — all this coupled with the airy and eccentric behavior of Father Bernard, who had been officiating as subprior, was more than poor Father Ignatius could tolerate.

On the 15th of June, 1861, he left with the announced intention of attending the General Chapter at La Grande Trappe, but when he was followed in his departure by Father Emmanuel and Brother Patrick, the two choir brothers who had arrived with him the previous October, it was evident to the community that he hoped his separation would be permanent. Because of his absence Father Bernard McCaffrey again became superior.

Thus the agitated affairs of the Iowa Trappist house and even the grave question of its very continuance became the matter of prime importance at the opening sessions of the General Chapter in France that early autumn of 1861. For the first time in its history New Melleray monastery was represented by its own superior at the capitular meeting, namely by Prior Ignatius, and also by its Father Immediate, Dom Bruno. The seriousness of the issue before the assembled fathers may well be understood from the wording of the minutes of the sessions. After an entire afternoon was devoted to the deliberations on "the house of New Melleray in America" it was finally decided that "as a result of an attentive examination of this delicate question, it has been agreed that there will be one more attempt made in order to save this community."

The minutes would further lead one to believe that the sympathetic capitular fathers regarded Father Ignatius as having almost been forced into exile by his community. He had been installed as Titular Prior by his Father Immediate, and here he was having left it discouraged and pleading not to return to that desolate and unfriendly land. If they were to believe a letter which had come from the Dubuque monastery, his community itself had actually consented willingly to his departure.

However: upon the entreaties of the General Chapter the Very Reverend Father Ignatius has graciously yielded; he will go back again to New Melleray; he will exert all his efforts in order to carry out for the good of religion what he had already commenced, so as to overcome misfortunes and prevent the monastery from perishing. Furthermore, the Reverendissimus Pater, Dom Bruno, will continue to do all in his power in order to accomplish the same end; notably, he will recall to Mount Melleray in Ireland the Reverend Father Bernard "who seems" [!] "to be an obstacle."

And further: two letters were ordered to be written, one to the Right Reverend Bishop of Dubuque, the former Titular Prior Clement Smyth of New Melleray; the other to the Iowa Trappist community. These letters are still extant today, brief and sincere, showing the affectionate solicitude of the capitular fathers over the fate of the struggling little Cistercian house, so remote from Europe and so far west, out beyond the storied Mississippi river. At these capitular meetings practically all the abbots were French, with an occasional Belgian or German present and one was English; to them, with no personal knowledge of America, the young republic was a strange land to be viewed if not with suspicion at least with diffidence. The Irish abbot, Dom Bruno, was up to this time the best authority they had on monastic matters in the United States, and to his advice they were perforce compelled to yield. And so to Bishop Smyth they wrote:

"Sir,

"The General Chapter of our Congregation has ever been very preoccupied with this dear House of New Melleray, to which, we are well aware, your Grace continues to bear always a lively interest.

"Some letters have come to us from this monastery; two religious, including the Reverend Father Ignatius whom we have sent there as Prior, have come to us; we have various sorts of information; we desire again to make an effort in the hopeful view of saving this community which to us seems so menaced. We shall send anew the Reverend Father Ignatius who began to do some good and will still continue to do it, and we recall, at least temporarily, the Father Bernard who might indeed prove an embarrassing stumbling-block.

"Permit us, Monseigneur, of counting upon your indispensable cooperation, be it either to make a try of the measure, or to encompass our Father Ignatius with your solicitude and your good counsels.

"The Religious of New Melleray have been your children, Monseigneur, they still are, and they always will be.

"Monseigneur

of your Grace

"The very humble and very devoted servants and Brethren in Jesus Christ, the members of the General Chapter" with their signatures.

And in equally stately Latin ran the letter to the Iowa community:

"The General Chapter of the Congregation of La Trappe, to our very dear brothers, the religious of Our Lady of New Melleray.

"Our very dear brothers,

"We have read your letters with attention and interest.

"We have also taken into consideration all the information we could otherwise obtain.

"Thus having examined everything well before God and having invoked the Holy Spirit, we send you again the Reverend Father Ignatius. Receive him as an envoy from God.

"The Reverend Father Ignatius is already favorably known to you; he is sweet, conciliating, charitable; he will not impose upon you heavy burdens; and he will help you to save your souls. We count upon you to aid him yourselves, so that in fulfilling his mission, you will render his task easy.

"We have confidence, you yourselves have confidence, and the good God will accomplish upon your dear house of New Melleray His designs of mercy.

"We are in the bosom of the Savior,

"Your very affectionate brothers in Jesus Christ."

As another indication of the profoundly serious view the capitular fathers took of this crisis in the life of the Iowa Cistercian institution, the fifth session of this convocation of 1861 was given over to the discussion of New Melleray and to Dom Bruno's proposals. It was decided that in agreement to Abbot Bruno's "wisdom for the directing of all things to the good" he should be empowered "to translate into Ireland the religious of New Melleray, if he can accomplish it." But a few years before Dom Bruno was solemnly planning to move the Irish abbacy to Iowa, and now he was faced with the possible necessity of transferring the Iowa colony back to Mount Melleray.

After all, however, the Dubuque monastery again safely weathered this crisis. At the Grand Chapter meetings in France the next year — in 1862 —the matter was briefly and soberly disposed of with the explanation that the letters which the General Chapter of 1861 had addressed to America to "our Fathers of New Melleray" and to the bishop of Dubuque had produced excellent results, and that "the Father Bernard of whom it was complained, followed the counsels which we gave him, and went to strengthen himself for a time at the Abbey of Mount Melleray." A far more interesting account of the effect of these missives comes in a letter from none other than the frank and incisive Brother Kieran to Bishop O'Gorman of Omaha who naturally was intensely interested in the successful emergence of his former priory from the turbulent and distressing circumstances in which it found itself. Writing on December 1st, 1861, from "Brother Francis Shop," Brother Kieran related: "There is neither abbot, Prior or Sub Prior here today. Poor Fr. Bernard, his blunder-gun blew him out of this monastery on Monday morning last, the 25th of Nov. The abbot of Mt. Melleray commanded him to report with speed to that monastery. So he is gone with the blessing of many. May he arrive there in safety. It is thought here that Fr. Ignatius now the Titular will again reach this monastery about Christmas.

"He was appointed last year and in coming to reform us he was accompanied by two choir monks, but in less than a year all of them had their backs to New Melleray, but the general chapter in its Paternal Solicitude for our double welfare condescends to inform us in their letter to the Bishop of Dubuque that they will make one effort more to save New Melleray so they are sending Father Ignatius back to us more encumbered now with authority than ever. We will wait and see . . .

"Dear Bishop, the community are well in health — only three in the infirmary — not very sick . . . Brother Ambrose is well — he has charge of the beer and gives us a fair measure daily for dinner. Br. Timothy is just the usual size if not fatter . . . Bro. Mary Bernard, housekeeper and co-jobber — the Bishop has put a final stop to his jobbing and all here are rejoiced at it. "And we will pray for you,
                    Your obedient and Humble Servant."

Father Ignatius did not return despite the deliberations and letters of the chapter and the fathers. It would be an understatement to describe the sentiments of the community as merely surprise when on February 25th, 1862, a new Titular Prior, Father Ephrem, appeared at New Melleray, and with him was none other than Father Bernard. Prior Ephrem had been Charles Joseph McDonnell, a native of County Mayo, who had entered the Mount Melleray Trappist house shortly before the death of its first abbot, Dom Vincent, in 1845. Now forty years of age, he was spoken of by the General Chapter in its reference to his appointment as superior of the Iowa foundation as "the best subject whom the Venerable Father Dom Bruno had." His incumbency of the superior's office was now the ninth in the twelve and a half years since New Melleray had been founded on that hot day of July of 1849. This incumbency was to last well over twenty-one years and was to occupy a significant niche in the historic structure of the Iowa cloister, not so much for its weal as for its woe. Brother Kieran testified fearlessly: "Many in the community (if not all) regret that he ever came. Though a more pious man was not, and could not be found in the whole Order, yet he suffered himself to be duped by designing men in this 'Traffic' business to such an extent as to ruin almost irretrievably our community."

Father Bernard was the new prior's friend, advisor and defender. Yet Father Bernard's activities from now on were to be centered mostly about the secular church; it had prospered under him before, and it was to continue growing and prospering under him for years in the future.

Each crisis of the many that occurred in the Iowa Trappist story had its own particular dramatic flavor and hue, and now an intriguing postscript must be added to the recital of the one in this chapter from which New Melleray had again successfully emerged. Another perplexity from the American Cistercians flustered the venerable capitular fathers at La Grande Trappe in 1862, but the threat this time came from Gethsemani Abbey in Kentucky and the Dubuque monastery was only indirectly involved. Abbot Benedict Berger proposed that a new province — the American Cistercian Province — should be erected, embracing the four houses in the United States and Canada: Gethsemani, New Melleray, Tracadie in Nova Scotia, and an expected affiliate of this latter house which was to be established near Quebec, Canada.[1]

[1] This was the short-lived Holy Ghost monastery, founded in 1862, closed in 1872. Today there is a Trappist monastery of Our Lady of the Holy Ghost, founded 1944, in the state of Georgia.

The reasons behind this proposal, then considered a quite radical one and which really startled the members of the General Chapter, were the inconveniences of time, travel and money facing the American superiors wishing to attend the La Grande Trappe convocations, the difficulties of European abbots — and now the American Civil War was on — of making annual visitations of American Trappist houses, and the advisability for American Trappist communities to meet together in order to discuss their own peculiar problems.

The deliberations and discussions of the Grand Chapter led to the following decision: the erection of an American Province should not be permitted as this would be contrary to the Constitution of the Cistercian Order, and as a consequence of this, the annual gathering of the four American superiors in a Provincial Chapter should likewise be prohibited. Bishop Clement Smyth of Dubuque, who discussed this matter personally with some of the abbots whom he met in Europe in 1862, joined in the opposition to the Gethsemani proposal, stating his firm conviction that a separation from the jurisdiction of the General Chapter would lead to the ruin of the New Melleray house of Iowa. However, the General Chapter granted a modification of the rules which had hitherto required the frequent attendance of American superiors at the La Grande Trappe meetings and also changed the rules affecting the visitation of American monasteries, but maintained that these latter, remaining in "the limits of the Chart of Charity" should constitute "the filiation of America united to the Congregation of La Trappe by their Father Immediate" of Europe.

In 1863 the capitular fathers noted with relief that Dom Benedict Berger had decided not to re-open the discussion of this embarrassingly delicate subject.

The Remains of What Was the Original New Melleray Abbey Building
Started in 1849.

The Chapter Room, La Grande Trappe Abbey, France

XIII

INTRODUCING BRIEFLY—
THE ABBEY!

The first years of Father Ephrem McDonnell's tenure of office as superior at New Melleray were auspicious and prosperous ones in almost every way, and this despite the fact of the ravaging Civil War and its aftermath.

The war had boomed the prices of all stocks and grains and other products, thus benefiting the monastery farms. New lands were purchased; a quarter section was bought from Lemuel Lytton, the owner of the Twelve Mile House, and another four hundred acres was secured from a New York land speculator. Another valuable purchase was the hundred and fifty acres of timber land known as "Langton's wood," purchased at an extremely low price by Brother Mary Bernard, the housekeeper. Langton and others in the vicinity who were anxious to escape the army draft disposed of their farms for any price and put out for parts unknown, most of them for Canada.

Needed improvements were made on the grounds. Brother Mark and a novice mason put up a splendid cut stone building, three stories high, for general utility purposes. Prior Ephrem saw the necessity

133

for a large stable and barn, and under Brother Joseph's directions, stone was obtained from the monastery quarries, lumber was brought out from the city, a large group of monks and generously helpful neighbors swarmed about the building project, and a huge thirty-six foot high structure finally rose up, over two hundred and thirty feet in length and fifty feet wide. The community in turn then assisted the farmers in erecting their new secular church.

As the war ran its course Brother Mary Bernard found more opportunities for his shrewdness in successful speculation and other business transactions. Shortly before the beginning of the year 1863 Dom Benedict of Gethsemani Abbey had made the visitation of New Melleray and although he found conditions both spiritually and materially very satisfactory he judged it necessary to express a word of caution about this vexatious activity. Yet the jobbing and the traffic, frowned on by all the superiors, continued with even greater vigor than before.

The war exercised some direct impact on the Dubuque Trappists. According to the laws prevailing at that time, the superior paid to the United States government five hundred dollars for each of those members of the community who were over twenty-one years of age and under forty-five to secure their exemption from military service. In the very first year of the conflict there was a flurry of excitement among the brethren when a report reached the monastery that their former prior, Bishop James Myles O'Gorman, had been arrested by General Nathaniel Lyon of the Union forces in Missouri. It was confirmed later that there was some basis to the rumor, but it was the Confederate forces who had held him prisoner. The steamboat on which he and other passengers were being carried on the Missouri river from St. Louis to Omaha reached Lexington, some forty miles east of Kansas City, just after General Sterling Price with his Southern army had captured the town and its Union defenders. The ship was seized and General Price ordered all on board to be made prisoners of war. The bishop, as the most prominent of the passengers, was personally interviewed by the commanding officer; the grey-clad Confederate general questioned the Trappist monk concerning his political leanings, and Bishop O'Gorman explained that he had always prayed for peace, that he was a loyal citizen of the United States and that he had nothing to say regarding the Southern Confederacy. Later, after an officers' council was held, and after being detained twenty-four hours, the bishop and most of the passengers were permitted to return aboard their boat and proceed on their journey. A strange historical coincidence may be remarked here: General Price only a month before had won the battle of Wilson's Creek in the Ozark foothills some miles south of Springfield, Missouri, — the battle in which the gallant Union leader, General Nathaniel Lyon, was killed; today, the brothers of the monastery, once presided over by the prior whom General Price had arrested, have established an affiliate in that very Ozark district but a few miles distant from the scene of the battle.

Now that the Iowa Trappist house was resting on a more secure financial foundation, plans for a new and beautiful stone monastery began to be discussed and even actively visualized. Already in the years of 1855 and 1856 preparations had been made toward the day when this building should be erected. Stones for that purpose were cut and hauled from the quarries; in the following years some funds were set aside from time to time in anticipation of the building of this structure. But before that day was to arrive, the older frame building was to have the grandeur of the status of an abbey thrust upon it.

Bishop Smyth of Dubuque in order to make his first *ad limina* visit to Rome left America about the middle of May, 1862, for Europe. He first stopped at his old Trappist home of Mount Melleray in Ireland for a short visit, but a few months later on his return voyage he spent a fortnight there with Bishop James Duggan of Chicago who had also just completed his first *ad limina* visit. The former Prior Clement of the Irish monastery who had been the first president of its famous seminary was entertained with enthusiastic affection by the abbot, the brethren and the students. The latter, in response to the bishop's address to them, presented him with a beautiful testimonial of compliments among which they stated: "We feel that the spectacle which greets your eyes today will be as gratifying to you as it is to the illustrious abbot of Melleray. You behold what colossal proportions this institution, which owes its origin to the generous impulse of your noble heart, has assumed . . . We freely and heartily offer the tribute of our reverent esteem and affectionate welcome to you as the reverend Founder of this Institution."

On the earlier part of this European voyage, when the bishop had travelled across the Continent and gone to Rome, he had addressed an entreaty to the General Chapter of La Grande Trappe for the erection of New Melleray monastery into an abbey. The day had passed when the now flourishing Iowa cloister could be in any way considered a precarious foundation tenanted by impoverished monks. No longer apparently was the consent of the American episcopacy required on this subject. The General Chapter declared that Dr. Smyth had given information on the community of New Melleray which was "so consoling that we do not hesitate to solicit the erection of the priory into an abbey. The Decree will be entrusted to the Very Reverend Visitor who will confer with the bishop for the opportunity either of its authoritative issuance, or the election of the abbot."

In Rome for the canonization of the twenty-six Japanese martyrs on June 8th, and for the consistory which followed it, Bishop Smyth obtained the privilege of a private audience with the celebrated pontiff, Pope Pius IX. Receiving the Trappist bishop with even more than his usual hearty geniality, the Holy Father — so it is related on the authority of one historian — stared for a moment at the bishop's white Cistercian cassock so closely resembling his own white papal soutane, and then exclaimed with a smile and a twinkle in his eye: *Ecce quam bonum et quam jucundum habitare fratres in unum.*[1] It was on this occasion that Bishop Smyth received from the pope himself the brief which raised the Dubuque house to the rank of an abbey.

When Dom Benedict of Gethsemani made his visitation of New Melleray in December of 1862 he had already received the documents from the General Chapter of the Cistercians as well as the authorization of Dom Bruno, the Father Immediate of the Iowa foundation, to preside at the election of an abbot. So in the chapter room of the pine board monastery on the 22nd day of December the monks of this trans-Mississippi Trappist community met to cast their votes, and their choice fell on Prior Ephrem McDonnell. The date for the ceremony of conferring the abbatial blessing was set indefinitely for the following spring when Bishop Smyth's return from Europe was expected. The bishop did not arrive until April 30th, and on the second Sunday following, May 10th, the solemnity was enacted in the Dubuque cathedral of St. Raphael's. The ceremony of the abbatial blessing differs very little from that of the consecration of a bishop, the only important change being the omission of the essentials of the episcopal order. Given here is a short descrip-

---

[1] "Behold how good and how pleasant it is for brethren to dwell together in unity." Ps. 132.

tion of this event — the first of its kind in the history of the western half of the American continent — from the diffident and bashful pen of a well-meaning non-Catholic writer in the Dubuque newspapers of that day:

As this ceremony is an unusual one for this country, it having taken place but once or twice before since the United States Government was organized, several Bishops and a number of clergymen were present and assisted at the ceremonies. Right Rev. Mr. Benedict, Abbot of Gethsemani Monastery, Kentucky, was the special guest for that purpose . . . During the Middle Ages many abbots, especially in England, were powerful feudal barons. In modern times they are simply superiors of religious houses . . .

We cannot give in detail all the ceremonies of the occasion, because in the 1st place, we do not understand them, and in the 2nd place, no mere description could do them justice — the splendor of the robes, the solemn yet beautiful chants . . . the sincerely religious demeanor of bishops and priests, and a score of other impressive pecularities connected with the consecration, we must not describe. There were present to assist Bishop Smyth in the ceremony, Bishop Duggan of Chicago, and the Rev. Frs. Clifford, Fendrick, Meis, McCabe and Cannon of Dubuque. The attendants of Rt. Rev. Benedict, the Kentucky abbot, were Fathers Robert and John of the monastery.

After the conclusion of the consecration ceremonies, Bishop Duggan entered the pulpit and preached one of the most eloquent sermons we have ever listened to. His subject was: "The Shame and the Glory of the Cross" . . . During the Mass of Mercadante a most elegant and difficult piece of vocalization was executed by Miss Linn Jones. Her voice is a beautiful, sweet, clear soprano, and no words of ours can pay her a higher compliment than did the immense audience in the painful stillness that reigned throughout the church during the time she was singing . . .

The name of Miss Linn Jones is an historic one both in its church and state connotations in Iowa. Two of the leading counties of the state were named after her. Her father, General George Wallace Jones, had been delegate to the United States Congress from both Iowa and Wisconsin Territories, and for many years senator from Iowa, and it was he who directed the naming of the counties of the new state. He had been an intimate friend of Bishop Loras, and now under Bishop Smyth he was the most prominent Catholic layman in Iowa. His daughter Linn, named after his affectionate colleague, United States Senator Linn of Missouri, had attended St. Joseph's Academy, the neighboring institution to New Melleray, and there she had become acquainted with the then Prior Smyth and later Prior O'Gorman, when they had frequently come to the convent to conduct retreats and other religious exercises.

Her father after his senatorial career had been appointed by President Buchanan as minister to Colombia, and now, but recently returned from South America, he listened with pride to his daughter's voice during the ceremonial blessing of the new Cistercian abbot of Dubuque; what added striking piquancy to his presence and Miss Linn's singing on this occasion was the fact that just two months previously he had been released from a short imprisonment in Fort Lafayette, New York, where he had been incarcerated by President Abraham Lincoln who suspected Jones of loyalty to the secessionist South as he had been a college mate and life-long friend of Jefferson Davis, its leader. And but a fortnight or so before the cathedral celebration of Abbot Ephrem's, General Jones had had the most unique celebration, in his honor, ever witnessed in Iowa. A tremendous crowd met him as he stepped off the steamboat in the harbor, the traces of his carriage horses were cut, and his enthusiastic admirers, welcoming him back from "the American Bastile" as the orators of the civic jubilation that day called his imprisonment, pulled his vehicle through the city's streets amidst the fireworks shot off on the Dubuque hills and the lusty ovations of the general public.

The first year of New Melleray's life as an abbey proved to be the last one on this side of heaven for five of the professed brothers, none of them old men; they were between the ages of forty-seven and fifty-five. Their deaths made more than a small breach in the ranks of the little more than sixty monks of the institution. Another year and a half passed and the news was brought to the abbey of the rather unexpected departure from this life of their first prior, Bishop Clement Smyth, at the age of fifty-seven years. The first Trappist bishop of the western world had never possessed a strong constitution and the war years had been hard on him. With his advance in age his illnesses had increased and a last arduous journey to Des Moines had planted in him the germs of the sickness which laid him low. His life had been quiet and saintly with little touch of the dramatic about it. And so was his death which occurred on September 23, 1865. At his solemn funeral Archbishop Kenrick of St. Louis was celebrant of the requiem mass, Bishop Henni of Milwaukee was in the sanctuary, and Bishop Duggan of Chicago preached the sermon.

The forthright scribe of the abbey annals, Brother Kieran, pronounced an epitaph that was somewhat bitterly worded: "He was twenty years and some months a member of our Order. As Bishop and [because] of his former connections with the Cistercian Order, he might have done something more than he did for his community. He had a good example set him by his predecessor, the Right Rev. Dr. Loras. What is here written of Bishop Smyth is applicable to Bishop O'Gorman — the difference being that the latter had a new diocese to form and was as poor as poverty itself could make it. Most likely each of them had plenty to do in their new mode of life without thinking of bestowing benefits on our community."

THE ABBEY

XIV

THE CHICAGO TRIBUNE AND
THE ABBEY

The existence of a strict monastic outpost, of a flourishing Cistercian abbey, in mid-America seemed quite incredible to the people of the 1860s and even of the following decades, but remained an amazingly obstinate fact. Telegraph wires at last stretching out entirely across the continent began to carry news stories; the railroads, throwing out their ribbons of steel from the Great Lakes to the Rockies and the Pacific coast, were now transporting people into sights and scenes hitherto only dreamed of. The appearance of this semi-mysterious religious institution, of this resurgent relic of ancient and mediaeval centuries, in the hardy and practical American West, in the heart of the modern Mesopotamia — today the veritable breadbasket of the world — was and is a matter of ever recurring peculiar interest. Articles and pamphlets and booklets have been written about New Melleray by Catholics and non-Catholics alike; stories about this monastery and its monks have appeared at frequent intervals in the newspapers from Minneapolis to Des Moines and from Chicago across to Omaha, and the public always appears intrigued.

One of the first articles — and one of the best — written about New Melleray Abbey was carried in the *Chicago Tribune* in October of 1863. The *Chicago Tribune* then as today was the principal vehicle of news and opinion in the central United States. This article from the pen of a cultured and broad-minded non-Catholic journalist, January Searle, gives a picture of New Melleray Abbey during the Civil War years with fascinating and intimate detail. It should be mentioned here that Abraham Lincoln was a faithful subscriber to and reader of the *Tribune* and it is easily probable that the Great Emancipator read this article with his usual chuckle and more than a modicum of interest. This contemporary story of the Iowa Trappists is told so well and with such disarming charm that it bears recounting almost in its entirety, even though it may be colored by the peculiar subjective dispositions of the writer.

THE MONKS OF LA TRAPPE IN IOWA
Description of the Monastery and How the Fathers Live
(Special Correspondent to the Chicago Tribune)

Dubuque, Oct. 26, 1863

I left Chicago a day or two since, to pay a visit to the La Trappe Monastery, ten miles over the river beyond Dubuque. As a preliminary to that visit, I called upon Clement Smyth, Bishop of Dubuque — a noble citizen and a most uncompromising Union man, and he was courteous enough to give a letter of introduction to the Abbot of the Monastery at New Melleray. I found him in the church grounds. He wore a mitre-shaped hat and the usual long robes of a priest in undress. He is a tall, handsome man, with an expression of great intelligence and general good humor in his face. His residence was the old house built for the Bishop of Dubuque, and was at that time the largest house in the city. It stands close to the new church, facing the mighty river, and backed by bluffs two hundred feet high. The revenues of the bishoprick are said to be immense, and out of them the church and a magnificent palatial residence for the Bishops have just been built. The latter, indeed, is not yet completed.

The old cemetery is situated on the top of the bluffs, amongst the trees overlooking the church and the precincts below. The new cemetery is three miles off, at Mount St. Bernard College.

After I had received my letter of introduction, I returned to the Julien Hotel where I put up — the most homely and hospitable of all the inns where I have lodged in the West — and hiring a pair of horses and a buggy, drove *straight* over the *crooked,* jaggy, uphill and downdale road to the Monastery. It was in many respects a dangerous ride, especially that part of the road for about two miles which led from the city to the wilderness of hills. To say that it was rough and narrow and jagged would give no idea of its terror and unpleasantness. A false step would have sent the horses plunging, pell mell, down the precipice into the river — by no means a pleasant thought! But as soon as I arrived amongst the hills and far inland valleys all that trouble vanished and all looked new and pretty in the midst of the glorious enjoyment which these new aspects of nature brought me.

It would be difficult to exaggerate the effects of the autumnal tints of the woods in their comminglings with the landscape. Grey and dark were the distant woods, and dun and yellow the prairies and the intermediate valleys; and the great belts of woodland and the tiny patches, and here and there the solitary trees, and the thick undercover of hazels were illuminated with such intense and gorgeous colors as to give the idea of an Arabian Nights' vision, so Eastern it looked in its dreamy haze! Pale orange, russet, dark yellow, crimson, ruby pink and fiery vermillion — these were some of the pigments wherewith nature had painted her autumnal scenery in these parts amongst the highlands of Iowa!

We passed many houses on the road, many of them isolated, and here and there a house of entertainment for man and beast. At last when I had arrived within a couple of miles of the monastery I came up to one of the most respectable looking of these houses — the Twelve Mile House; and remembering that my friends, the Monks, had no relish for the flesh-pots of Egypt, and that their food consisted for the most part of roots and herbs such as hermits in the older time did eat and no more; it struck me that the rural hostel might possibly supply my own wants and those of the noble horses which I had brought with me. For the idea of roots and herbs (raw relishes, peradventure, and cabbage innocent of the cook pot) was not very savoury or tempting to a hungry stomach. So I pulled up and dined well there.

My route now, for two miles, lay through some thick hilly woods where the path was execrable, having a water rut down the middle of it and large boulder stones down each side of it. For about a mile the road descended rather precipitately, and at the bottom of the hills I came to a stream of running water which I had to cross nearly axle deep. From this point the road ascends until on a sudden we came out of the woods, most of which belong to the Abbey; and the moment we were clear of them the broad, open farm lands of the Abbey spread before us in glorious upland sweeps, rising gradually from the well cultivated valleys. The whole appearance of these lands gave the impression of long culture and reminded me of some of the old Eastern farms. Good fences of solid rail enclosed these vast fields, many of which looked forlorn and desolate with the ragged and frost-bitten corn. Further on to the right were some fine pieces of prairie which had the appearance of old park lands belonging to some noble estate in Europe. Whilst I was looking over these fair landscapes, there came riding up to me on horseback a remarkable figure in a long woolen robe and a slouched hood on his head in the place of a cap. He pulled up on my whip hand and I saw clearly enough that he was a monk belonging to the Abbey at Melleray. I afterwards learned that he was the post-man of the establishment. He inquired eagerly after the election news which I was the first to carry into that wilderness. He did not rejoice over the intelligence which I gave him, but muffled his speech as if he were going to a funeral. He departed on his way and my heart did not go with him.

A quarter of a mile further to the left, on a gentle eminence, stood a large white-washed church built of wood, lighted up by four large windows, with a belfry and two crosses, one at each end of the building. It is a secular church built for the worship of the neighboring farmers and settlers. The ordinary attendance on Sunday is about 600; and during the festivals of the nation — the Thanksgiving Day and the 4th of July — the church is usually crowded. It stands a little off the main road and nearly opposite to it, on the right hand, are the entrance gates of the Abbey.

These are of simple wooden structure, altogether unlike the ruins of similar gateways which the traveller meets in Europe; but the fac-similes of those which are first erected in every new country where Christianity obtains a foothold. It was only after religious fraternities had grown rich that they sought to beautify their houses and build them up in cultured stone. What is now going up in this Abbey at Melleray is precisely what transpired during the early history of every European Abbey, and on going over it, one seems transported back fourteen hundred years and to be present at the founding of Christianity itself.

The gates are old and dilapidated and the carriage road leading to the Abbey is planted with five rows of poplars on each side of it. To the right running from the gates are the kitchen gardens; to the left open fields; the drive to the house is about a quarter of a mile. It is fenced all round with a substantial railing and here I tied the horses whilst I went and announced myself.

The Abbey is a long wooden building containing all of the rooms and religious apartments necessary for the proper conduct of such an establishment. The lodge faces the second entrance gates and one ascends it on wooden steps. There is first of all a kind of stoop or porch, extending from the main building with several chairs in it for travellers to rest on. Beyond this is the Abbey Lodge kept by Brother Augustine, the porter. There was no one in it when I entered and I was profane enough to take stock of the apartment. It consisted of a table under the window, where without ceremony I ensconced my gun and travelling gear. A number of chairs — three or four — a stove, a clock on the wall and four or five pictures — The Marvellous Ascension, The Sacred Heart of Our Lord, Giving the Habit, Crucifixion of Our Lord — these were some of the subjects.

Presently Brother Augustine entered and I delivered to him my letter of introduction. He vanished out of a side door instanter and returned with the Prior of the house, Father Bernard, the Abbot being at his devotions. This good Father was a genuine, good-natured Irishman, a tall, stout man, a scholar of course as all such are, and a man of intelligence and ready wit with much simplicity of manner. He was very agreeable and very communicative and hospitable. He called upon Brother Augustine who was a short, round-bodied man with a remarkable, shrewd expression of face and genial withal, to bring me bread, cheese and ale; all of which after sufficient trial I found excellent food; especially the ale which had a rich flavor of the malt in it and not too much hop; nor was it too strong — a little flat, if it had a fault, but very welcome to thirsty lips.

I told Father Bernard that I had come all that long distance to see the Abbey and to make a report of what I saw in the Chicago Tribune, whereupon he went with me directly to the gardens which I found interesting enough. They occupied ten acres. There were upwards of 300 apple trees on the ground; above 100 pear trees; 7 or 8,000 plum trees; an acre of strawberry plants from which last year they gathered nearly 100 wagon loads of fruit. The berries are nearly as large as a plum — their name "Wilson's Albany Seedling." The fault of them is that they are too acid. Hundreds of current and gooseberry bushes were ranged in rows all along the garden. The garden itself is surrounded by poplars forty feet high most of which are four years old. The garden walk within the enclosure is walled also with poplars. At the top of the garden near the house is the Apiary containing about fifty hives — well sheltered.

The Abbot was making many improvements in the garden — and among them was the erection of a large garden house with a green-house attached, the foundations of which were dug and partly laid when I was there.

The nurseries were also large, mostly of poplars, with which they proposed to make fences all around the farm. At one time all the hedges on this vast estate were composed of Osage orange shrubs; they had four miles of these shrubs on the grounds. But the winter last year killed them all except a strong thick piece at the top of the garden which had withstood all its shafts and the bitings of the frost.

I noticed that the garden contained everything which the monks could possibly require for their use in the house. Father Bernard showed me the tobacco patch with a good deal of pride. They had raised a fine crop from it and he was evidently looking forward to much enjoyment from a participation in its sedative fascination.

When I said to him, "Dear Father, I thought the rules of your Order forbade you from smoking?"

He said, "Yes! but not from sniffing! We rise every morning at two o'clock and go to bed at seven in the evening. When we rise it is good to taste the titilating narcotic in the olfactories! It rouses us up thoroughly and other successive pinches keep us awake."

"Rise at two o'clock," said I; "that is surely a very early hour!"

"Not a bit too early," he replied, "to praise God! We pray, more or less, from that hour to eight o'clock. There are intervals during those six hours which a Monk can fill up as he pleases; either by praying or reading in the Chapter House."

I saw some rows of fine plum trees and there were extensive graperies laid out and framed.

After making a survey of the upper part of the garden, we walked to the lower end of it towards the entrance gates. I asked how many acres the estate contained and the Father told me there were 1600 acres in a compact body round the house, 1000 of which were cultivated, 400 in timber and the rest wild.

The number of brothers in the Abbey was sixty; and there were six priests to attend to their spiritual necessities.

At the foot of the garden near the entrance gates was the graveyard of the Abbey; and to meet it was a very touching sight to see the clustered graves of the six dead brothers who reposed there. There was something very patriarchal in thus gathering them together in that quiet and secluded garden. They still seemed to be a part of the Abbey family and were only separated from the living by a few feet of earth. Here came every day one or more of the good monks to hold commune with God over their ashes; so that although they were no longer familiar objects on earth, they were not forgotten, but affectionately remembered and many prayers were said for their souls' rest.

Father Bernard related to me the names of these dead monks who slept so well under the open heavens, far away from the proud fanes of European cities. These were all the monks who had died within the walls of the Abbey during fourteen years. There were two graves close to them, ranged indeed in the same row with them, of seculars who had visited the Abbey and died there during their sojourn. All the graves were simple hillocks, having wooden crosses at the heads of them on which the names of the departed were inscribed with their ages when they died.

The monks' names are as follows:

Brother Lawrence, aged 60
Brother Benedict, aged 55
Brother Francis, aged 55
Brother Robert, aged 70
Brother Andrew, aged 40
Brother Stanislaus, aged 27

The seculars were:

Mr. Nolan, aged 70
Mr. Casey, aged 35
Both from Ireland.

When the Father had pointed out these graves to me, he paused a moment and with much earnestness said: "I knew all these Brothers intimately well; and if it be possible for men to live without sin, those who lie here were sinless!"

We went from the garden to the washing and drying grounds which were about a quarter of an acre in extent, surrounded by poplar trees. One man washed and dried for the whole community.

It may be as well to state here that every trade required in the service of the abbey is represented by some member of the fraternity; and I saw the various shops of the carpenter, tailor, shoemaker, watchmaker, blacksmith, etc.

I was much interested in the bakery which supplied the food for so much godliness. The entrance is by a side door which leads into a narrow and thoroughly monastic passage way having a window looking into the garden and piles of wood ranged along the outer wall. A door to the left leads down a short flight of steps into the large and open room where Brother Jerome makes all the bread for the monks and the chance visitors. It differs in no wise from any other bakery that I am aware of, except that the oven is probably larger than most, being capable of baking three or four barrels of flour at a time. Brother Jerome seemed very delighted to see me and I have no doubt he would have been equally delighted to see the very devil in that wild seclusion of his; so that I take no credit to myself on that account. He wore a white cap — did Brother Jerome — and he grabbed my hand at parting with the grip of an iron vise, grinning from ear to ear with a most comical expression of laughter on his white face.

From the bakery we crossed the courtyard to make the inspection of the house. At one corner of it I saw two brothers in their monastic habits, chopping and piling wood, whilst others cast side-long glimpses at the Chicago stranger and vanished under the arches of sojourning outhouses. The habit of this Order, — vulgarly called La Trappe, from the original monks in France whose house stood in a valley and was then nicknamed La Trappe — the habit of this Order is precisely that which was worn by the old Romans 1400 years ago. It is the veritable Toga Virilis; but although warm and picturesque it is not the best adapted to the hard work of modern times. Like the Toga, however, there are brass rings attached to it which, by the aid of a string, draw up the folds and leave the limbs tolerably free for action. The Romans called this *arta cinctus* — highly girt up, ready for knuckling and mauling. A heavy hood covered the entire head — and when not wanted for protection was thrown over the neck, upon the back, between the shoulders.

We entered the house by the front porch and passed through a narrow passage to a private chapel on the right where a monk was kneeling before the Crucifix on the dimly lighted altar. The ghastly appearance of the man, clothed from head to foot in white woolen garments, kneeling there so motionless, did not affect me in the pleasantest manner and reminded me of a vision I once saw in an opium dream when recovering from a sickness. Neither was the close odor which greeted my nostrils the most agreeable perfume which I had tasted. It would be easy to remedy this if the good monks would only admit the fresh air — and I take the liberty to make this suggestion for their benefit and in part payment for their kindness to me.

Immediately behind this private oratory was the Church of the Abbey. Every morning at two o'clock the great bell rings and all the brothers turn out of their dormitory and repair at once to the Church where they pray in silence for two hours. The Church is dimly lighted with candles and the High Altar is illuminated with numerous wax tapers. At such a time it is a very imposing spectacle to behold. The front stalls are occupied by the monks in their white habits; the back stalls by the lay-brothers who are clothed with black garments. At four o'clock Mass is celebrated and it is optional to the Brothers either to be present at this sacred rite, or to retire to private devotions, or to go read and meditate in the Chapter House. The breakfast, however, varies according to the season. At eight o'clock the secular business commences. Teams are driven afield — either to plow, or sow, or reap, as the case may be. The stock is duly provided for; the pigs and poultry are fed; the horses groomed and provisioned; the working carpenters, the smith, the baker, the tailor, the shoemakers, the woodchopper, the cook, the brewers — have each their task allotted to them.

The watchmaker repairs all wrong-going time pieces; the physician attends to the sick in the hospitals; the lawyer — if his services are required — attends to the Abbey interests; and indeed this secluded establishment is a busy world in miniature, and man, however much he may be restrained by religious doctrine and discipline, is still the same old mole that he is in the out-of-door world, animated by the same feelings and subject to the same passions.

I saw no difference except in dress between these Benedictine Monks and the ordinary people of our cities. They very evidently do not allow their religious devotions to interfere with their secular affairs, but are good, shrewd business men who look well after their own interests. They seem to thrive on their vegetable diet; and their field hands perform as much labor and work as long without fatigue as any other farmers. This is rather surprising because the articles of their day's provender are not of the most substantial kind, often consisting of nothing more than boiled beets and coarse brown bread with a pint or so of cold coffee.

I questioned Father Bernard as to the health of the Monks and their capability of endurance. He replied by calling to one of two Monks who were returning with a wagon and a yoke of oxen from the fields where they had been husking corn all day to come and speak to him. The man, whose name was Brother Merry (sic), jumped down from the wagon like a young, lusty fellow of twenty-five and soon stood before us in his working garb.

"How old are you, Brother Merry?" asked the Father.

"Eighty years within a few months," was the reply.

"And do you feel well and hearty?"

The man gave a round, horse laugh at this question, gathered up his long garments, arta cinctus, and began to dance about like a lamp-lighter. He was clearly booked for a long lease of life yet; and there did not appear in him any of the usual signs of extreme old age.

I thought, however, that the monks whose avocations confined them mostly to the Abbey did not look solid, substantial men although most of them were stout and fleshy. They seemed puffed and flabby, if I may use such expressions without offence, and lacked that hard, healthy look which the field hands possessed.

One thing struck me on going over the Abbey yards and grounds, namely the silence that enveloped them like an atmosphere. Signs of busy life and activity were abundant, and monks were moving about here and there and everywhere. But there was no noise — no shouts nor laughter. All was as still as death, broken only by the occasional sharp ring of the hammer on the smithy anvil, and by the lowing of the cattle on the hills.

The only glimpse I got of the Abbot was in the Church, and then I only saw his skull-cap. He was praying there and I could just see it over the railing; and a little to the right of him was another monk — a very old man, upwards of eighty years, who was also occupied at his devotions. The Father told me that these two monks were, to use his own words "at it all the time; week in, week out, morning and night; and they'll soon be in heaven," he added. The height of the Church was twenty-five feet, the length about eighty feet and the breadth thirty-five.

From the Church we went to the Chapter house, a long, low, narrow room, where the monks read and write during their leisure. I could not help contrasting this humble apartment with the magnificent structures of York, Peterboro, Ely, Lincoln and Durnam, all which I have had the supreme pleasure of beholding. In a short time, however, the present Abbey will give place to a majestic stone building and this matter with many others will be remedied. All around the room seats were arranged and under them were little recésses, each containing a few pious books and a copy of the holy Scriptures. On the walls were hung several mediocre engravings of sacred subjects and tables of church duties with the names of the officers appointed to perform them. These were altered every week; and there was a similar table for serving Mass with a weekly directory of saints' festivals. At the end of the room was the symbol of the Cross. The refectory was a large room capable of containing all the monks. It was sixty feet long and twenty-five feet wide containing three rows of tables, and in each brother's place, there with the brother's name printed on it, was a napkin, a knife and fork, a spoon and a drinking cup. In the middle of the room was a desk for the lector whose duty it was to read from the Acta Sanctorum whilst the dinner was progressing.

The bill of fare in the refectory is not the most tempting which an epicure could desire. It consists entirely as I said of vegetables, — namely: boiled potatoes, beets, onions, parsnips and mangle wurtzel; relieved occasionally by batter puddings, apple and plum pastries and great bowls of milk. In the fruit season the dinner table is laden with strawberries, raspberries, currants, gooseberries, apples, plums, grapes — as the case may be — and some of the finest wheaten bread I have ever tasted. It is a curious sight to see the monks at dinner in their antique dresses and to watch the expression of their faces as they discuss the viands before them. Not a word is spoken by anyone present from first to last. The lector reads in a dreary, monotonous tone of voice, his passages from the Lives of the Saints and the thoughts of each particular brother are supposed to be occupied all the while with divine things.

The dormitory contained some forty beds and was in no way remarkable. The apartment for strangers is capable of accommodating eight sleepers.

Having visited the inner apartments of the Abbey we returned to the Lodge where Brother Augustine insisted that we should partake once more of his malt brews. A jovial monk this! — who evidently desires to keep up the olden tradition of monkish hospitality.

In conclusion I may say that there was everywhere the appearance of tranquillity and happiness. I asked the Father if any of the Monks had run away.

"No!" he said. "They are all perfectly happy here and contented. It is true that they work hard; and they live on vegetable food, never tasting meat except when they are sick, but no one ever utters a complaint. Of course," he added, "nothing but the inspiration and grace of God could keep men here. They can all leave if they like. I have a horse," he said, "worth a hundred dollars, in the stable. What is to prevent me from getting into the saddle and riding off? Nothing, my friend, nothing at all, but the restraining grace of God."

And I believe it is all true.

January Searle[1]

---

[1] A few of the details of Mr. Searle's otherwise accurate article are not quite correct: 1) the ages of the brothers buried in the cemetery: that of Brother Stanislaus is correct, that of Brother Andrew too low, and those of the others too high; 2) likewise neither the abbot nor the other monk "praying in the church" were "upwards of eighty years," for the records reveal that among the sixty or more members of the community at that time three were dividing the honor of being the oldest at the age of sixty-four; 3) of the two seculars buried in the cemetery, the Cemetery Record shows that the name of the one is not "Casey" but John Flinn; (incidentally, the other — Mr. Nolan — was the father of Brothers Joseph and Peter Nolan of the monastery); 4) the age of "Brother Merry" of whom there is no record as well as the entire incident about him seems to be an exaggeration, and is a typical example of the ability of that eccentric and inveterate jokester, Father Bernard McCaffrey, of pulling the leg of an inquisitive stranger, no matter how distinguished he might be.

XV

MATERIAL PROGRESS

* * * * * * * * * * *

The frame buildings — stoutly constructed as they were — which housed the community of New Melleray Abbey were naturally regarded by the monks as only temporary dwellings which some day would be replaced by a stone monastery worthy of its name. That day finally arrived; the expansion of the holdings of the institution and the prosperity it enjoyed during the Civil War and the years of its immediate aftermath, due to the toil and frugality and patience of the brothers, placed it in a financially favorable position where its wholesome ambitions could be realized on a lofty scale. Money had been set aside; stones and lumber had been gathered for years; the plans were sent by Abbot Ephrem to the General Chapter and came back approved.

Fortunate was New Melleray in securing the competent services of John Mullany. This Dubuque architect was the brother of Brother Stanislaus Mullany, the first member of the community to die at New Melleray. John Mullany had been for three years in England on the staff of Augustus Welby Pugin, the architectural genius of the nineteenth century who at his death left England studded with his cathedrals, parliamentary buildings, colleges and monasteries, among the latter Downside of the Benedictines and Mount Saint Bernard's of the Cistercians. Pugin more than anyone else restored architecture in England and revived the mediaeval forms which since his day have covered that land. Mullany successfully carried over Pugin's Gothic spirit and his embodiment of Gothic art into the building he erected at New Melleray. The two wings of the proposed huge quadrangular edifice erected according to his designs — the north wing two hundred and twelve feet in length and the east wing one hundred and twenty feet — were of the Pointed Gothic style of the thirteenth century. These designs, for the major part unchanged, are still today being gradually carried out toward the completion of the quadrangle. The two wings begun in March of 1868 were completed on the 1st of November, 1870, at a cost of just under one hundred thousand dollars, and without a single cent of indebtedness remaining. This amount by no means represented the real cost, for no account was made of the materials and labor provided by the monks themselves which probably far exceeded another hundred thousand. Because of delays and difficulties due principally to problems of heating and ventilation, the structure much to the understandable disappointment of every member of the community was not occupied for habitancy until 1875. By that time another important addition, one hundred and twelve feet in length, known as the kitchen-wing, was constructed.[1]

The gray, limestone cloister-walls were firmly and carefully laid and soon the ivy was growing upon them. Today — and even since shortly after 1875 — the abbey beneath its steepled crosses and sturdily graceful stone water tower fifty feet in height has assumed an appearance of antiquity and hoary venerability.

Dom Bruno of Mount Melleray returned to America and Iowa in October of 1870 just as the two Gothic wings were being completed in all their pristine loveliness. It had been ten years since his last visitation. Astonished and gratified at the prosperity of the hitherto often tottering Dubuque institution he launched out on a paean of rapture and praise on his visitation card of that year:

---

[1] The principal contractor who assisted John Mullany in the building of New Melleray Abbey was John Keenan of Dubuque who during over half a century of building activities had erected churches and public buildings in various localities in the state of Iowa. In 1850-51 he had built Mount St. Bernard's College and Seminary for Bishop Loras at Table Mound just south of Dubuque, and exactly fifty years later he constructed Hennessy Hall, which today is the Science Building of Loras College, the successor to Mount St. Bernard's College.

"We find a great source of joy in the actual condition of New Melleray. Little more than twenty years ago, Ireland being then in a sea of confusion, we made choice of your present Prior (Father Bernard) as a fit and proper person to act as Pioneer in this Country, with a view to the Foundation of a monastery. We gave him a letter, in which, as we recollect, we expressed a hope that we might live to see a Majestic Monastery of the Cistercian Order rising up in the midst of one of the vast solitudes of America. That bright vision is become a still brighter reality.

"Let a traveller from Europe take his stand upon the eminence known here as Mount Carmel. Tell him to fix his steady gaze upon the Buildings and the Land, upon the Live Stock, the Trees and the Fences. Tell him that all the improvements, the cultivation of the Farm, and the splendid stock are all, without exception, the fruits of Monastic industry; that the Monks worked morning, noon and night, sometimes at 2 o'clock in the morning, sometimes at 10 o'clock at night; that they travelled night and day in all kinds of weather, collecting, not money, but cattle to make money; that the Superiors never sent out begging Brothers or begging letters, never made appeals to the public in any Newspaper, and scarcely ever received even a small donation from any Benefactor.

"The Traveller will naturally ask: what was the number of Brothers, and what the number of years, since the Foundation of this Monastery? When informed that New Melleray was not founded until late in the summer of 1849, and that the average number of Brothers throughout the whole period was under fifty, we can imagine his amazement. Well might he exclaim: 'Incredible! Incredible! . . . The truth appears to me stranger than fiction. When or where, in what country or in what Century since the Foundation of Christianity, was there ever a stone Monastery built otherwise than by subscription and collection? New Melleray must be one of the wonders of the Roman Catholic Church. It must be the wonder of the Cistercian & of every Religious Order, of the Trappist & of every Religious Congregation!'

"Your reply should be 'Non nobis, Domine, non Nobis.' 'Not to us, O Lord, not to us, but to Thy Name give glory!'"

And then with a touch of justifiable pride, Dom Bruno, the Father Immediate, spoke of one of the great distinctions of his still youthful affiliate: "We find another source of joy in the extraordinary esteem and predilection exhibited by His Holiness, the Pope, towards this

Community. The name of New Melleray has been mentioned in his presence only to be honored. Once, and only once in Europe, since the time of De Rancé, who this day 200 years was Abbot of la Grande Trappe, — once only was a Trappist monk chosen to be Bishop. Father Malachy became Bishop of Carpentras and continued as far as possible to lead the life of a Trappist Monk . . .

"Passing from Europe to the new world, what do we behold? A small Community, scarcely beyond the age of infancy, living in a Frame House, glorying in the Cross of Christ, and in that calm, holy obscurity which is the true element of the Monks of La Trappe. From that one little Monastery the Holy See was pleased to take two Bishops within three years . . .

"Rejoice in this that their names are, as we confidently hope, written in the book of life, and that Our Holy Father the Pope was pleased to select two Monks of New Melleray out of nearly two thousand Priests then officiating in the United States."

It was well that the brethren had this period of rejoicing with Dom Bruno; in less than a decade the day of catastrophe and desolation — the worst in their history — was to be upon them, and that bitter day was to stretch out into many sad years for the Dubuque Trappist house.

The monk who at this time was more responsible than any other for the material growth and prosperity of the Iowa monastery was undoubtedly Brother Mary Bernard Murphy. This housekeeper or business manager or bursar of the establishment — he was actually all three — enjoyed the complete confidence and trust of the abbot. Abbot Ephrem was a pious, an extremely pious, man. *The Chicago Tribune* correspondent had heard correctly when he was told that the abbot spent so much of his time in prayer in the monastery church. Physically, he was by no means strong in body or health. Because of this, he delegated much of his authority in directing the abbey to the prior, Father Bernard McCaffrey, and to the housekeeper, Brother Mary Bernard. The abbot's physician recommended drives in the fresh air, and of this means for preserving his health, Brother Kieran wrote slyly and somewhat waspishly: "For this purpose the housekeeper bought for the Abbot's exclusive use a grand buggy. This was used by him only in the summer and fall. For his winter drives was purchased a splendid sleigh-cutter. Glittering in the sunshine with its brilliant varnish, horse and harness were well mated to these vehicles. The horse invariably was the best pacer in our stables. To complete the turn-out a beautiful string of musical sleigh-bells had to be added. With these, cushions and buffalo-coverings, the rig was perfect.

"Now all this was meant for the Abbot's health, of course, and at all events it is well known the Abbot's health was very delicate and most likely he needed this exercise. Indeed, it is well known too that he was suffering from serious infirmities, and so kept on to his drives until within a few months of his departure to Mount Melleray, the 29th of August, 1883."

This solicitude for the infirm abbot by the housekeeper, Brother Mary Bernard, was without any doubt perfectly justifiable in the circumstances, but it also brought about in return an intensification of the trust and affection which the abbot entertained for him. Brother Mary Bernard was a redoubtable character and possessed a colorful personality, and from all that can be learned about him one must conclude that he was a good and pious monk. He showed for years a wonderful business ability, and the clever resourcefulness that was displayed in many important undertakings never reflected in the slightest on his honesty and integrity.

Brother Mary Bernard had been one of the younger monks on the steamboat *Constitution* in 1849 when the cholera had struck down so many of the passengers including six of his Trappist brethren, and the heroic assistance he had rendered to the afflicted during that voyage had won for him high commendation from Father Patrick and the other members of the colony. During the early bitter years of the New Melleray foundation he had been a loyal and faithful worker in the community, and his sterling talents had finally caused him to be singled out for the important office of housekeeper. In the Iowa of his day he had shrewdly discovered that on the broad acres of his monastic house the livestock industry could be very profitably developed, and among his many activities it was this particular field that he exploited more than any other.

In the early 1860's he had already won a creditable name for the Dubuque monastery farm as a cattle and oxen ranch. The *Chicago Tribune* correspondent had written in glowing terms of the monastery cattle, as this interesting excerpt shows: "In the Cattle Yard I saw some of the finest Durham stock I had ever beheld. I had a good view of the estate from this yard; and was pleased to see that the hills and prairies were well stocked with cattle. — They give a pretty, pastoral aspect to the landscape. There were hundreds of well selected pigs, and lots of poultry in the yard. The noble part of the stock, however, were the Durham oxen. They have twenty-four pedigree Durhams on the estate. Those which struck me as being the noblest of these animals, were, the one a red and white, from Sangamon County, Illinois, and the other, all red, to which the first premium had been awarded at the late Dubuque fair. I was so fascinated by the last animal that I studied his points long enough to describe him — if only I had the ability to do it."[2]

The fame of the farms of New Melleray Abbey and of their products and livestock spread throughout the West, and at the time it was a well-earned and wholesome fame. But beneath this material prosperity of the institution lay constantly an uneasy feeling, a feeling of incipient threat toward the quiet spiritual order that should be the Trappist way of life.

This lurking danger was not entirely hidden from the kindly solicitous eyes of the various visitators, possessed of the austere and penitential character of St. Benedict and Citeaux. During this cycle of years there appeared at the Iowa abbey on official visits besides Dom Bruno of Mount Melleray, Dom Anthony of Melleray, France, Abbot Benedict of Kentucky's Gethsemani, Father James, prior of Little Clairvaux of Tracadie in Canada, and finally Dom Eugene of France's ancient Melleray. Not like old monastic patriarchs nor with stentorian voices did they denounce the ever growing threat

[2] Searles later judged he had the ability to depict this prize ox, and for those who are interested in pedigreed cattle, — and especially in the splendid type of livestock possessed by New Melleray Abbey in the 1860s and 1870s —, his following description is herewith given:

"The Monk whose business it was to attend to him roused him from his stall, and brought him out with a halter tied to his horns. There he stood, that vast Leviathan of beef! on those four short legs, which looked as if they were not half strong enough to bear the ponderous weight of his immense carcass.

"His sides like solid walls; his broad, enormous rear quarters, flanked by a fine tail, with a silky brush, which showed the breeding of a long ancestry of noble sires. The line along the back rising to a high arched ridge over the neck, close to the small and beautifully formed head. The ears and horns small; the eyes large, dark and fiery, the nose delicately moulded. The depth from the top of the neck to the base of the chest, and from thence to the extreme peak of the huge lap that hangs from it and joins the concave line of the belly between the forelegs, is really a mighty measurement, which no man could compass with his outstretched arms and hands. A neck like that of the warhorse spoken of in Job — literally 'clothed with thunder.'

"I walked more than once or twice all around this splendid animal so finely proportioned in all its parts, and thought I had never before seen so much beauty and so much mammoth power combined in any living creature. Brother Romuald, his keeper, who was more than half afraid of him, said he weighed upwards of 2,500 pounds."

to the peaceful life of the cloister; but gently and tenderly they made their cautiously worded but none the less pointed suggestions about avoiding the commerce and traffic of a noisome world. Plainest spoken of all was Abbot Eugene of France. Although unable to speak English, and accompanied by Abbot Benedict of Gethsemani to serve as his interpreter, he made his prudent observations clear: the intensive business traffic was spiritually unhealthy for the order; several of the farms owned or rented were too remote from the abbey for supervision; the frequent travellings by the brothers were dangerous to the quiet contemplative life; too much was spent for the various machines, whose complex operations were not well understood and which were soon abandoned.

These admonitions were hearkened to by the pious Abbot Ephrem of New Melleray with due humility but apparently were not well understood; worrying little about temporal affairs, he passed these admonitions over to Father Bernard, the prior, and Brother Mary Bernard, the procurator, but both of these monks failed to see the necessity of their close and immediate application.

In the long and bitter and acrimonious aftermath that followed the financial collapse of the Iowa Trappist institution in 1879 and 1880 it has been customary for the writers describing that hectic episode to pillory Brother Mary Bernard Murphy as the arch-perpetrator of the disaster, and many acid-tinged shafts were directed by Brother Kieran, the fearless annalist, at "Brother Murphy," as he was then widely known. But in the heyday of the abbey's prosperous fame in the '60s and '70s no one was more highly and more deservedly respected for his honesty, zeal and business genius than this same Trappist brother. His activities reveal an intelligence and acumen in farming and commercial methods that in another walk of life would have made him one of the American captains of agricultural industry of his day. Brother Mary Bernard possessed the respect and admiration of business leaders and bankers from Omaha to Chicago.

In the early 1860s despite the depressing days of the Civil War he began the profitable work that was almost entirely responsible for the eventual erection of the lovely stone monastery building. In the year 1863 he purchased for the brothers their first large flock of sheep — Cotswolds — in central Illinois. Living in an old fashioned canvas-covered wagon for three weeks, he drove the sheep on foot all the way to New Melleray. It was at about this period also that Brother Mary Bernard started to raise the purebred Durham cattle for which the monastery was noted all over the West; he had gone to Kentucky and bought his first herd there. During the Civil War years he commenced the policy of buying hogs and cattle from neighboring farmers in order to fatten them and sell them to the Ryan Packing Company of Galena, Illinois, the largest packing house on the upper Mississippi at that time. The hogs were driven all the way to Galena on foot with a horse-drawn wagon or two accompanying them in order to pick up the tired-out stragglers. This trip from New Melleray to Galena usually took three days. During the winter the task of driving the large herds of hogs across the frozen Mississippi to Galena presented quite a problem. Each brother at hour intervals started over the ice with a small group of hogs. Should the earlier groups become contrary and turn back and meet the later groups coming over there was too much congestion of weight at one spot and danger of the entire herd going to the bottom of the river. On one occasion there was a drove of seven hundred hogs going to the Ryan Packing Company; at another time two hundred and fifty head of cattle were driven over.

During the years Brother Mary Bernard bought a few small farms and rented several others; some of this acreage was tilled to raise grain but most of it was used for grazing purposes for the herds now grown so large that even the monastery lands could not feed them. Various brothers were stationed for certain seasons of the year at these farms to care for the livestock. Most of these farms were in Dubuque County not too many miles distant from the abbey, but about the year 1870 Brother Mary Bernard acquired a large tract of land in Mills County. This county — sparsely settled at that time — is in the southwest corner of Iowa bordering the Missouri river some miles south of the city of Council Bluffs. For years several brothers had to maintain a home in Mills County in order to look after the herds that were grazed there. Brother Mary Bernard and Brother Barnaby lived there an entire year themselves. Many of the Mills County cattle were taken to Omaha to be fed in the distillery there and when fat were shipped to Chicago for sale. The Sisters of Charity owned five hundred acres of wild and unfenced prairie land adjoining the monastery domain and here the brothers herded large droves of cattle. A brother minded the cattle by day, coming home after dark when the cattle would lie down; and he was off again in the morning by daylight.

The procurator's successful endeavors reached out into other fields, too. In the year 1872 he bought forty acres of woodland in South Garryowen, fifteen miles south of the monastery, and for four winters — until 1875 — the brothers made excursions there with horse and mule teams to obtain cord wood and fence posts. Ten thousand posts and five hundred cords of wood were hauled away from those forty acres. The round trip was thirty miles, and in order to complete it in a day, the brethren rose at two o'clock in the morning, went to the stables to feed and harness the teams, came back to the monastery to attend holy mass at three o'clock, ate their breakfast at four and then hitching up their steeds were eight or ten miles away by sunrise — "often a cold winter's morning with the glass perhaps 20 degrees below zero."

Cooperating with Brother Mary Bernard in those years the fathers and brothers performed all their own work on the abbey domain without any hired men. When necessary, in harvest time as many as forty-eight persons, — choir and lay brothers — worked in the field. Of these, eight were regular horse teamsters and two were ox teamsters.

Occasionally, one or other of the Trappist procurator's business exploits was written up in the press. Thus, the Dubuque *Daily Herald* of Sunday, September 12, 1875, proclaimed:

Sale of Short Horns

The Brothers Purchase one of the most Valuable Herds in Illinois for $23,500.

One of the most important purchases of short horn cattle that had been made in Iowa for some time was transacted in this city yesterday. J. B. Murphy, of the Brothers, New Melleray, Dubuque County, has purchased the noted show herd of A. A. Funk, McLean County, Ill., a herd which we venture to say has been looked upon with envy by every stockman in the Northwest. The show herd consists of the First Duke of Vermillion and five cows. The Duke is the prize winner of Kentucky, Ohio and Illinois in his own ring and sweepstakes. Last year this animal was displayed in Indiana and took the 1st prize over the renowned Breastplate in the 4 year old ring in sweepstakes, and all others . . .

In addition to the above herd, the Brothers purchased of A. A. Funk nine other cows as well bred as any in the United States, tracing through the American herd books to the

English herd book. The price paid was $23,500.00. This
herd was originally from Kentucky, was selected with the
utmost care and caution, and was considered one of the
most successful prize winners. We understand that they
will be taken for exhibition to the state fair of Nebraska
which meets on the 21st inst.

It is a matter of record that for fifteen years from 1862 on, the
Trappist brothers of New Melleray successfully entered their purebred cattle at state and county fairs; for several weeks before each
fair there was washing and currying and feeding the animals to
embellish their appearance; two or three brothers accompanied the
bullocks and oxen and were usually gone for a fortnight; they seldom
returned from a fair without coming away with both first and second
prizes and red and blue ribbons on the cattle's horns.

During all this time Abbot Ephrem, zealously wrapped up in the
spiritual affairs of the monastery, never questioned the methods of
Brother Mary Bernard. In the course of his profitable transactions
it was probably inevitable but that the procurator should finally become imbued with the fever of speculation, and should indulge in an
occasional plunge on the Chicago board of trade. He had made the
acquaintance of Armour and others of the great packing industries.
He was the representative of New Melleray, and that now highly re-
puted corporation had an extensive line of credit.

XVI

DEBACLE AND DELIVERANCE

It was not until the spring of 1877 that the authorities of New Melleray Abbey — that is, Abbot Ephrem and the prior, Father Bernard — became uneasy about the financial affairs and structure of the Iowa Trappist institution, and began to challenge and check the business activities of Brother Mary Bernard. That the frenzied finance and traffic had hitherto borne no rank or distasteful fruits was due to the continuance of inflation after the Civil War. The national panic of 1873 did not appear to affect New Melleray at the time, but from that year on the debts of the monastery began to increase rapidly. In 1874 the amount owed was $115,000.00 but the brothers then had enough to meet any demands. Brother Mary Bernard began to show a reluctance and a hesitancy in turning in the accounts and in revealing the bills that were presented for payment. Then in 1877 the abbot and the prior were frightened when they discovered that the indebtedness amounted to $170,000.00. To meet this they had — entirely exclusive of the new monastery itself and the two thousand acres of land around it — assets, mostly in land and some in livestock, between $140,000.00 and $150,000.00. This would have left them, they believed, in debt only to the amount of $20,000.00 or $30,000.00 and this they then hoped to be able to pay off by good management in a few years — should no financial crisis or new panic occur.

The causes of the steady and rapid rise in indebtedness were not obscure and could be bracketed under two principal headings. The one was the heavy interest the monks were compelled to pay for the outstanding obligations. The interest paid to creditors varied, some receiving eight, others ten and a few as high as twelve and a half per cent. Add to this the fact that much of the interest was compounded, and it will be seen how quickly the deficit grew. The other causes were due to a constant and persistent loss in the selling of live stock — in which so much of the monastery's holdings were invested — since the year 1873. Winter feeding of cattle in Iowa had suddenly become a losing venture since the states to the southwest had become cattle raising areas. Kansas, Texas, Colorado and other states became more populated due to the rapid extension of the railroads, and since there was little or no winter there, cattle could be matured without corn or hay. It took sixty bushels of corn worth from $12.00 to $18.00 to fatten an ox in Iowa. In the Southwest men could mature their herds of steers and oxen without corn or hay by merely letting them graze in the fields. The supply of fat cattle carried to the eastern markets from these regions by the new railroads was greater than the demand and ruined all chances for profits by the great Iowa livestock raisers such as the New Melleray corporation.

It became apparent that only a severe tightening, spiritually and corporally, of the monastic belts might save the day — and it was doubtful if even this heroic measure would stave off the threatening catastrophe. In desperation Father Bernard wrote to Dom Bruno in Ireland: "It is with a sad and heavy heart I write this letter to you. When you were here seven years ago, you imposed a law in your visitation card on Brother Mary Bernard to give an accounting to the Abbot, every time he returned home, on how our financial affairs stood. Until the great fall in cattle came 3 or 4 years ago the Abbot did not urge him much. But though often asked, he deferred until 1874 when he gave a statement that our debts were then $115,000.00." After a long recital of the almost insuperable difficulties facing the monastery, Father Bernard made his final plea. "The Abbot and I wish you to make arrangements with the General Chapter to come yourself and visit our house as soon as you can after the Chapter is over. There is no use of sending Abbot Dominic of Tracadie or any one else. None but yourself can do us any good this time. Our debt is not yet too far gone, but if allowed to accumulate for 4 or 5 years more in the ratio it has accumulated for 4 or 5 years past, we may lose all we have. The sooner a remedy is applied, the better."

Of course, Dom Bruno came — but not until a year and a half had elapsed. Toward the end of November, 1879, he arrived at New Melleray accompanied by his sub-prior, Father Lewis Carew. Now in his sixty-sixth year, and still erect and slender of physique, he was as vigorous as ever in the service of the Lord. Old Brother Kieran wrote mournfully in his annals: "He found our affairs much changed, and not for the better, since his last visit in 1870. It was a very different affair from former visitations. There was an atmosphere of dejection and gloom on all sides. The effects of the 'traffic' was felt, — it was more than felt, it took the sorrowful shape of a dark, impenetrable cloud hanging over our monastery, and meant to remain. But our good Visitor told us that the dark, impenetrable cloud must be penetrated by humble incessant prayers. He prescribed special prayers to be said in our community every evening for this purpose, and to continue them until the next Visitation be made. When it was made, the prayers were continued, yes, and even to the Visitation that again followed that."[1]

In addition to his mandate of storming Heaven by prayer, the Father Immediate advocated in this crisis poverty and sacrifice. "If ever you were bound to practice holy Poverty," he urged, "now is the time . . . If you have to wear old, patched boots and shoes; old, patched cowls and cloaks, robes, scapulars and stockings; be content; and let there be no murmur in your heart, or on your lips, or fingers; no sadness, or displeasure, in your eyes, or countenance." And in his appeal for personal sacrifice, the eloquent abbot attacked the use of tobacco with an argument that is such a classic of startling novelty that we dare not forbear quoting it here: "If tobacco was made for Man, it is rather strange that the world had existed for five thousand five hundred years before its use was known. Tobacco, and Martin Luther, and Henry the Eighth, and the so-called Reformation came before Europe much about the same time. To take snuff is bad enough. To smoke, with pipe or cigar, is worse. But to chew is worst of all. Happy is the Monk who never uses tobacco in any

---

[1] These special prayers have not only been continued to the present day but have even been enlarged upon.

shape or form ! Turn away from it, you who are young, as you would turn away from sparks of fire!"

Matters were worse, though, than Dom Bruno dreamed. Prayer and sacrifice are not miracles, and only a miracle could have prevented the culminating calamity from breaking into public news and causing a local panic. Hardly had the Irish abbot and his sub-prior returned to Europe, when matters came to a climax. The sad state of affairs, which month by month had grown worse since the day that Abbot Ephram and Father Bernard had first taken alarm, was now noised far and wide. Creditors came storming out to the abbey grounds in crowds. The monastery resembled a broken savings bank, the only difference being that the doors were left open and all had free entrance.

In desperation Father Bernard sent out eight hundred letters to friends and charitably inclined persons; he received seventy-five replies and only eight hundred dollars. He penned an urgent letter to Father Daniel Hudson of Notre Dame, Indiana, explaining that sixty thousand dollars had to be raised immediately if the Abbey of New Melleray was to be saved, and requesting him to insert an enclosure with a moving appeal in each copy of the *Ave Maria* magazine's next issue, except to "the residents of Dubuque County, Bishops and priests."

In the meantime, the procurator, Brother Mary Bernard, by then thoroughly frightened and feverish, again risked his chances on the Chicago board of trade, rashly hoping for some measure of success. Reverses came fast and he was beaten in the market. In an effort to recoup his losses he went more deeply into debt. 'Although now removed from office and replaced as housekeeper by the able Father Alberic Madigan, he displayed great courage during the stress and strain of the next few months, and it was due to his efforts, aided by Father Alberic, that the monastery land and farm stock were saved from being auctioned off at less than half of their value by the clamoring creditors.

According to Brother Kieran and others the indebtedness had reached the figure of $230,000.00. Due to some remission by friends and to a fortunate legacy by Father James Sweeney of Buchanan County, Iowa, who came to the monastery as a postulant in 1879 and died within a year, the actual figure probably did not far exceed the two hundred thousand dollar mark. But with this huge debt confronting them the monks of New Melleray looked for the end of their

Iowa foundation. The loss to them was everything, and rumors were rife that preliminary arrangements had already been made to close the Trappist cloister and return to Ireland.

Here again Brother Mary Bernard Murphy exerted himself effectively. His staunch friends in the business world came to the rescue. Mr. William J. Knight, one of the most prominent attorneys of the West and for years a state senator of Iowa, who had occasionally represented Brother Mary Bernard in legal affairs; Mr. William Ryan of the Ryan Packing Companies of Dubuque and Galena whose business relations with the former monastery procurator had covered a score of years; and Mr. Patrick Clarke of Dubuque — these three gentlemen freely offered to serve as a committee to represent the New Melleray corporation in settling its affairs with its creditors. The brothers gladly appointed them as the legal trustees of all their properties. The committee published letters and notices that it was deciding upon a bond issue as a solution of the financial problem. The bonds would run for five years, and were renewable, and the high interest rates would have to be reduced to a uniform six per cent. The creditors were assured that in this way — and in this way only — would they all be ultimately repaid.

Preliminary meetings were held, excitement ran high, but the confidence inspired by the high calibre of gentlemen who composed the committee tended to ease the strain of the affair. Finally a general meeting of all the creditors was called at the monastery,. and bonds aggregating two hundred thousand dollars were issued. This meeting, however, promised to be a turbulent one; objections and complaints, long, loud and profanely emphatic, were shouted, and the element that hitherto had been receiving the highest interest proved to be the most difficult to please. An Irish farmer from the northern part of Dubuque County was very violent in his denunciations, using such terms as "swindlers" and "robbers." But when an Englishman rose up and joined him in his abuse of the monks, the Irishman angrily resented his remarks as a Protestant attack on the Faith, and for a moment there was danger of a physical encounter. As a by-play and a piece of very becoming Celtic consistency the episode struck everyone as a refreshing oasis in a desert of dry details. Harmony soon prevailed and the able trustees then guided the meeting to a successful conclusion. "Thus was averted through God's goodness," piously commented Brother Kieran, "the dread of being thrown out of house and home of our beloved New Melleray." But every member of the community was profoundly conscious of the fact that sleeves had to be rolled up and loins girded to meet the labor and economy and sacrifice of the years ahead.

Meanwhile, the former housekeeper, Brother Mary Bernard, bore the overwhelming reverse bravely for a while but as the enormity of the loss dawned upon him and he realized the disastrous effect it had on his Cistercian house, he weakened. It is reported that he died of a broken heart, torn by the anguish of the calamity he brought upon his beloved abbey.

It was inevitable perhaps but that legal haggling should be continued somewhat intermittently by those disappointed with the terms of the Dubuque monastery settlement. Thirteen years after the settlement, in 1893, the final case was disposed of by the courts. The Dubuque *Daily Telegraph* then wrote a special editorial dealing with the matter, indicating how honorable and adequately the monks had fulfilled their obligations.

The McNamara-Melleray Case.

The case of Michael McNamara against the monastic corporation of New Melleray was on Wednesday last, for the second time, decided in favor of the defendant . . .

Regarded from any standpoint this is a complete exoneration of the monastery. If there had been the slightest equitable liability on the part of the corporation, there would have been no suit, for the brothers would have paid every dollar of the claim if the settlement had taken their last acre of land. If proof of this were required, better could not be asked than the fact that the corporation voluntarily assumed the unauthorized debts contracted by Mary Bernard Murphy when it could easily have escaped their payment by resorting to law. It is a splendid tribute to its conscience and character that trying and manifold as have been its financial difficulties, it has uniformly and persistently disdained to avail itself of legal technicalities to escape any debt for which it regarded itself as in the least morally obligated . . .

The case is a very interesting one, and its interest is the justification for this special editorial reference. It has intensified public respect for and confidence in the New Melleray community by making prominent the fact that in its dealings with its creditors the corporation has been governed by a delicate sense of honor and a most scrupulous, high-minded conscientiousness.

This case wrote *finis* to the litigation and to the most desperate and publicly embarrassing crisis in the history of the Iowa Trappist house. But years of heroic labor and struggle had made this honorable denouement possible, and other years of struggle still lay ahead.

Nearly all the monks who had come to America in 1849 and 1850 were surprisingly still alive. They had weathered many a storm and many a crisis and were now venerable and bent and grey. Since 1863 when five of the professed brothers had been laid away in the little monastery cemetery there had not been a death among them. Then in 1882 the pendulum of life slowed up and stood still for seven professed lay brothers of New Melleray. Among them was Brother Philemon, the last survivor of the band of Trappists who were expelled from Melleray Abbey in France in 1831 by Louis Phillipe, King of the French. Brother Philemon had entered the French cloister in 1826 and at the time of his death had been a member of the Cistercian order for over fifty-six years.

The next year, 1883, saw the passing of the first of the Irish monks who had come to the American shores with the definite purpose of establishing a Trappist colony here. He was Father Bernard Mc-Caffrey, the former superior and prior, the staunch but erratically grounded pillar upon whom the simple and pious Abbot Ephrem had leaned during all his years in Dubuque. From the day of Father Bernard's death, March 3d, the abbot himself began to decline, and a few months later, resigning his office, he departed for Mount Melleray, Ireland, on August 29th. Here he survived, however, for another fifteen years, finishing his holy life in 1898.

The last official visitor delegated by the Father Immediate, Dom Bruno, to inspect the Iowa monastery before the resignation of Abbot Ephrem, was none other than a son of France, Dom Jean Marie, abbot of Our Lady of Bellefontaine, France. Arriving in New Melleray in June of 1883, he found the community somewhat reduced in numbers, there being fifty-one members including novices and postulants. Encouraging them he wrote on his visitation card: "We knew what a heavy debt weighed upon you, and one of our first cares has been to inquire into this matter. We have been very happy to learn and to feel assured ourselves, that, thank God, you are henceforth out of all danger and that with the Blessing of God, the resources of the

Farm and proper management, you may be free from debt and may even begin again to think of completing your new monastery. Without any doubt the severe lesson you have received will preserve you from future danger . . . We must in truth, my very dear Brethren, congratulate you on your excellent dispositions, your piety and the desire you have to be faithful to the Holy Rule. But we cannot be silent on the object of our grief — your numbers decline more and more, especially the members of the Choir . . ."

Such was the status of New Melleray, when on the feast of St. Michael, the Archangel, September 29th, 1883, there arrived a new superior, Father Alberic Dunlea, with five companions, Father Placid Flynn, Father Gregory Pendergast, Brother Francis Bransfield, Brother Patrick Fitzgerald — these latter two soon to be ordained priests — and Brother Malachy Coghlan. New blood, it was apparently judged, was needed at the Dubuque monastery; for lack of Trappist vocations in America, the mother house in Ireland was willing to send some of her finest sons. And indeed, as time was to show, Father Alberic was the savior providentially chosen by Dom Bruno for his Iowa affiliate. He found a monastery with a load of enormous debts and with crushed hopes for the future. A man of fifty years of age, Father Alberic was tall and of commanding appearance, and from the day of his arrival he inspired a confidence that always remained with the community — a community that now had lost the privilege of having a mitred abbot because of its debts and the paucity of its members.

Probably ignorance was bliss in Father Alberic's case, for with no real knowledge of the difficulties that lay before him and simply by placing all his confidence in God, he went to work with an energy that was surprising. Meticulously careful management became the rule; needless expenses and doubtful ventures were eliminated. A bit of news that must have heartened him and his brethren appeared toward the end of his first year as superior, in the Dubuque *Daily Herald* of August 26, 1884:

The trustees of the New Melleray monastery, the Hon. W. J. Knight, Mr. Wm. Ryan and Mr. Patrick Clarke, held a meeting Sunday to consider its financial affairs. The brothers, five years ago, to meet a sudden financial disaster issued bonds to cover the indebtedness. They have since extinguished $75,000.00 of the debts and the bonds are at par. The new ones will be issued for five years and will draw six per cent interest. Their amount will be $130,000.00.

Nearly all will be negotiated in this city where they will find a ready sale.

A splendid lieutenant of the superior in his able efforts for the welfare of the community was his prior, who also acted as his housekeeper and bursar — and who was his namesake — Father Alberic Madigan. Besides the outlay for the retirement of the debt, current expenses had to be met, new farm and out-buildings had to be erected, new green-houses built, new trees planted. Many years later one of the surviving monks wrote of this period: "As far as manual labor was concerned I think it is true to say that the Religious of New Melleray, during the last twenty years of the nineteenth century and the beginning of the twentieth, were the most hard-working Religious in the Church. In fact, no laboring men in Europe or the United States worked harder than they did. Efforts such as these were bound to be crowned with success."

What was both helpful and consoling to the depressed brethren in this their severe hour of trial was the evidence of loyalty among the rank and file of the faithful in many parts of the country who now rallied to their cause. Hundreds of people either brought or mailed donations of from one to ten or more dollars. Nuns and laborers and small merchants, many of them anonymous, sent in their pittances. Many others sent in stipends for mass intentions that were to be fulfilled at the future convenience of the fathers at the monastery. One surprising feature of all this help from the humble and lowly friends of New Melleray was the number of mass stipends and money offerings — all of these latter quite slender, it is true — which came from Mexico across the Rio Grande. These kept on arriving during the years of 1883 and 1884; and on the old records one reads with a measure of wonder and curiosity the mellifluous Spanish names of the collectors of these funds for the hard-pressed Iowa monks: Manuel Cortina Valdovinos, Donna Ramona Cortina, Alberto Alvarez, Dnā Ana Yermo, Agustia Rodriguez, Dōna Amadora Santacruz, J. Mariano Duarte, Don Victorio Carillo and Ignacio de la Torre. They had forwarded contributions from two hundred and eighty-seven individuals in Mexico.

The official visitor of New Melleray in 1886 was Dom Mary Eugene of Melleray in France — the first time Iowa saw the Vicar General of the "Congregation of the Cistercians of the New Reform of La Trappe" as he signed himself on this visit, the Vicar General being the supreme executive officer of the Trappists. Both he and the succeeding visitor in 1887, Albert Eugene of Bellefontaine, emphasized the caution that should be displayed toward a new type of inmates of this monastic house; they looked askance at the practice of some western bishops who began at this time to send certain recalcitrant clerics to the Dubuque monastery for periods of penance and recollection. In particular, however, they asked that the postulant oblates should be carefully screened and should be accepted only if they had the sincere intention of remaining and of submitting to the Rule, especially that part of it that pertained to silence. An oblate is a lay-person who desires to share, to some extent, in the life of prayer and the spiritual benefits of a monastic order. In the Cistercian order oblates live in the monastery and, with some modifications, lead the life of the monks, but take no vows or other formal religious obligations. Those requesting admission under these conditions were to be turned away unless they were candidates of the best character and would submit to thorough probation.

Father Alberic carried out these latter recommendations with scrupulous care. In 1887, including novices, postulants and oblates, there had been sixty-seven members in the community. Two years later, in April of 1889, when the Father Immediate, Dom Bruno, arrived from Ireland the number had been reduced to fifty-three. Of these monks ten were priests.

This visit of Abbot Bruno's was his sixth. It was forty years before, in a hot month of July, 1849, that he had arrived in Iowa for the first time. This sixth visit was to be his last. There had not been many physical changes between these two visits. True, the ivy-clad stone monastery of Augustus Welby Pugin's artistic design stood there, but it was only half-built, and financially it was shakier than the humble frame and log dwellings that had housed the first Trappist colony. Crisis after crisis had been successfully weathered, but now after these bitterly won victories with all the sacrifices they entailed, the American affiliate was as weak as ever. In numbers, the institution had barely held its own; indeed, were it not for the constant transfer of brothers from Mount Melleray, the New Melleray house might not have survived. The volatile nature of Dom Bruno could not be restrained from a touch of impatience; he was an old man now, seventy-six years of age, and his grizzled beard was white and hoary.

"The main object of a Visitation," he told the fathers and brethren of New Melleray, "is the correction of abuses. We proceed, at once, to point them out clearly and briefly." It was apparently hard for him to understand the delicate and difficult tasks that poor Father Alberic Dunlea and his monks were facing in these still critical years, and he probably believed that a change in administrative personnel was needed. His concluding appeal to the brothers on his visitation card was both prophetic and pathetic: "We ask special prayers for Ourselves, who now bid you farewell forever, in this world."

XVII

THE SECOND ABBOT

* * * * * * * * * * * * * *

$\mathbf{F}$ather Lewis Gonzaga Carew became superior of the Iowa Trappist house at Dubuque on September 27th, 1889. An experienced and able monk, now in his fortieth year, he had already served as master of novices, sub-prior and procurator at Mount Melleray Abbey in Ireland before his appointment to the American post. He was not entirely a stranger to the United States, for in 1878 he had been the travelling companion to Dom Bruno on his visitation of that year, and had journeyed as far west as Nebraska City, Nebraska, to visit relatives there. Of particular note was Father Lewis' ability as a medical practitioner. He had studied medicine and surgery but had never been granted a degree; at Mount Melleray he had acted as chief infirmarian and pharmacist and had been regarded in the community as a highly successful doctor.

Immediately upon assuming his duties as superior, Father Lewis, recognizing the talents of Father Alberic, his predecessor, — who, incidentally, was sixteen years his senior — appointed him his acting prior.

We must here diverge for a moment from the particular story of the Iowa Trappists to recount a major event occurring during these

173

years among the Trappists of the entire world. Since 1879 there had been a movement manifested, especially through petitions to Rome, for a reunion of the scattered Trappist congregations into one order, with one head and a uniform observance. In 1892 that great pope, Leo XIII, took the matter out of the hands of the cardinal consultors and cutting through all the difficulties and red tape, he summoned all the abbots of the four strict congregations to an extraordinary General Chapter in Rome. Every professed choir religious in the houses of these congregations was invited to give his opinion and vote on the subject, and in Dubuque as practically everywhere else the votes declared decidedly for union. On October 1st, 1892, fifty-four superiors of Trappist monasteries, of whom thirty-two were mitred abbots, met in the Eternal City under the presidency of the Jesuit Cardinal Mazella. The final amalgamation so earnestly desired by the Trappists and the Church, after a number of peaceful discussions, was brought to a happy completion, with only three houses of a small Italian congregation refusing to participate.

At first it was decided by the General Chapter that the now happily fused and reunited order should be officially known as the "Order of Reformed Cistercians of Our Lady of La Grande Trappe." In the next few years, the buildings still left standing of the ancient mother abbey of the Cistercian order, Citeaux in France, after the political and physical storms of the centuries, were bought back again, and the abbot of Citeaux became the abbot general of the united Trappist congregations. "Once again," wrote Thomas Merton, "the abbot of Citeaux was the temporal and spiritual head of a worldwide family of monasteries where the monastic life was lived in its perfection." The name of La Trappe was then dropped entirely from the title, and as has been previously explained, the official designation now is "Order of Cistercians of the Strict Observance." A Cistercian house of studies was organized in Rome, and a group of advisers to the abbot general, called definitors, representing the different countries in which the order has taken root, reside there also with him.

This permanent bond of union has made the order more fully conscious of its great heritage, and the six decades that have passed since the reunion was enacted have seen a constant growth of the fervent, contemplative spirit that prevailed in the mediaeval monasteries of Citeaux and Clairvaux.

And now, ambling back from Citeaux to Iowa once more, we find Father Lewis, the superior, in April of 1892 receiving his first official visitor in the person of Dom Jean Marie of Bellfontaine, France. The latter found that at the urgent insistence of Bishop John Hennessy of Dubuque the fathers of the monastery had for several years been obliged to care for a second secular parish, that of St. Joseph, a few short miles away, and had also been given the duties of the spiritual direction of the Sisters of Charity of the B.V.M. at their mother-house nearby. But as the Sisters were soon to move to their new convent at Mount Carmel on the banks of the Mississippi, Dom Jean Marie arranged that both of these charges would within a few years be removed from the care of the monastery. The abbatial visitor expressed himself as highly astonished at the large number of lay people who daily brought their sick to the porter's lodge seeking the medical ministrations of Father Lewis. He gently admonished the superior to refrain from medical affairs, especially those concerning remedies and consultations for the general public, — these being incompatible with the obligations of his office, — and to devote his time to monastic matters and to the brothers of his community.

It was during this same year of 1892 that New Melleray had received another notable visitor — William Rufus Perkins, professor of history in the State University of Iowa, — who abided there for a while in order to secure material for his historical monograph on the abbey which was later that year published and sold under the auspices of the State University of Iowa Publications. "Few men engaged in historical researches," he wrote in the preface of his monograph, "have met with so cordial and hearty appreciation as has been vouchsafed by the monks of New Melleray to the author." Father Lewis gave him every assistance on this visit and of the superior Professor Perkins remarked: "The character of Father Lewis can be described in a few words. He has wonderful self control, he is never taken by surprise. He seems always prepared for any emergency and his temper is never ruffled . . . His self-possession, his gentleness and his firmness make his government efficient, and a light yoke on the community."

From the county court house records the professor prepared a list of the holdings of New Melleray Abbey at that time but pointed out that the monetary valuation is based on an "assessment of 33 1/3 per cent of actual value." Here is the list:

	Number	Value
Acres	2441.93	$30,666.00
Horses	54	1,000.00
Cattle	285	1,735.00
Sheep	270	270.00
Swine	90	100.00
Vehicles	3	30.00

Grand Total of All Property........$33,801.00

By 1892, the day of the oxen as draft animals had apparently passed.

Perkins was informed that the number of the members of the community was fifty-four, eleven of whom were American born, the others Irish by birth. He pointed out, however, that whereas thirty years before in 1862 there had been forty-eight professed members, there were in 1892 only forty-two. It was because of this failure in growth of numbers as well as of other reasons which he adduced that Professor Perkins took a dark view of the future stability of the Iowa abbey: "It is strange in the nineteenth century and on the banks of the Mississippi, in the midst of the new and vigorous west, to see the usages of thirteen centuries ago still active and fruitful — to behold the white robe of Citeaux and the brown scapular of Benedict, to know that within the walls of New Melleray the canonical offices of the Ancient Church are chanted, and that the community preserves the customs of mediaeval times. The question cannot but present itself as to what will be the future of the Abbey. Will its members increase in number, will the American monk replace the one of foreign birth, will the cross which now heralds a Cistercian house be thrown down, or will it multiply itself? These questions time alone can fully answer. But like all other religious communities which seclude themselves from the world and build barriers against its stress of progress, it is not unlikely that this may find its isolation fatal, and that it may prove to be the first and last Trappist Abbey west of the Mississippi."

Toward the end of December, 1893, the sad news reached the brethren of New Melleray that Dom Bruno Fitzpatrick, their beloved Father Immediate, had at last passed away. For two score and four years he had been the Iowa Trappists' hope and prop and pride. On December 4th, the great abbot of Mount Melleray, the victim of influenza in his eighty-first year, had gone to his eternal reward. The celebrated Cardinal Logue mournfully proclaimed that the entire Catholic world had suffered loss by the abbot's death. In the abbey's little cemetery a handsome Celtic cross surmounting his grave has inscribed on it, in classic Latin, the story of his heroic life and labors.

His successor as abbot of Mount Melleray and Father Immediate of New Melleray was Dom Carthage Delaney. One of the first acts of Dom Carthage was to delegate in 1894 Abbot Eugene of Melleray in France — who was also to visit Gethsemani in Kentucky — to act as the official visitor of his Iowa affiliate. When Abbot Eugene, who spoke little English, arrived in Dubuque he was accompanied by Dom Edward Chaix-Bourbon, abbot of Gethsemani, who served as interpreter. Dom Eugene discovered that it was the almost unanimous prayer of the brethren of New Melleray that an abbot should be elected to preside over their institution, and this ardent desire of theirs he promised to transmit both to Dom Carthage and to the General Chapter. The material conditions of this American house had now become more favorable and the monastic spirit had never been more fervent.

The prayers of the brethren were answered. In June of 1897 Dom Carthage made his first visit to America and to the Iowa monastery, and with him from Europe had returned Dom Eugene of Melleray in France. On Whit Monday, June 7th, the canonical election was held in the chapter room, and the choice of the monks fell on the prior, Father Alberic Dunlea. The holy and self-sacrificing work of this Trappist monk that had so inspired them during the years before the arrival of Father Lewis and latterly while he served as prior, won their approval of him as their new abbot.

The formal abbatial investiture of Abbot Alberic did not take place until the following October 29th, almost five months later. The abbot of Gethsemani was ill and as there was no other Trappist abbot in the country to assist with the abbatial blessing, Archbishop John Hennessy of Dubuque was delegated to perform the ceremony alone, aided by two priests acting as substitutes for the abbots. This was a singular situation and it is doubtful if another similar function ever took place in the ritualistic history of the Church. In order not to be guilty of deviating from the age old customs and rule of the Cistercian order, the perplexed abbot-elect, Father Alberic, had written to Rome for counsel, and on September 25, 1897, a letter from the Holy See addressed "Au Révérénd Père Dom Alberic, Abbé de la Trappe de Nouvelle Melleray par Dubuque, Iowa," arrived at the monastery permitting two priests to act as assistants in the conferring of the abbatial blessing — something hitherto entirely unprecedented and since then never duplicated. During the month following the receipt of this letter, it was decided to hold the ceremony in the secular parish church nearby which was under the spiritual care of the fathers of the monastery, and to which the general public, both men and women, could be invited — the latter not being permitted to enter the abbey church or even go within the abbey walls.

Except for the pontifical mass it was a modest and simple affair — extremely modest when compared with the elaborate celebration on the occasion of the abbatial blessing of Abbot Ephrem in the Dubuque cathedral thirty-four years before. Even the decorations of the little church were very simple, consisting of evergreens and leaves. No prelates, religious or secular, were present except Archbishop Hennessy. Except for the monastery fathers only a handful of priests attended — to be exact, there were twelve. One of these, the Very Rev. P. J. McGrath, a former president of Loras College, delivered a long and erudite sermon, terminating with this expression of his felicitations: "Permit me, my Lord Abbot, to offer to you and your true and faithful and tried brothers — now that you have passed through your dark night of temporal bondage — my heart's sincerest congratulations on this happy day; and in the name of his Grace, and of you, my Lord Abbot, and your devoted monks, I tender my friend, the Honorable William J. Knight, undying thanks for his judicious and charitable and superhuman efforts in bringing, under God, the deplorable financial condition of the monastery to so felicitous a termination. May God inspire us all with a true zeal for His work so that we may enjoy forever the rewards of our holy labors. Amen."

Father Lewis Carew returned to Europe with Dom Carthage and was shortly afterwards appointed by the General Chapter of the Cistercians as one of their definitors for the English-speaking monasteries. He held this ofifce for two successive terms of five years each, residing during this time at Rome with the abbot general of the order, the abbot of Citeaux. Not long after his return to Mount Melleray, Ireland, he was chosen as the provisional superior of Mount St. Bernard's Abbey in Leicestershire, England, and while acting in this capacity he died in 1927 in his seventy-eighth year.

It is almost incredible but it is certainly true that the New Melleray monastery after having through its first half century of existence emerged from one perplexing crisis after another, now for almost another thirty years under its new mitred abbot, the extraordinarily able and pious Alberic Dunlea and his capable successor, faced yet again an emergency — a very protracted and a very tenuous crisis this time — in its long history of acute crises. Materially and financially the abbey was on a sound basis, in piety and good works its life-blood never pulsed more ardently, and yet strangely enough it began to face the ever growing danger, year by year, of death by strangulation — strangulation simply due to utter dearth of vocations.

During this period the Iowa abbey seemed to lead the life of an isolated, half-abandoned outpost of the monastic world. From 1897 on for over twenty years it received only four official visitations from the abbatial officers of the Cistercian order. There seemed, outwardly at least, during these long years of spiritual distress, to be no intimately sympathetic interest displayed by the episcopal leaders of the Dubuque and other Iowa dioceses in the affairs of New Melleray Abbey. It may have merely seemed so — in comparison with the fiercely affectionate and paternal support of Bishop Mathias Loras and the ever ready assistance of the Trappist bishop of Dubuque, Clement Smyth, in the early years of the monastery's life, and the renewed kindly interest of the archbishops of Dubuque in these last two decades of our day. There is no doubt but that among the public it was regarded as a foreign colony, strangely surviving on the Iowa prairies, written up periodically by newspapers and magazines, usually in favorable language, as something very wonderful indeed, but hinting that its members were probably pious paranoiacs, and the entire monastic group was quite out of this world, and after all a bit foreign and fantastic.

It was in the first year of the twentieth century, 1901, that the distinguished superior of Gethsemani, Abbot Edmond Obrecht, who had been sent to Kentucky by the abbot general himself, made an official visit to the Dubuque monastery. Somewhat dismayed when he learned that the members of the community had shrunk to only thirty-four, Abbot Edmond addressed them: "We thank God that we have found among you a true religious spirit and a real zeal for your sanctification. However, we cannot conceal from you that, with

many of you, we are most deeply impressed and worried about the
scarcity of vocations and about the future of the personnel of this
house. Is it only a trial sent by our Lord to you? We hope so
from the bottom of our heart." And Abbot Alberic accepted it as
a trial. Leading a mortified and an austere life himself, he was the
soul of patience, ever considerate and kind towards his brothers of
whom everyone loved him dearly. At the common manual labor
he bent his tall frame and worked as hard as any of his perspiring
monks. "Though there were several confessors in the house," wrote
one of these monks, "most members of the Community of their own
free choice selected the Abbot for their confessor and spiritual director. His room opened on a public corridor along which both
religious and guests frequently passed. Nevertheless, at a certain
hour every Saturday evening after the end of work, the members
of the Community were to be seen kneeling on the corridor outside
the Abbot's room waiting for their turn, and I saw some with tears
flowing from their eyes as they were preparing for Confession."

The prayers for an increase of vocations continued, patiently, un-
ceasingly — but so did "the trial sent by the Lord."

And then in May of 1909 came a distinguished visitor indeed who
signed his name on the official visitation card — "✝ F. Augustinus
Marre, Episcopus, Cisterciensis Abbas Generalis" — and was the abbot of Citeaux himself, arrived from Rome to inspect New Melleray
and the other American monasteries. To the brethren he read in
making his formal address to them: "We, Brother Augustine Marre,
Titular Bishop of Constance and Abbot General of the Order of
Reformed Cistercians, visiting the Abbey of New Melleray in the
Archdiocese of Dubuque, have found under the direction of the
Right Rev. Father Dom Alberic, its venerable Abbot, 5 Choir Religious, 1 Novice, 2 oblates, 16 Lay-Brothers, 1 non-stabiliated, 2 lay
oblates, in all 27 persons."

The discouraging decline: twenty-seven members, and most of them
grizzled old men grown gray with Grace! In humble silence they
listened attentively to their abbot general: "Now, my dear Sons,
We are happy to visit you for the first time, and We do not regret
the length and trouble of the difficult voyage, because We desire to
become personally acquainted with all the members of our Order.
We are compelled to confess that Our first impression has been a
little sad, since We find the number of both Choir Religious and Lay
Brothers to be so small. This gives Us serious fears for the future

of your Monastery. We wish to call your attention in a most special manner to the strict necessity under which you labor, of meriting, by your fervour and regularity in the observance of the Rules, that God may send you good vocations to continue the good work you have commenced."

But had not these veteran soldiers of the Trappist monastic army shown fervor and regularity in the observance of the Rules? Wasn't this the "trial sent by the Lord?" Continued the abbot general who had come from Rome: "It is not sufficient to have merely temporal prosperity, to own a large amount of land; to have a monastery at least one half completed; all these you have; but you must also have religious to dwell therein, otherwise there is nothing but ruin, at least from a spiritual point of view, for all your work. We see that amongst you the greater part are well advanced in age; it needs, therefore, almost a miracle from God to hinder the Abbey of New Melleray from falling, and that very soon."

A miracle was needed to save New Melleray!

In fatherly language the abbot general then counselled them gently: in a small community there was danger of everyone being overburdened with work which in large communities is nicely distributed, so care must be taken that the spiritual should always hold the first place. The brothers have not come to the Iowa cloister merely to work — all have entered it in order to sanctify themselves by means of the regular pious exercises. Therefore, a goodly number of laymen — "seculars" — should be employed to lift the burden of labor from the monks sufficiently to permit them to assist at all the spiritual exercises prescribed by the Rule.

And furthermore, something must be said about picnics, he explained — "Pic-nics," it was spelled. This was a word that on the last three or four official visits had represented something a bit mysterious, possibly a bit reprehensible, to the puzzled French and Irish abbots coming to Dubuque. It seems that for a number of years in the nearby cities excursions had been arranged to bring crowds to New Melleray where the well-kept grounds and lovely woodlands, hospitably offered to the public by the monks, were ideal for large scale picnic dinners and the playing of baseball and other games. The proximity of the crowds to the monastery buildings, their noise and din and music, greatly disturbed the monastic quiet, especially on Sundays. The reasonable suggestion was made by the abbot general that these affairs should be restricted; the pleasure parties should be kept at a distance from the enclosure, from the cemetery, and especially from the brothers in the fields on working days.

There was one visiting monk present on this occasion who understood the American urge for outdoor picnics. He was acting as secretary to the abbot general during his tour of visits in the United States and he subscribed his name to that of the Abbot Augustine Marre on the visitation card at Dubuque as Frater Frederick M. Dunne. Born and reared in Ohio, he was the first American choir monk to come to Gethsemani Abbey in Kentucky and remain — and he remained for over fifty years. He was likewise the first native American to become a Trappist abbot, and under him from 1935 to 1948, New Melleray's sister abbey, older by one year, Gethsemani, attained along with its filiations the greatest expansion and prosperity in its history.

The growing crisis in the affairs of the Iowa Trappist monastery was obvious, of course, to the public and to the press. A Dubuque newspaper with the headline "Recruits the Crying Need of the New Melleray Monastery" wrote in its Sunday issue of March 21, 1909:

. . . With three thousands of acres of land now under the control of the Abbey and with its temporal position more than exalted, it is nevertheless a waning institution, in the heart of a cold, modern world, looking back over the passing centuries, seeking the spiritual strength of men willing to forsake the world and its pleasures to live the life of the Trappist monk, the life ordained by St. Benedict and followed by thousands for the last 1300 years. The disintegration is marked. The Abbey calls for recruits . . .

With all its interesting history New Melleray today occupies a threatened position. The young men who instilled strength into the order two score years ago are old men. New blood has not appeared for many years. To work the immense farm it is necessary to employ assistance. With hired help they have no little trouble. Time and again the abbey has appealed for recruits. It now needs them badly and must have them to preserve the institution.

The mother house is aware of the condition. A brief time ago — and this is the first publication of the fact — notice was received by Abbot Alberic to stop adding land. Here-

after, New Melleray will purchase no more ground. Recruits
to work the vast acreage now possessed is the crying need.

The decline at New Melleray continued. When the new Father
Immediate, the recently elected Abbot Maurus Phelan of Mount Melleray, came to Iowa for his first visitation in June of 1911 the members numbered twenty-five. "Alas," exclaimed Dom Maurus, "that
your community is so small, and that year by year it is growing
smaller still. May God Who can grow up children to Abraham
from the stones of the earth come to your aid, and preserve your
life as a Community by sending numbers to strengthen your ranks."

A few years later the number of monks in the New Melleray Abbey
fell below the twenty mark. Yet, through all these years under
Abbot Alberic, except for the growth in the number of vocations,
there was progress of every other sort — in the conduct of temporal
and spiritual affairs, in the introduction of modern farming methods
and machinery, in completely wiping out every vestige of debt and
adding to the monastery's lands and assets — progress and peace and
piety were there. Much of the material well being of the monastery was due to the splendid work of the zealous procurator,
Father David O'Sullivan. During most of these years Father David
served as the pastor of the secular parish attached to the abbey, and
under his wise direction a beautiful brick church was built for the
flourishing congregation of Iowa farmers.

XVIII

DARKNESS—THEN DAWN!

. . . .

It was during the second decade of the 1900s especially that rumors
were rife about the impending doom of New Melleray Abbey. Due
to the steady decline in the number of its monks and to the fact
that so many winters weighted down the hoary heads of the devoted
survivors it was inevitable but that among the public in general
and among the monastery's friends in particular the belief had
arisen that the institution would soon be forced to close its doors.
When the visitors beheld the extensive lands of the estate with so
few hands to care for it, when they saw the vacant cells in the
large dormitory and the empty stalls in the choir, they were naturally
inclined to credit a widely circulated report that a Canadian religious
order was to make an exchange with the Trappist brothers and establish an experimental farm at New Melleray. Then in the summer of 1912 several newspapers carried a similar story and gave
chapter and verse: the Sacred Heart Missionary Society of Sparta,
Wisconsin, was to be transferred to the Dubuque Cistercian foundation; the society was to open up an agricultural college for boys
and young men; the buildings and lands were to be leased by the
missionary organization. It was further explained, however, that

complications might delay the transfer, because a group of French Trappist monks was already on its way to New Melleray to assist in the farming operations and in the conduct of the work of the order, and furthermore the change would have to be approved by the "Abbot in France."

Under the impulse of these unsubstantiated rumors one of the newspapers of that city most interested in the abbey as a neighboring institution, Dubuque, published an editorial on the subject as illogical as it was wanton, and it revealed the usual popular misconception of the purpose of contemplative monastic life. Apparently irked by the refusal of the community to grow in numbers, and looking only toward utilitarian and pragmatic results, the impatient editor wrote in the *Telegraph-Herald* on August 23d, 1912:

The Trappist Monastery

A Catholic missionary society is reported to be seeking the lease of the Trappist Monastery and farm at Melleray for a boys' college with an agricultural department.

All thoughtful persons will wish the society success in its efforts. The monks at Melleray are thinning out and the order is contributing little or nothing to the welfare of society. Since its founding here over seventy years ago it has done little more than serve itself in piling up titles to land. Its spiritual influence, to be sure, has been felt in the countryside, but a missionary society would exercise the same influence and serve social welfare at the same time.

A monastery may by silent suggestion remind men of the need of saving their souls, and offer to penitents a place of retreat for contemplation and penance, but this monastery doesn't do the latter. It exists for the spiritual benefit of the members and the material benefit of the order.

In this day and age they are accounted truly religious who are in line of service, who are taking part of the burden off men's backs, helping struggling men up the path, and opening the door of opportunity to children. With this conception in mind, one speaks truly of orders of Sisters which care for the sick, the superannuated, the aged and which instruct the young, as truly religious.

The serviceability of such monastic orders as that at Melleray passed with the Dark Ages. They are anachronisms in this age.

One of the few things Abbot Alberic Dunlea had ever written in his life for publication was his forthright reply to this editorial:

Dear Mr. Editor: — An article appeared here in a local paper regarding this monastery which was not written with a friendly hand. In what school of asceticism the writer qualified as a competent judge of the utility of our lives, I know not. Our serviceability, he says, passes with the dark ages; someone had told him of dark ages and he actually believes they were dark. Our Order reaches far back in history, that is true; the famous Abbey of Citeaux in France is the birthplace of the Order. The wonderful diffusion of the Trappists — more properly called Cistercians — is due in great measure to St. Bernard, the last of the Fathers of the Church. During his life-time (1091-1153) the order had spread so rapidly and so widely that it was said "All Europe is Cistercian." Throughout their history its members won renown as agriculturists. In this connection Europe owes to them a greater debt of gratitude than to any other religious institute.

This sage of ours informs the public that we are contributing little or nothing to the welfare of society; that for seventy years we have done little more than serving ourselves and piling up titles to land. What does he think of the mountains of food and provisions which we laboriously produced and furnished to keep alive the multitudes in this nation during those near-to seventy years — whilst in all probability he did not produce a spoonful?

Our people came here at an early date, forty or fifty in number, hardy, industrious men, more given to labor than to traducing their neighbors, and the signs of their industry could soon be seen all around them. The country being a wilderness at that time and land being had almost for the fencing, these enterprising men acquired title to a considerable share of it. Several of those titles we have given up and some we retain but both those which we have held and those which we now hold have been obtained through our own hard labor and industry like those of other honest people and like the members of our Order all over the world. These possess lands according to our rules, that laboring in them and earning their bread by the sweat of their brows, they may not be a burden on the Church or on the people and that they may live in peace and be out of reach of malevolent critics. If their lives seem not useful to persons of a certain stamp, it is not their fault.

For our old and grand Order and its practices I make no apology to this writer nor to anyone else, and if this light of the twentieth century go back to the so-called dark ages, he can find much in them wholesome and profitable to his poor soul. As for us, I think we have as much right to live in solitude if we so please, as others have to keep out of it, and that right we assert. The world and its agents have ever been a trouble to monks, ever thrusting themselves upon their solitude, and trying to draw them out of it lest here they meet with failure. Our help is in the name of the Lord!

The rumors died away — but not the Iowa anachronism. It persisted with an obstinately robust spirituality; it persisted because Providence was pleased with it and with the prayerful devotions that were offered up daily, yes, hourly for a world of editors and others who just would not understand.

There were occasionally other items of news in the press about New Melleray, but most of them during this period dealt with a subject that struck the popular fancy — that of a medical monk whose fame as a healer far surpassed that of Father Lewis Carew who had been the successful physician for the whole countryside during his years of superiorship. Brother Paul was a lay brother who previous to his entrance into the Dubuque monastery had studied medicine and for years had interned in several Chicago and St. Louis hospitals. Thousands of people from all northeastern Iowa, poor and wealthy, Protestant and Catholic, flocked to the abbey to receive treatment for their bodily ills from the hands of Brother Paul.

In 1915 when his fame was at its height it was estimated by newspaper reporters and taxi drivers that not less than one hundred automobiles called there on favorable days to disgorge passengers seeking aid from the brother, and on Sundays and holidays there was twice that number. On these days crowds were scattered about the grounds waiting for an appointment; some of the people were seated on the grass eating lunches and picnic dinners which they had brought with them, while others hovered about the doors of the institution patiently awaiting their turn for admission. In all those years Brother Paul and the monastery refused to accept a cent of financial payment, judging the services merely as a Christian labor of love for humanity. These ministrations were later terminated with the sudden decline of Brother Paul's health and strength.

In the face of steady decline, frequent discouragement and occasional denunciation the soul of venerable, old Abbot Alberic was imperturbable. He knew that at several meetings of the General Chapter the fate of New Melleray had been discussed and mournful apprehensions had been manifested. But serenely and, thus far, safely he had held the destinies of his beloved house in his gnarled and withered hands that were so often clasped in prayer in chapel and cell. On a Sunday morning of early February, 1917, the angel of death cordially grasped those withered hands of the zealous monk, then in his eighty-fifth year, and on the following morning the obituary mass was offered up in the monastery chapel by the prior, Father Bruno Ryan.

Then for the first time in the trans-Mississippi history of America was an abbot buried — in the abbey cemetery, in Iowa soil, Abbot Alberic was laid away in the rough habiliments of his silent, toilsome days, with the surviving members — only seventeen! — of the Dubuque Trappist house grouped about his grave.

Father Bruno Ryan was immediately appointed as head of the New Melleray institution. The new fifty-one year old superior had entered Mount Melleray Abbey in Ireland as a postulant in 1888 and had been ordained to the priesthood in 1896. While acting as master of novices to the lay brothers, he was sent in July, 1914, to America to serve as prior under Abbot Alberic in the administration of the Iowa foundation.

When in 1918 Abbot Pacomius Gaboury of Our Lady of the Lake Abbey near Montreal, Canada, made the official visit for Abbot Maurus of Mount Melleray to the Dubuque cloister and found Father Bruno surrounded by his sixteen lonely monks, he exhorted them: "Your dear monastery is at the turning point which causes you great anxiety. Your lists are growing smaller by degrees, many of you are very old and must bear the burden of labor. The future appears to you full of uncertainty . . . But fear not. How could Providence abandon those who renounce all things for His sake?"

These pious words bespeak the zeal of Dom Pacome. But with all his zeal and piety he was outstandingly an abbot who today would be called progressive. On his monastic lands at Oka near Montreal were then the finest blooded livestock in Canada; on his abbatial domain he had introduced for the use of his monks the then last word in modern farm machinery. Father Bruno, naturally anxious to restore again to New Melleray the good name it had once enjoyed for its famed cattle and agricultural products, broached the subject of the introduction of pedigreed stock and new agricultural machines to the Canadian abbot. But the cautious and monitory advice of Dom Pacome discouraged him. Indeed, so disheartened did he become over the ever saddening prospects that, according to his younger contemporaries still living today, he assumed a fatalistic attitude during the first years of his spiritual rule at New Melleray, believing firmly that the Iowa monastery was doomed and that his surviving monks would soon return to Ireland. His laudable dream of restocking the Iowa monastic estate with blooded cattle and modernizing its machinery was finally to be carried out later under the favorable direction of Abbot Eugene Martin.

In both years of 1919 and 1920 the Father Immediate of the Dubuque monastery, Abbot Maurus, personally made the visitation. On the earlier visit he stated it as his conviction that the introduction of a fresh contingent of young, active monks from Ireland or elsewhere was a necessity, and he promised to do his utmost to bring this about. He sent over five good brothers from Mount Melleray, and on his second visit to Iowa was pleased to note that with the addition of a couple of American novices the community now numbered twenty-five. In return he asked for prayers for Ireland, which in 1920 was desperately wrestling for independence against English troops and Black-and-tans. His next visit to the American filiation was in 1924, when he was accompanied by Father Celsus O'Connell, (today — 1952 — the Father Immediate of New Melleray and happily presiding over Mount Melleray as its abbot) and on this occasion he found the community unchanged in numbers as well as in its excellent spirit of piety and austerity.

The visitation card of this year of 1924 reveals itself to the research student with the impact of a mild shock. What is this? Where is the scroll on the mustily fragrant parchments of the earlier visiting abbots? Where are the flourishes of the pen as the often eloquently worded exhortations were written out? This card is typewritten! From Citeaux and Clairvaux to the Royal and the Underwood — from the scratch of the quill-pen in the cell of the monk to the clack and ring of the modern machine in the monastic halls, — why, this is an attack on the alleged monkish anachronisms.

But this was not the end of treason to Cistercian mediaevalism — there was still further mischief afoot. At the General Chapter meeting in ancient Cistercium — Citeaux — in 1921 New Melleray Abbey in the United States was authorized to introduce electric lighting and heating in its corridors, rooms, halls, and during the next few years Father Bruno proceeded with the complete modern installation of electricity. But even this did not terminate the wonders, for in its final session of that year of 1921 the staid and venerable fathers of the General Chapter after a favorable vote, then a reconsideration, and then a second favorable vote permitted the superior of New Melleray the use of an automobile! Vehicles of the de luxe type, though, were interdicted.

The interest of writers in the Iowa Trappist foundation, whether feature specialists for newspapers or professors of learned societies, did not flag in the least during all these years. In 1906 a Professor Loos of the college of political science in the University of Iowa made a visit, with some fan-fare, to the abbey and gave out a public announcement that he was to write an authoritative account of the institution for the Iowa State Historical Society. He was to return later for a week of study and observation and would be a guest of the monks. Professor Perkins' account of the monastery in 1892, the announcement continued, had contained inaccuracies, but an entirely new and correct story was to be written and published by Professor Loos. The records on hand today, however, fail to reveal any such published work.

But in 1922 one of the journals of the Historical Society, *The Palimpsest,* devoted an entire issue to the monastery, the articles appearing under the title of "A Day at New Melleray." The editor in his short article took a rather gloomy view of the future of the Dubuque Trappist "anachronism," and concluded with the statement: "The asceticism of the silent monks at New Melleray does not appeal to American youth. Religious zeal is not a prominent trait of the times. Monastic life in Iowa seems to be an anachronism." The principal articles of the journal which dealt with the oft treated features of monastic life which usually interest the public, were written by an able professor on the staff of the university, Dr. Bruce Mahan, and with a fortuitous note of prophecy, he made the query:

"One wonders if this settlement of the Trappists in the Mississippi Valley will repeat the story of Citeaux. Will New Melleray Abbey, which now seems to languish, wax vigorous in the future, spreading its influence afar and contributing to a revival of monasticism?"

It was in 1926 that the *Chicago Tribune*, — "The World's Greatest Newspaper," it styles itself — again ran a series of articles on New Melleray Abbey, written this time by that incomparable artist, James O'Donnell Bennett, who had no peer in the newspaper world of his day. "Tis the nearest to an absolutely unique shrine place in all Chicagoland," he commented, and then philosophized: "And there I was in a different world and in another age of the world. I was in the premier seat in our country of the kind of healing the unaging Dumas prescribes in that unaging book of his, 'Monte Christo': 'All earthly ills yield to two all potent remedies — time and silence.' For at New Melleray stands, amid rich fields and stately groves and numerous graves, a Trappist monastery of the Roman Catholic Church, and there they have abundant silence and all the time there is — from generation unto generation, from age unto age. Saecula saeculorum is no hollow formula within those long, cool corridors of silence.

"For seven and seventy years that monastery has stood there, and what was happening there in the year of our Lord 1849 was happening there yesterday and today, and will be happening there in the year of our Lord 2003.

"I mean an unhalting, unvexed, unhurried and unhurrying routine of prayer and praise, of digging the soil for the kindly fruits of the earth and digging the soil for the kindly grave that shall at last enwrap us all in the everlasting silence."

During this same year Father Bruno decided to put into effect a project that he had been mentally nurturing for some time — a project that had been frequently mentioned to him by friends of the community, both clerical and lay. This was the erection of a guest and retreat house. The purpose of a guest house in all Trappist monasteries is to provide accommodations for gentlemen — both priests and laymen — where they may spend a number of days in retirement and seclusion, apart from business, home and social duties, to attend to life's most important affair — the salvation of one's immortal soul. Although service buildings had been erected on the grounds, there had been no major addition to the large and lovely

Gothic semi-quadrangle whose construction was completed fifty-
seven years previously. Work was started on the guest and retreat
house in 1927 and was finished toward the end of 1928. Erected
on the grand scale it forms part of the third side of the contemplated
huge quadrangle. Along with this project a new abbey church was
installed in the north wing of the quadrangle on the second floor,
running almost its entire length east and west. A screen separates
it into two unequal sections, the larger part forming the community
chapel, and the smaller section, with altars and confessionals and
pews for two hundred people, accommodating the laity. It was thus
arranged so that the monastic church and the divine services would
be accessible to the general public, and thereby the laity of both
sexes could have the opportunity of satisfying their devotion by
visiting the church and assisting at the various liturgical services.

On October 28, 1928, Archbishop James J. Keane of Dubuque
blessed the new buildings and delivered the sermon of the occasion,
while Bishop Henry P. Rohlman, then the chief shepherd of the
Davenport diocese, offered up the pontifical mass.

These and other necessary improvements left a debt of $30,000.00
on the Trappist institution, but under the careful management of
Father Bruno this was paid off during the next few years in the face
of the severe depression which struck the nation in 1929.

When in 1928 the abbot general of the Cistercian order, Dom Jean
Baptiste Ollitrault de Keryvallen of Citeaux, arrived for his visitation of New Melleray he was quite pleased with what he saw. The
monastery was at least holding its own in numbers — the community
had twenty-seven members. He wished that he could visit them
more often in order to assist them. "Unfortunately you are so far
distant from your Mother House that you cannot enjoy the assistance
of regular visitations," he said. "In fact, this is the fourth year since
you received the visit of your venerated Father Immediate and it is
nineteen years since you have seen the Abbot General!" He lauded
the building of the guest house and then suggested the erection of
stone walls for an enclosure, that is, a high barrier with locked doors,
about the immediate grounds surrounding the monastery "to protect
your interior life from the interference of the world of outsiders."

The last visit of Abbot Maurus occurred in 1930, and the next year
the Iowa house was honored with the visit of the new abbot general
of the Cistercian Order of the Strict Observance — Dom Herman

Joseph Smets. What he saw gave rise to sentiments of optimism — thirty-eight members and a sincere zeal for monastic observances! "We thank God," he exclaimed, "for having found here a community few in numbers, it is true, but about to increase! Your monastery has taken on new additions and is blessed with a goodly number of novices seeking therein the peace of God and way of perfection according to the Rule of our Father St. Benedict."

The shrewd abbot general correctly sensed that here at last was the critical yet propitious turning of the scale. Probably the chief factor in the election of Father Bruno Ryan a few years later to the abbatial dignity was the increase of native vocations under his superiorship. The increase was small at first but kept growing during the years, and after his death it became an avalanche. For eighty years Mount Melleray had been sending its monks to America to help staff the Iowa filiation; under Father Bruno affairs seemed finally to be shaping themselves in such a manner as to promise the complete emancipation of the daughter house both in regard to material administration and to vocations.

The same phase of history had been passed through some years earlier by New Melleray's sister abbey, Gethsemani in Kentucky. For the first thirty or forty years at that Trappist house there had been only eight native Americans at the monastery, and they had all run away. Had it not been for the French and German and Irish and even French Canadian novices who came from time to time the foundation might not have kept going, but finally that great problem of home vocations was solved. Extraordinarily odd it was that the first of a long list of native Americans to enter Gethsemani — this was in 1885 — and take the Rule and remain to the end was a Texas cowboy, John Hanning, who became Brother Joachim, *The Man Who Got Even with God.*[1] By the early 1920s the Kentucky cloister housed a thoroughly homogeneous "American" community, although there were still many monks who had come from foreign lands.

This metamorphosis developed a little later in the Iowa Trappist story. When Dom Celsus O'Connell of Mount Melleray, the Father Immediate, was present at the Dubuque monastery in 1935 for the

---

[1] By M. Raymond, O.C.S.O. (Milwaukee, 1941). — John Hanning was the first American lay brother to stay on, and Frederick Dunne. later Abbot Frederick, who entered in 1894, was the first American choir brother to remain.

election at which Father Bruno was chosen the third abbot of New
Melleray, he made it clear that from then on this American affiliate
was to strike out entirely for itself.

The abbatial blessing of Father Bruno followed his installation
as the third abbot of the Dubuque Trappist cloister; this took place
on May 23d of 1935, and formed an epochal event in the annals
of the abbey. It was the most colorful and impressive function that
had ever hitherto taken place at the monastery. Archbishop Francis
J. Beckman of Dubuque pontificated at the blessing of the new
abbot and at the solemn high mass. Seven bishops, twelve mon-
signori, three scores of priests and many members of religious orders
and of the laity attended the ceremonies. Three abbots of the Cistercian order were present: Dom Celsus O'Connell of Ireland; Dom
Pacome Gaboury of Oka, Canada; and Dom Frederick Dunne, the
recently installed abbot of Gethsemani. Because of the predominance
of the natives of Ireland at New Melleray it was only appropriate
that prominent among the special guests should be the Irish consul
at Chicago, D. J. McGrath, as representative of the Irish Free State.
The sermon on this occasion was preached by Bishop Henry P. Rohlman of Davenport.

Frederick L. Holmes, the distinguished Wisconsin lawyer and
publicist, and for years the managing editor of that lively periodical,
LaFollette's *Weekly*, called at New Melleray about a year after
Abbot Bruno had been installed, and after a visit through the
grounds and buildings of the abbey asked permission to interview
the abbot. A moment later Abbot Bruno appeared. Smiling, he
said he was glad to have Mr. Holmes as a guest. The conversation continued for some minutes.

"You wanted to ask me something, I believe?" the abbot finally
remarked.

"It is an important question, but I think you have answered it with
your appearance," Holmes rejoined. "Out in the world it is said
that the Trappist tortures his body by insufficient food and lack of
sleep. I came —"

"You came to find out for yourself," interrupted Abbot Bruno.
"Take a good look at me. I have been a member of the order for
over fifty years; do I look as if I were suffering from loss of sleep
or starving for food?"

Holmes was forced to confess that he had seldom met a man over
seventy with so robust a physique. He learned, too, that no special

treatment was accorded to the abbot. He rose at the same hour of two o'clock, ate the same as others, and scrupulously performed the same services, including four daily hours of manual tasks.

"Do the monks dig their own graves?" Holmes asked.

"The grave-digging story is like Banquo's ghost," the abbot explained good-naturedly. "That is only one of the many untruthful stories told about us to excite the curiosity of strangers. Many visitors show keen disappointment when disillusioned. Ours is a life of happiness and not of gloom."

The healthy progress of New Melleray under Abbot Bruno may be indicated by the growth of vocations: the number of brothers grew to fifty-one in 1938 and to fifty-four in 1941; by the improvements and renovations on the lands and in the monastery buildings; by the introduction of special courses in theological training for the priests and candidates for the priesthood among the increasing number of choir monks — this was done on the suggestion of Dom Celsus, the Father Immediate; and also on his advice the organization of classes for all the brethren to sing the holy office under the direction of the cantors.

Then came World War II, and the monks of New Melleray suffered no more than the rest of the nation except for one spiritual embarrassment: the drafting of all available men into the military services temporarily stopped the flow of new novices and postulants into the monastery. Some of the younger ordained monks were seized by the prevailing martial fever; two of them obtained dispensations to serve as army chaplains, and three others were granted leaves to help various bishops by replacing other priests who had volunteered as chaplains with the military forces.

In 1943 Abbot Bruno conceived the idea of establishing a Trappistine convent in or near Dubuque. Numerous nuns and lay-women had written to the abbey inquiring about the availability of such an institution with its holy and austere mode of life. The Trappistines — Cistercian nuns — follow substantially the same rule as do the Trappist monks. Prayer, especially the divine office, reading and manual work, are fused in a way that does not burden the spirit. The seven hours each day spent in manual labor include in most convents the making of vestments, altar linens, altar breads, rosary beads, etc. Although Canada already had several Trappistine convents, all composed of French-speaking nuns, there was no such establishment in the United States.

Abbot Celsus of Mount Melleray Abbey, when he learned of the number of American ladies definitely interested in Trappistine vocations, consented to the venture and even promised additional vocations from Ireland. Archbishop Beckman of Dubuque also gave his approval to Abbot Bruno in the matter, provided that a suitable site and sufficient endowment could be secured. Father Flanagan of Boys Town in Omaha sent the first check, a sizable one, in support of the cause for which he promised enthusiastic support. But with his death in 1944 Abbot Bruno's ambitious plan came to an end.

Still, this same plan of the Dubuque abbot was later revived by Archbishop Cushing of Boston, and in October of 1949 he brought a group of Trappistine nuns from Ireland to establish a convent in Wrentham, Massachusetts, the first community of this order in the United States.

On August 2nd, 1944, the Trappist brethren were saddened by the passing of Abbot Bruno Ryan, then in his seventy-ninth year, after having served his community selflessly and zealously for more than a quarter of a century. Archbishop Beckman officiated at the requiem mass for the repose of his soul three days later. Dom Celsus O'Connell at Mount Melleray wanted to come to America to be with his daughter-house during this period and to preside at the election of a new abbot. But a world war was on, all normal transportation and communication was interrupted, and an ocean full of hostile surface warships and U-boats separated him from the United States and Iowa. Nothing daunted, he obtained passage on an army troopship and crossed the perilous seas in the late fall arriving safely at Dubuque in time to be present at the choosing of a fourth abbot of New Melleray on December 12th, 1944.

XIX

THE SECOND CENTURY OF THE
IOWA TRAPPISTS

· ·

Prior Albert Beston, graduate and master of arts of the National University of Ireland, professed choir monk and priest of the Trappist order, professor in Mount Melleray seminary and sub-prior of Mount Melleray Abbey, had come to America in 1920. At New Melleray he had served as master of novices, professor of moral and dogmatic theology and as prior at the time of the death of Abbot Bruno; and as successor to the latter he was elected to abbatial honor on December 12th, 1944. He was installed on December 14th, at which time each professed member of the community made his promise of obedience to the newly elected superior. He was blessed on December 28th, in the presence of two archbishops, three other Cistercian abbots, eleven bishops, and a great number of priests, religious and laity. The three visiting abbots were the Father Immediate, Dom Celsus O'Connell of Ireland, Dom Pacome Gaboury of Notre Dame du Lac, Canada, and Abbot Stephen Schappler, a Benedictine, of Conception Abbey, Clyde, Missouri. Archbishop Rohlman, formerly bishop of Davenport and now coadjutor arch-

bishop of Dubuque, pontificated at the mass, and Archbishop Beckman in his eloquent sermon paid this tribute among many others:
"This venerable Abbey, its roots embedded deep in the sacred dust
of generations of its forebears and inextricably intertwined with
those of the Old World, is a living symbol of the Christian life at
its best, an example of Christ-like sacrifice shining forth like a signet
of hope in a pleasure-jaded, war-surfeited world.   What untold
wealth of blessings has this Archdiocese reaped from within the
hallowed walls of New Melleray where, if nowhere else in these
parts, giant saints are in the making!"

A few days before, in his visitation address to the Trappist brethren,
Dom Celsus after congratulating Abbot Albert Beston on his elevation and the community on having him as their superior, declared
that New Melleray Abbey must appeal to the American world as
the home of God where men spend themselves and are spent in
His service. And then calling on them as monks with arms and armor,
he said: "You must fully realize that you are Christ's ambassadors on
earth; His elite bodyguard, his valiant soldiers.   The arms of your
warfare are, not the deadly weapons of militarism, but the spiritual
armor of Faith, Hope and Charity daily, to a high degree, exercised
in your community duties; in penance and prayer, and in the full
imitation of your Divine Master."

Abbot Albert's term of office lasted not even two years, but they
were years crowded with colossal occupations both spiritual and
material. As the first months of 1945 were ushered in it became apparent to everyone that the Fascist might of Germany and Japan
was doomed, and that the long war would soon be followed by an
era of peace. Then the holy example of Abbot Albert and his monks
not only drew in more vocations but inspired the growing number
of novices already in the cloister. When Abbot Albert was installed as superior in December of 1944 the community numbered
fifty-one; at his death in September of 1946 it had grown to sixty-
seven, by far the greatest increase in the history of the Iowa Trappist
foundation. It was apparent that the flood of vocations was just
starting. When Archbishop Rohlman at the conclusion of the pontifical mass on December 8th — the feast of the Immaculate Conception — 1945, during which he had ordained two of the young and
fervent monks to the priesthood, delivered a beautiful sermonette
and said: "What a wonderful culmination if at your centennial in
1949 you had a hundred monks at New Melleray — one monk for

each year of the abbey's existence!" he prophesied better than he knew. Incidentally, the two brothers who had been ordained were Alphonsus Layeaux of Minneapolis and Basil Zavadskis of Cleveland — their names and origins indicated the new trend of American vocations to the Trappist monastery.

Another colossal work of Abbot Albert's was the inauguration of the building program to complete New Melleray Abbey. The ideas for this mammoth undertaking were submitted to the community for their consideration and by a unanimous vote of all those monks who had been solemnly professed it was decided to launch the program. The labor and finances which previously had been intended to be used toward the erection of a Trappistine convent would now be employed toward the work on New Melleray Abbey itself. The very growth of the numbers of the community demanded this. The mediaeval Gothic designs and dreams of Augustus Welby Pugin and John Mullaney would be carried out and even be extended. All useless expenditures from now on were to be cut down and all efforts were to be concentrated on this great work. Due permissions were soon obtained from the General Chapter and from the Holy See, and immediate arrangements were begun for the completion of the plans and the letting of the contracts.

Then for months — and for years, too, for that matter, as the work is painstakingly but surely progressing today — a small army of monks aided by all that modern mechanical contrivances can do, went to work with a will. New basements were dug under the older cloister wings; land was cleared as the forest of trees to the south and east fell beneath the ringing blows of monastic axes. Graders large and small. powerful caterpillars, cranes, trucks, scrapers and shovels all added to the joyful noise and apparent confusion of excavating and preparatory building of the new wings and extensions of the huge Gothic quadrangular pile. Father Michael Holland, a former Canadian "mountie" as well as a building expert, was drafted into service as director of construction; and it should be added here that at the beginning of 1952 he celebrated his thirty-fourth anniversary as a Trappist happily recovering from being crushed under a concrete wall which his fellow monks were building. Father Holland had come to New Melleray for this specialized work from the monastery of Our Lady of the Valley, Valley Falls, Rhode Island. This monastery, since that time destroyed by fire, has been rebuilt at Spencer, Massachusetts.

After the war auto-trucks were being sold from army surplus materials and at a large discount to educational institutions. These strong vehicles were needed at New Melleray for construction work as well as for other operations on the abbey lands. Prior Vincent Daly travelled to Washington and convinced government officials that as the Iowa institution had a school of philosophy and theology for its priestly candidates it correctly came under the proper classification for the discounts. In the spring of 1946 Prior Vincent accompanied by two other brothers and two laymen made a triumphal arrival at New Melleray from the East with four new army trucks.

Naturally the World War had interfered with the movements and travel of Trappist abbots and superiors, just as it had with everyone else, and had prevented their capitular meetings since 1938. So when in 1946 a convening of the General Chapter of the Cistercian Order of the Strict Observance was to be held at the abbey at Citeaux in France on May 1st, Abbot Albert considered it his duty to attend, and the more so, because a new abbot general was to be elected. That great son of Flanders, the Most Reverend Herman Joseph Smets, the abbot general who had visited America and New Melleray in 1931, and at that time had so prophetically discerned the latter's coming growth and vitality, had been dead since January of 1943. To arrive in Europe on time Abbot Albert flew from New York to Ireland by plane — another colossal affair and sufficiently of a novelty at that time to appear as quite a blow to those who considered Trappist methods anachronistic. But what was still more striking and something which had never occurred before in history was the sight of four Cistercian abbots together flying from Shannon airport, Ireland, to Paris, from where they motored to Citeaux. This quartet, much photographed and commented on in the world press on that occasion, consisted of Dom Celsus O'Connell, Dom Camillus Claffey of Mount St. Joseph Abbey, Roscrea, Ireland, Dom Benignus Hickey of New Melfont Abbey, Ireland, and Abbot Albert Beston.

There at the eight centuries old Citeaux Abbey the Iowa Trappist monk, Abbot Albert, met Cistercian abbots from all over the world. There with the other white-robed prelates he marched from solemn votive mass in the chapel to the spacious chapter room. Massive oak double doors closed behind the monks as they took their seats for the opening of the balloting for the new abbot general. The chapter room at Citeaux is a simple room furnished only by two rows of chairs and green-topped tables. Only two pictures hang on the walls

— of two great monks to whom we referred in the early chapters of this Iowa Trappist story: the one is of Abbot de Rancé, the great reformer of LaGrande Trappe, and the other is of the handsome Dom Augustin de Lestrange, among whose followers was the Prior Joseph Dunand who had made the missionary visit to the Iowa Country and the Upper Mississippi valley in 1817, coming from St. Louis and Monks' Mound.

At the head of the chapter room sat the vicar general with his secretary and "scrutators" or examiners on a slightly raised platform. At the green-topped tables along with Abbot Albert were forty-three other chapter members from France, Belgium, Ireland, Italy, Canada, England, Spain, Holland and the United States. This chapter meeting of 1946 was not a full one — across from Abbot Albert were nine vacant seats. Abbots from Japan and China were unable to come, and the French military authorities, still actuated by the feelings of *la revanche*, had refused to permit entry to the abbots from Germany.

Before each member present lay a white ballot paper. But before he wrote the name of his choice on it, the Iowa monk walked to the vicar general, president of the General Chapter, knelt before him and swore that he would vote for the man he thought most worthy. Each of the other abbots present did the same. One by one the capitular members completed their papers, walked to the secretary's table and dropped them into an ancient urn that had witnessed these elections for hundreds of years. One by one they returned to their places.

Three hours later the abbots filed out singing the Te Deum, and announcement was made that by one of the largest majorities in the history of the order Dom Dominic Nogues, a white-haired monk from Brittany, the former abbot of Thymoduc in France, and for seventeen years the vicar general of the order, was elected the new abbot general.[1]

[6] In 1951 a new abbot general was elected at Citeaux Abbey as successor to Dom Dominic Nogues who resigned at the General Chapter of September 12th, 1951. The present abbot general of the Cistercian Order of the Strict Observance is Dom Gabriel Sortais, formerly abbot of Bellefontaine, near Angers, France, who was elected at the extraordinary General Chapter of November 7th, 1951. Several abbots of Bellefontaine were official visitors of New Melleray during this past century of its existence.

The new abbot general, Dom Gabriel Sortais, is renowned in France for his conduct during the last World War. In 1940 he rescued wounded men of the 38th Infantry regiment, an action for which he was awarded the Croix de Guerre.

After a week of strenuous meetings Abbot Albert flew back for a visit to Ireland and then returned to New Melleray. But not for long; always active — he himself had helped to dig the foundation for the abbey expansion — he was now hospitalized from an illness that followed his return journey to America. On September 5th the shy and gentle Abbot Albert passed into eternity, and two days later Coadjutor Archbishop Rohlman of Dubuque who had blessed him as abbot twenty months before celebrated the pontifical mass of requiem at his funeral obsequies in the abbey chapel.

Until the election of a new abbot which was to take place the next month when the Father Immediate, Dom Celsus of Mount Melleray, was expected to be present, Prior Vincent Daly acted as provisional superior. After the arrival of Dom Celsus the election was held in the chapter room on October 3d following the mass of the Holy Ghost. Several ballots were required among the seventeen solemnly professed choir monks present, for in the election of an abbot there must be an absolute majority of votes. Father Eugene Martin, the abbey procurator and sub-prior, was their choice.

For almost a century — a century lacking only three years — every superior of New Melleray had been a professed monk who had made his vow of stability in Mount Melleray Abbey at Cappoquin in Waterford, Ireland. Father Eugene Martin has been — and is — the only exception. He was received into the order and made his vows at Mount St. Joseph's Abbey at Roscrea in Tipperary, but this institution like New Melleray of Iowa had been founded by the illustrious Dom Bruno Fitzpatrick of Mount Melleray — so he was a grandson of Mount Melleray by filiation. After serving in various administrative offices in Mount St. Joseph's, Father Eugene came to the Iowa Trappist house in 1920 and at the time of his election was sixty-eight years of age — the oldest to be elevated to the abbatial office at New Melleray with the one exception of Abbot Bruno Ryan who had been in his seventieth year at the time of his election.

He was made a member of the underground Liberation Committee of the Maine et Loire department after he gave sanctuary in his monastery to hundreds of Allied parachutists.

His successor at Bellefontaine Abbey is Dom Emmanuel (René) Coutant, a twenty-eight year old monk, believed to be the youngest monk ever elected to head a Trappist community. He had been the prior since the time of his solemn vows before being ordained to the priesthood. It was at this monastery that the nephews of Bishop Mathias Loras had made their vows in the early part of the last century.

The ceremony of the abbatial blessing of Abbot Eugene was a major ecclesiastical function with national and even international undertones. The abbot had served as the monastery's active procurator for twenty-five years and his engaging personality had won him a wide circle of friends throughout the country. It was learned immediately after his election that many of these friends intended to be present at the ceremonial affair. Because of the limited capacity of the abbey chapel it was decided that the blessing should be held in the nearby secular church as on previous historical occasions. This proved to be a wise decision for — despite a two hour downpour of rain at the time of the ceremonies on October 24th, 1946 — five hundred and sixty people from all walks of life were present. Four Benedictine abbots from United States monasteries were in attendance as well as three bishops, and four Cistercian abbots, these latter being the Father Immediate, Dom Celsus O'Connell of Mount Melleray, Ireland; Dom Camillus Claffery, the Lord Abbot of Mount St. Joseph's, Roscrea, Ireland, who had come to America to see the son of his abbey elevated to the dignity of the abbatial office; Abbot Frederick Dunne of Gethsemani, Kentucky; and Abbot James Fox of Our Lady of the Holy Ghost, Conyers, Georgia.

Archbishop Rohlman again pontificated at the mass, and at the conferring of the abbatial benediction he delivered the sermon of the occasion. After the ceremony all were guests of the community at dinner and about one hundred and fifty remained that evening for supper. Many of these were relatives of the New Melleray brethren, and among them was Mr. Joseph Martin of New York City, the new abbot's brother, who had come to Iowa with his wife and two sons to witness this signal function. Incidentally, this is the only record in New Melleray's history of the members of an abbot's family being present to witness his reception of the honors.

(The abbatial titular prefixes of "Dom" and "Lord" possibly prove somewhat of a puzzle to the interested American reader. In democratic America, abbots prudently refrain from translating the "Dom" in front of their name to its English equivalent of "Lord." As Thomas Merton aptly explains, in England and Ireland the abbots are *Lord* abbots (*Dom'ni abbates*). In England it is a title. In Catholic Ireland it is not merely a title; it is something more of a fact. The superior of New Melleray in mid-America will be referred to by the title by which he is so well known to his many friends and acquaintances — Abbot Eugene.)

The blessings of God continued to be heaped upon the Dubuque Trappist monastery, and as the first century of its existence was being rounded out it found itself entering an era of ardent spiritual vigor and unprecedented temporal progress and well-being. The guest and retreat house, built in 1928, had spiritually as well as materially justified its existence a thousand times over. For years hardly a week went by that some organized group of laymen from Iowa or the surrounding states was not attending a week-end retreat. One of the neighboring dioceses conducted the annual retreat of its priests at the abbey. During the week there were annually hundreds of other persons — priests and, more often, laymen — who sought in the consoling quietude of the guest house and the abbey chapel and the monastic walks the divine unction needed for their souls.

Under Abbot Eugene the work on the new oratory and church and the other wings of the great Gothic quadrangle has been steadily and earnestly continued. The constant influx of vocations has made the execution of the building program more imperative than ever. The monks carry on the construction of the addition themselves using outside labor only when special skills not available among the members are needed. By doing the work themselves the brothers are fulfilling a double purpose — they do the four hours of manual work a day required as a minimum by the law of their Trappist monastic life and at the same time they are slashing today's inflated building costs.

When the original plans were made — and the various wings must have offices and refectories, kitchens and dormitories, a monastic library, a scriptorium, large, airy classrooms, a community infirmary, sanitary facilities, special quarters for choir brothers and also for lay brothers, for novices and postulants — the contractors estimated the cost at about $2,500,000.00, an enormous sum for the monks, and one which because of the lessons learned from the past financial history of the Dubuque abbey, they eyed with almost suspicious horror. By doing the work themselves, however, the silent Trappists in white and brown have cut the estimate drastically to $1,000,000.00, still a formidable sum for the cautious but yet daring brothers working on the Gothic halls in the Iowa countryside.

So — with earnestness and even relish, pouring concrete, cutting pipe, digging foundations, cutting and setting tile, pushing wheelbarrows are the occupation for at least four hours a day for men, some of whom can also read easily ancient languages, others of whom can wrestle with abstract problems in philosophy and still others can give evidence of their scholarship in diverse fields of learning. These ambitious activities of the Dubuque Trappist brothers were considered so newsworthy by both the secular and the Catholic press that from time to time feature articles, some of them accompanied by photo-illustrations, appeared all the way from the front page of the New York *Mirror* to the Chicago *Sun-Times*, *News* and *Tribune*, as well as in a number of Iowa papers and on out to the Rocky Mountains where the Denver *Register* also ran pictures and by-lined stories.

The real invasion of New Melleray by the new postulants commenced after Abbot Eugene had only become just comfortably ensconced in his abbatial seat. It was headed by young men, some still wearing their uniforms, who not so long before had been in the North African campaign against Marshal Rommel, the Desert Fox, or who had taken part in the bloody battle of the Bulge or who had been island hopping in the Pacific under Douglas MacArthur. How strange the puzzle is when one looks at it from merely the human viewpoint. For from 1919 to 1926 when America was peaceful and serene as never before only five of the applicants who knocked at the doors of the nigh vacant New Melleray Abbey persevered in their monastic calling. A quarter of a century later in a new day of radio, jet plane, television and hydrogen bombs the manly youth of America turned to the great anachronism, in numbers.

The records show that in 1946 Abbot Eugene had the spiritual direction of sixty-seven members of the Iowa Trappist community. In 1947 there were seventy-three members; in 1948 the number had grown to eighty-four; in 1949, the centennial year, the prophecy of Archbishop Rohlman had been fulfilled and surpassed — the number was one hundred and eight! And in 1950 one hundred and thirty-five!

Today, in 1952, the numbers have gone still higher and the Dubuque cloister would have little elbow room were it not for the fact that a new filiation in Missouri is now receiving its own generous quota of members from New Melleray. They come from all walks of life; and although we have spoken of some who have mastered ancient languages and others who have delved deeply into philosophy and the natural sciences, we do not wish to convey the impression by any means that any great part of them is "learned" men.

An Omaha street car conductor will have his monastic cubicle next to a Milwaukee high school graduate. During the past two years a Negro from Chicago's South Side area and a Filipino from the West were admitted, the first non-Caucasians ever to enter the Iowa monastery. Trappist cloisters have no racial or national discriminations. Anyone is admitted without question provided he meets only the physical, mental and educational standards required of all

XX

THE DAUGHTER HOUSE: OUR STORY'S FINALE

. . . .

During the last century many another Trappist abbey has established an affiliate — a daughter house — from the overflow of its members. In the face of its many acute crises New Melleray was under the providence of God fortunate enough to survive itself without daring to dream of erecting filiations. It will be recalled that back in 1856 an experimental attempt was made to carry on an annex at Wexford, Iowa, on the land deeded over to New Melleray by Father Thomas Hore, but this effort died abornin'.

While Abbot Eugene was in Europe during the summer of 1950 to attend for the first time the meeting of the General Chapter at Citeaux Abbey in France, an event of tremendous importance occurred at Dubuque during his absence. In 1849 on a hot July day the monastery of New Melleray had been formally established in Iowa. Now, on another hot day in July, just as the Dubuque Trappist foundation was completing the first year of its second century of existence something almost incredible — even for Cistercians, whose faith in the Lord's power is profound, indeed, — took place in the reception room of New Melleray's guest house. Reference has been made several times to the interest the Chicago *Tribune* through its feature writers has displayed in the story of New Melleray Abbey. One day a gentleman called at the abbey and in the absence of Abbot Eugene was received by Prior Vincent. The gentleman, after introducing himself as Mr. Joseph Pierson, a retired foreign correspondent for the *Chicago Tribune,* explained that he had a thirty-six hundred acre ranch in the foothills of the Ozark Mountains in Missouri which he would like to extend as a gift to the Iowa Trappist monks.

It is no exaggeration to say that Prior Vincent could scarcely trust his ears as he listened, first with amazement and then with gratitude to the good God, to the words of Mr. Pierson. These words of explanation were brief: his age and the calling of his sons into the military service had first disposed him to sell the property; but he had often heard of the Cistercian brotherhood and although he was a non-Catholic he had long admired their holy lives of solitude, prayer and work, and God in His mercy had inspired him to seek out the monks of New Melleray to offer them this land and to induce them to come and make a new foundation.

With most sincere praise to God and gracious acknowledgment to Mr. Pierson, the Iowa community accepted this princely gift. Abbot Eugene, apprised of the proposal, had cabled Prior Vincent from Europe to receive gratefully the benevolent offer. All the legal requirements for taking it over were expedited and Bishop Edwin V. O'Hara of Kansas City welcomed with enthusiasm the coming of the Trappists to his diocese. On this widespread estate, most of which is still virgin forest, seventy-five miles east of Springfield and twenty miles north of the Arkansas line, is a main building of stone and concrete with five thousand square feet of floor space. This is connected with a large workroom and garage, and nearby are barns and other outbuildings. The location is in the ideal tradition of the Rule and polity of St. Benedict — far from the haunts of men and well adapted to monastic life. Catholicism is little known in this part of Missouri — there was but one Catholic church in the entire county — but this was an added incentive to the monks to let their flame of Faith gleam openly from the Ozark hills.

The initial group of monks which left New Melleray for their new home was a well-seasoned staff of young Trappists, eleven in all, three priests and eight brothers — skillful and able to face the vicissitudes of the strange hill country and the problems of a new foundation. Recruits from the Iowa parent house have been steadily arriving and the original number has now been more than doubled.

Eight and a half centuries ago twenty-two monks, headed by Robert of Moslesme, left the abbey of Moslesme to found a world renowned monastery — famed Citeaux — in the marshy woodlands of Burgundy. Twenty-five monks today, of whom six are priests, under their superior, Father Canice Keneally, have left the abbey of New Melleray to found a monastery on the hilly woodlands of Missouri. At Citeaux the Duke of Burgundy had ceded in 1098 the sparsely settled and practically useless land to the monastic colonists, believing that they alone could ever cultivate it. Today, a modern duke of charity has donated his estate in the primitive Ozark highlands to poor and penitent monks because of his confidence in them and because of his admiration of the Trappist way of life.

In this foundation the monks have grimly set to work with a will. Their first problem was that of rearrangement of the rooms of the main building to comply with the requirements of Trappist community life. The long, low garage and workshop connected with the main building was converted into a pleasing monastic chapel soon after their arrival. A new and modern heating-plant was installed. The poor roads which impeded travel and transport have been considerably improved. There had been no electricity for a time but light and power have now been introduced through the agency of the Rural Electrification Administration. It had been necessary to make a four-mile trip to Evans, Missouri, each day for the mail, but the mailing address has now been changed to the town of Sweden from where there is Rural Free Delivery. One gains an idea of the monastery's primitive remoteness on learning that there is as yet no telephone service. A small saw mill is now being operated by the brethren in the shady forests about their home; they have already planted orchards and vineyards; and the bucolic science of apiculture or beekeeping is here being developed just as at Dubuque.

In the woodland chapel of this Trappist Arcadia every morning and every evening there rises up the soft chant of monastic voices as the brethren praise the Lord and pray for the world. Under the benign blessing of God Almighty this pioneer Missouri Trappist cloister — the monastery of Our Lady of the Assumption — will grow and prosper; it was appropriately named in honor of the great dogma of the Assumption of the Virgin promulgated to the world in the Holy Year of 1950, the year of its founding.[1]

At New Melleray itself, just as in most of the Cistercian abbeys of America and of the world at large, the year 1952 sees the measure of new vocations still flourishing near the flood mark. Of course, there are some who perforce must leave, and, according to the law written for all men, there are some who die. Of these latter there was one at the Iowa Trappist abbey who in February of 1952 passed away in his eighty-fourth year — Father Placid Magee, for more than forty-one years the pastor of the secular church, the "monastery parish" of the Holy Family. For all these breaches in the ranks of the monastic heroes, the grace of God working in the hearts of young men, sends more than commensurate replacements; "good measure and pressed down and shaken together and running over."

At the one hundred and third anniversary of their abbey's penetential existence, the priests and brothers of New Melleray rejoice in the evidence they behold on all sides of God's benign acceptance of the greatest gift they can put at His feet — their lives.

*　*　*　*

This is the Iowa Trappist story. It is the story of the austerely humble monks in white and brown who for over a century have carried the weapons and armor of Jesus Christ in the modern agricultural and industrial valley of the Upper Mississippi.

Our Lady of New Melleray had a slow and painful growth — building on a foundation of poverty and sacrifice. Crises and calamities were its ever recurring portion, and as the pages of this book clearly show, its constant survival was almost miraculous. Yet today the monastery is compelled to expand by the press of vocations and is prospering more than ever before in its long history.

The writer can well recall when as a lad with his parents, driving out on summer or fall afternoons from Dubuque in the old family carriage, they approached the vicinity of New Melleray. There, a short distance away, stood the monastery with its whitish-grey stone walls with arched windows, with its buttresses and spires and

---

[1] History records an earlier attempt at establishing a Cistercian monastery in Missouri in the early 1870s. Several monks from the short-lived Holy Ghost monastery in the Province of Quebec, Canada — which was an offshoot of Petit Clairvaux, Nova Scotia — founded the monastery of the Immaculate Conception at Old Monroe, Missouri, with Father Gerard Fuerstenburg as superior. After a short and stormy existence the foundation was abandoned as hopeless in 1875.

ornamental chimneys, set on the crest of a rise within a frame of trees and green fields. There it stood, a bit of mystery and even somewhat of an American anomaly; to us of Dubuque and to folk in general it was still mediaeval, still foreign; what we saw of the institution — the monks, with their dust-covered habits tucked in about their hips, working silently in the fields as we passed —, what we read and heard about their austere life, fell just short in those days of making a practical appeal to American Catholic youth for vocations. At the end of World War I an idealistic West Point graduate returning from France with the writer and dismayed by what he had witnessed at Chateau-Thierry and in the Argonne forest essayed a postulancy at the monastery; after two months' trial he, like a number of others through those years, withdrew.

But of late a new breath of the Holy Spirit is astir in the ranks of our Catholic people. What a transformation among the youth of America in regard to Cistercian monastic life in the last score of years! New Melleray Abbey and other Trappist cloisters seem to be revitalized centers of spiritual attraction, throwing out their mystic life-lines to the increasing number who are seeking a regimen of Benedictine inspiration — a life of monastic obedience and labor and fasting and silence. They "See God's world through the rags of this."

Catholicism has always held the prayerful, contemplative life as an ideal one; the critics of the Catholic Church have in the past condemned such a life as a useless one. Today the critical pendulum is swinging in the other direction. In the national weekly, *Time Magazine,* for January 21, 1952, is a reprint of an article by an alleged Catholic which originally appeared in the Protestant *Christian Herald,* berating American Catholicism because it is "totally non-mystical; it is booming, aggressive, materialstic." Non-mystical! The Catholic Church in the United States? Behold the mysticism and prayerfulness found today in America in the growing number of contemplative monasteries, convents, the lay retreat houses and various apostolic movements such as Catholic Action! The marked increase of theological interest and spiritual reading among American Catholics in recent years indicates the strong growth of the mystical movement. St. Teresa of Avila and St. John of the Cross have been rediscovered by clergy and laity. But in the forefront of it all just as in bygone centuries is the Cistercian contemplative life of today. Trappist asceticism practiced in the abbey of New Melleray for over a century, and today more powerfully attractive than ever before, is a conclusive proof of the healthy mystic life of Catholicism, especially in mid-America.

"Arms and the Monk!" It is the end of the day at New Melleray; the monastic militia files out from the Gothic structure which to them is their Rule and their Fortress, and in their hands they carry their weapons, — the rosary, the divine office, the book of general devotions. During the supper period in the refectory they had been listening to the brother reading over the public address system an article dealing with another onslaught against the Church of Christ behind the Iron Curtain. They are a bit depressed but outside here everything is golden. The setting sun is gilding the trees in the woodlands about them. One of its rays flashes on an airplane high in the skies speeding on to Chicago. An ex-aviator pulls his cowl over his eyes to shield them from the sun as he stares at the plane. It's a large airplane; it reminds him of the C-47s he used to fly. From a nearby tower rings a soft, wistful, silvery but insistent bell. The monks pass back within the monastery along corridors hung with placards lettered with the word "Silence."

Slowly they mount the stairway leading to their chapel. Strains of organ music fill the air. There is a mumur of voices, an intoning, and a lift of song, *Salve Regina*, and lo, these monks of the centuried Iowa cloister are wrapped up in the blissful devotions with their brethren throughout the world and with their predecessors from Monte Cassino to Citeaux and Clairvaux, and down the ages, to New Melleray, "ad majorem Dei gloriam."

Arma, Monachum Cano!

XXI

HISTORICAL SIDELIGHTS

1. MONASTERY RETREATS

The impetus given the spiritual retreat movement by the erection of the guest and retreat house at New Melleray Abbey and described in the later chapters of this volume continues to this day. The schedule for retreats for groups of laymen for the first half of the year 1952 is herewith given, and it may be pointed out that it included not only parish groups from Iowa, Wisconsin and Illinois, but other particular groups: the Newman Club, University of Wisconsin, Madison; the Phi Kappa Fraternity, Iowa State College, Ames, Iowa; Chevrolet Motor Division of Milwaukee and Iowa; the Dubuque Business and Professional Men's group. The schedule follows:

January 18-20—Tennyson, Wis.
January 25-27—Darlington, Wis.
February 1-3—Cuba City and Potosi, Wis.
February 8-10—St. Mary's and St. Patrick's, Dubuque.
February 15-17—Monastery Retreat.
February 22-24—Newman Club, Madison, Wis.
February 29-March 2—Lancaster, Wis.
March 7-9—Cascade, Iowa.
March 14-16—Farley, Iowa.
March 21-23—Monastery Retreat.
March 28-30—Phi Kappa Fraternity, Iowa State College, Ames, Ia.

April 4-6—Palm Sunday group.

April 18-20—Chevrolet Motor Division, Milwaukee, Wis., and
　　Waterloo, Iowa.

April 25-27—Dubuque Business and Professional Men.

May 2-4—Holy Ghost, Dubuque.

May 9-11—Plymouth, Wis.

May 16-18—St. Columbkille's, Dubuque.

May 23-25—Dyersville, Iowa.

May 30-June 1—East Dubuque, Illinois.

June 6-8—Business and Professional Men, West Allis, Wis.

June 13-15—Business and Professional Men, Fond du Lac, Wis.

2. ST. PHILOMENA AND NEW MELLERAY

The enthusiasm for the cult of the St. Philomena devotions which
prevailed in the earlier decades of the nineteenth century was carried from Europe to Iowa by two of the founders of New Melleray
monastry, Bishop Mathias Loras of Dubuque and Father James
Myles O'Gorman, superior of the monastery from 1849 to 1850 and
prior from 1857 to 1859. Bishop Loras' sister, a nun of the Visitation
Convent in Condrien, France, his oldest living sister, and his "Maraine
et seconde Mère," as she signed herself, bore the name of Soeur
Philomene. One of the parishes he organized near Dubuque at
Asbury he named St. Philomena's.

Prior James O'Gorman encouraged the devotion in his cloister
and when he went to Omaha as bishop of the Nebraska vicariate,
he named his first cathedral St. Philomena's, and this parish still
flourishes today. That the cult of the "saintly Princess" continued
from his time on is proven by the profusion of pictures and prayer
leaflets left in the various books of the brothers who passed away.
During the gloomy days of the threatened bankruptcy of New Melleray in the 1880s novenas of masses in honor of St. Philomena were
said and the happy escape from ultimate extinction was frequently
attributed to her intercession. From 1903 on Father John Burns
was the leader of the devotees of St. Philomena, and on his death
his mantle fell on the shoulders of Brother Timothy Westemeyer whose
family gave several members to New Melleray, among them Abbot
Bruno Ryan. Due to Brother Timothy's zealous activities, especially
in recent years, this devotion has spread from the monastery to many
other localities. Only since November of 1947 this Trappist brother
has sent devotional articles to every state of the Union, as well as to

Guam and Alaska, Canada, Ireland, Italy, West and South Africa and to India.

These articles include nine thousand copies of the booklet, "Saint Philomena, the Wonderworker," seventeen thousand medals, approximately fifteen thousand cords, two thousand six hundred pictures, about forty-five thousand prayer leaflets, and nine hundred third class relics.

In March of 1952 Father W. H. Dunphy, the Command Chaplain of the Royal Canadian Air Force, wrote a letter to the abbey explaining how he, through the influence of Brother Timothy, has spread the devotion to St. Philomena not only among his fellow chaplains but among the airmen, airwomen, their dependents and all others entrusted to his care. In April Bishop John Collins of Monrovia, capital of Liberia, West Africa, wrote: "May God bless and reward you and the Client of Saint Philomena who defrayed the expense of sending this last box of articles."

3. A PROPHECY OF WORLD WAR III?

Among the priests of New Melleray Abbey who enlisted in the army to serve as chaplains in World War II was Father Gregory Kennedy. In a letter in the abbey archives received from Father Kennedy from Seoul, Korea, and written on March 8, 1948, is a rather remarkable passage: "It is nearly two years since I arrived in Korea, the land of missionaries and martyrs. It is a very troubled place and it has accurately been called 'the powder-keg of the world — a place that can easily explode and plunge the whole world into the agony of World War III.' I see daily the terrible struggle between Communism and the forces of Christ — and the holy monks at New Melleray should use every means of their prayerful lives to halt the inroads of this dreadful enemy." — This was written well over two years before the North Korean aggression across the 38th parallel in the summer of 1950.

4. BURIALS AT NEW MELLERAY

What is of bizarre interest even to Catholics is the method of burials of the Trappist monks. The fact that they are buried in their monastic habits instead of in coffins brings at first a recoiling impact of distaste and aversion to those accustomed to the un-Christian world's policy of gilding over and softening what should be to us the wholesome lesson of the shock of death. Yet, this interring of the monk in the earth from which he sprang is as logical as it is touching.

From the *Histoire de Notre Dame de la Grande Trappe* (Bordeaux, 1903), the following beautiful description is taken:

Les cloches s'associent au deuil de la famille religieuse. Au cimetière le supérieur récite quelques oraisons, bénit la fosse, asperge et encense le corps et la tombe; ensuite les quatre frères qui le portaient le descendent avec des bandelettes dans la fosse, où le Père infirmier est déjà descendu. L'infirmier reçoit le corps, l'étend avec respect, arrange ses vêtements, lui rabat le capuce sur le visage, et remonte après avoir accompli ce devoir suprême envers son frère défunt. On sait que les Trappistes pratiquent la pauvreté jusque dans leur sépulture; voilà pourquoi on les enterre sans cercueil. L'infirmier étant remonté de la fosse, le supérieur asperge et encense une dernière fois le défunt, jette sur lui un peu de terre, puis les frères remplissent la fosse.

Which means — that amidst the tolling of the abbey bells and the pious recitation of the prayers of the brothers, the grave is blessed and the body is sprinkled with holy water and the fragrant clouds from the burning incense are wafted over it. "The Father infirmarian standing in the grave receives the body as it is lowered to him, stretches it out with reverence, arranges the habit, draws the cowl over the countenance of the deceased, and ascends from the tomb having performed this supreme duty towards his dead brother. Just as it is well known that the Trappists practice poverty until their very sepulture, so it is understood why they are buried without coffins. Once again the superior blesses the deceased with holy water and incense, tosses upon him a bit of earth, and then the brothers fill up the grave.

"The religious then sing seven psalms as though asking pardon from God for the faults their brother may have committed through the seven capital sins . . .

"Among the Trappists, the cemetery is contiguous to their church, contrary to the modern innovation, which under pretext of public health but in reality in order to erase from man the thought of death, locates the cemetery as far away as possible from the centers of population . . .

"After the death of a Trappist, following an ancient and venerable custom of the order of Citeaux, the place which he had occupied in the refectory is served his repast as though he were still present; a little cross of wood is placed on his napkin."

This pious practice continues for a month. And during this month — the Tricenary it is called — masses, prayers and good work are offered up in behalf of the deceased.

5. LIST OF ABBOTS, PRIORS AND SUPERIORS AT NEW MELLERAY

1. Father CLEMENT
(Timothy Smyth)
Born Feb. 24, 1810
Professed: Nov. 1, 1839

Prior: July 16, 1849-Aug. 18, 1849
Resigned his first appointment as Titular Prior. (See No. 4 below)
Died: Sept. 22, 1865

2. Father JAMES
(James Myles O'Gorman)
Born Oct. 16, 1804
Professed: Mar. 25, 1841

Superior: Aug. 18, 1849-Apr. 12, 1850
Appointed temporary superior until the arrival of new Titular Prior from Mount Melleray. (See No. 5)
Died: July 4, 1874

3. Father FRANCIS
(Thomas Walsh)
Born ...., 1813
Professed: Feb. 2, 1834

Prior: Apr. 12, 1850-Dec. 6, 1852
Removed by Dom Bruno Fitzpatrick when monastery reached critical stage. Worked thirty years on Iowa missions by dispensation.
Died: October 29, 1893

4. Father CLEMENT
(Timothy Smyth)
Born Feb. 24, 1810
Professed: Nov. 1, 1839

Prior: Dec. 6, 1852-Apr. 16, 1857
Left New Melleray to become second bishop of diocese of Dubuque.
Died: Sept. 22, 1865

5. Father JAMES
(James Myles O'Gorman)
Born Oct. 16, 1804
Professed: Mar. 25, 1841

Prior: Apr. 16, 1857-May 2, 1859
Left New Melleray to become first resident Vicar-Apostolic of Nebraska, later Diocese of Omaha.
Died: July 4, 1874

6. Father BERNARD
(Hugh McCaffrey)
Born: Aug. 6, 1813
Professed: Nov. 1, 1837

Superior: May 2, 1859-Oct. 2, 1860
Appointed temporary superior until arrival of new Titular Prior from Mount Melleray.
Died: March 3, 1883

7. Father IGNATIUS
   (Michael Foley)
   Born: ...., 1824
   Professed: Sept. 8, 1848

   Prior: Oct. 2, 1860-June 15, 1861
   Returned to Mount Melleray Abbey to become president of Mount Melleray Seminary. Later, Prior of Mount St. Joseph's, Roscrea.
   Died: May 6, 1912

8. Father BERNARD
   (Hugh McCaffrey)
   Born: Aug. 6, 1813
   Professed: Nov. 1, 1837

   Superior: June 15, 1861-Nov. 2, 1861
   Served as temporary superior until arrival of new Titular Prior from Mount Melleray.
   Died: March 3, 1883

9. Father ALBERIC
   (Hugh Madigan)

   Superior: Nov. 2, 1861-Feb. 25, 1862
   Served as temporary superior until arrival of new Titular Prior from Mount Melleray.

10. Abbot EPHREM
    (Charles Joseph McDonnell)
    Born: Feb. 12, 1822
    Professed: Nov. 1, 1846

    Prior and Abbot: Feb. 25, 1862-Sept. 29, 1883
    Elected 1st Abbot of New Melleray. Blessed May 10, 1863. Resigned office and returned to Mount Melleray.
    Died: March 13, 1898

11. Father ALBERIC
    (Denis Dunlea)
    Born: March 8, 1833
    Professed: Dec. 8, 1860

    Superior: Sept. 29, 1883-Sept. 27, 1889
    Election of new abbot postponed because of heavy debt and lack of vocations.
    Died: February 4, 1917

12. Father LEWIS
    (Peter Carew)
    Born: June 9, 1850
    Professed: Dec. 8, 1871

    Superior: Sept. 27, 1889-June 7, 1897
    Aided in reducing the debt and left New Melleray to serve as Trappist Definitor in Rome.
    Died: June 2, 1927

13. Abbot ALBERIC
    (Denis Dunlea)
    Born: March 8, 1833
    Professed: Dec. 8, 1860

    Abbot: June 7, 1897-Feb. 4, 1917
    Elected 2nd Abbot of New Melleray. Blessed Oct. 28, 1897. Cleared the debt and enlarged the domain.
    Died: February 4, 1917

14. Abbot BRUNO
    (James Ryan)
    Born: Dec. 19, 1865
    Professed: Dec. 14, 1890

Superior and Abbot: Feb. 4, 1917-Aug. 2, 1944

Elected 3rd Abbot of New Melleray. Blessed May 23, 1935. Built guest house in 1928. Farm and buildings modernly equipped.

Died: August 2, 1944

15. Abbot ALBERT
    (John Beston)
    Born: Nov. 15, 1880
    Professed: Aug. 25, 1901

Abbot: Aug. 2,1944-Sept. 5, 1946

Elected 4th Abbot of New Melleray. Blessed Dec. 28, 1944. Inaugurated building program to complete the monastery.

Died: Sept. 5, 1946

16. Father VINCENT
    (Vincent Daly)
    Born: January 4, 1911
    Professed: Dec. 8, 1932

Superior: Sept. 5, 1946 until election of Abbot Eugene. Now, Claustral Prior of New Melleray Abbey.

17. Abbot EUGENE
    (John Joseph Martin)
    Baptized: July 17, 1878
    Professed: Feb. 28, 1904

Abbot: Sept. 5, 1946

Elected 5th Abbot of New Melleray. Blessed Oct. 24, 1946. Continuing the building program. Sent colony to the Ozarks in Missouri, Sept. 25, 1950.

Died: Nov. 10, 1952

(Researches of Bro. Timothy Westemeyer, O.C.S.O.)

6. STATISTICAL PERSONNEL OF NEW MELLERAY

When the Iowa Trappist foundation was commenced by Dom Bruno Fitzpatrick in July of 1849 its membership consisted of two priests and four lay brothers. Toward the end of that year, despite the tragedy on the Mississippi which took the lives of six of the monks, the number rose to six choir brothers of whom four were priests, and eleven lay brothers. The following numbers are taken from the records in the stated years:

Year	CHOIR BROTHERS			LAY BROTHERS			Total	Priests
	Professed	Novices	Oblates and Postulants	Professed	Novices	Oblates and Postulants		
1851	18	7		20	5		50	5
1860	13	2		37	9		61	7
1870	8		3	38	3	4	56	7
1878	7	1	4	40	3	5	60	6
1889	6		6	31	4	6	53	10
1892	8		6	33			54	9
1901	5		4	21		4	34	8
1909	5	1	2	17		2	27	6
1911	6		2	15		2	25	6
1918	5		1	10	1		17	5
1920	8	1	1	13	2		25	7
1924	9	2		11	4		26	7
1930	7	8	1	15	2	5	38	4
1934	15	6		15	1	2	39	8
1941	19	6	2	21	3	3	54	16
1944	21	5	1	21		3	51	14
1946	24	12	3	20		8	67	15
1947	27	9	4	22	7	4	73	17
1948	32	12	1	20	13	6	84	19
1949	38	20	10	26	9	5	108	23
1950	45	28	3	27	15	17	135	24

7. "WESTWARD DOES THE STAR OF EMPIRE . . ."

Bishop Mathias Loras of Iowa, encouraged and pleased by the lives of the Cistercians whom he had helped to establish on the banks of the Mississippi, sought in the middle 1850s to bring their monastic cousins, the Benedictines, into his diocese also. One Benedictine house had been commenced as far west as Indiana — at St. Meinrad's — in 1854, and another near what is now Collegeville, Minnesota, in 1856.

The correspondence in connection with this effort between Dr. Loras and the celebrated Archabbot Boniface Wimmer of St. Vincent's Archabbey in Pennsylvania, found in the Dubuque archdiocesan archives, is both edifying and amusing. Much as he admired the archabbot and the Benedictines, Bishop Loras was such an advocate of Temperance — spelled with a capital T — as this historical study has already shown when speaking of the bishop's relations with Father Mathew, the giant Apostle of Temperance, that he hesitated about an outright invitation because he feared the introduction of a monastic brewery in his diocese. The Bavarian monks of various orders were famous for their brews of beer in Munich, and the phantom of a possible Benedictine brewery proved too much for Loras — really somewhat of a Prohibitionist at heart — and he withheld the invitation.

This did not hinder the penetration of various other parts of the West by the Benedictine monks. Even today's press relates how these followers of the Rule of St. Benedict, commonly known as the "black monks," have now established an abbey high in the Coteau hills of northeastern South Dakota. A 576-acre farm is being transformed into a monastic setting, and from now on will serve as headquarters for the Benedictine missions to the Indians. Hitherto, the administration of these missions was handled at the founding abbey, St. Meinrad's of Indiana. For more than seventy years these monks have labored among the Indian tribes of the Dakotas.

8. FORMAL VISITORS AT NEW MELLERAY

In general, all Cistercian monasteries are visited by their Father Immediate or his delegate, unless the Abbot General has already visited them. It is chiefly on the Visitation, properly made, that the preservation of regular discipline depends. Here is the list of Formal or Regular Visitors to New Melleray during its centuried existence taken from the Visitation Cards; the Visitation Cards are letters, sometimes lengthy, written by the Visitors containing solicitous paternal admonitions which are to be read on the ember days of the four seasons of the year until the next Visitation:

1849 — Dom Bruno Fitzpatrick, Founder and Father Immediate, Abbot of Mount Melleray, Ireland.

1857 — Dom Bruno Fitzpatrick.

1860 — Dom Bruno Fitzpatrick.

1862 — Dom Benedict Berger, Abbot of Gethsemani, Kentucky.

1867 — Dom Benedict Berger.

1868 — Dom Anthony, Abbot of Our Lady of La Trappe, Melleray, (Nantes) France.

1870 — Dom Bruno Fitzpatrick, Father Immediate and Abbot of Mount Melleray, Ireland.

1875 — Father James Deportement, Prior of Petit Clairvaux Monastery, Tracadie, Nova Scotia, Canada.

1876 — Dom Eugene Vachette, Abbot of Our Lady of La Trappe, Melleray, (Nantes) France.

1878 — Dom Bruno Fitzpatrick, Father Immediate, Abbot of Mount Melleray, Ireland.

1882 — Dom Dominic Schietecatte, Abbot of Petit Clairvaux, Tracadie, Nova Scotia, Canada.

1883 — Dom Jean Marie, Abbot of Notre Dame de Bellefontaine, France.

1886 — Dom Eugene Vachette, Abbot of Melleray, France.

1887 — Dom Jean Marie, Abbot of Bellefontaine, France.

1889 — Dom Bruno Fitzpatrick, Abbot of Mount Melleray, Ireland. (Sixth, and Last, Visitation of the Founder before his death.)

1892 — Dom Jean Marie, Abbot of Bellefontaine, France.

1894 — Dom Eugene Vachette, Abbot of Melleray, France.

1897 — Dom Carthage Delaney, Father Immediate, Abbot of Mount Melleray, Ireland, and Dom Eugene Vachette, Abbot of Melleray, France.

1901 — Dom Edmund Obrecht, Abbot of Gethsemani, Kentucky.

1909 — Dom Augustine Marre, Titular Bishop of Constance, Abbot of Citeaux, France, and Abbot General of the Order of Reformed Cistercians. (First Visitation by the Abbot General of the Order.)

1911 — Dom Maurus Phelan, Father Immediate, Abbot of Mount Melleray, Ireland.

1918 — Dom Pacome Gaboury, Abbot of Notre Dame du Lac, Oka, Montreal, Quebec Province, Canada.

1919 — Dom Maurus Phelan, Father Immediate, Abbot of Mount Melleray, Ireland.

1920 — Dom Maurus Phelan.

1924 — Dom Maurus Phelan.

1928 — Dom Jean Baptiste Ollitrault Keryvallan, Abbot of Citeaux, France, and Abbot General of the Order of Cistercians of the Strict Observance. (Second Visitation by an Abbot General.)

1930 — Dom Maurus Phelan, Father Immediate, Abbot of Mount Melleray, Ireland.

1931 — Dom Herman Joseph Smets, Abbot of Citeaux, France, and Abbot General of the Order of Cistercians of the Strict Observance. (Third Visitation by an Abbot General.)

1934 — Dom Celsus O'Connell, Father Immediate, Abbot of Mount Melleray, Ireland.

1935 — Dom Celsus O'Connell.

1938 — Dom Celsus O'Connell.

1941 — Dom Pacome Gaboury, Abbot of Notre Dame du Lac, Montreal, Canada.

1944 — Dom Celsus O'Connell, Father Immediate, Abbot of Mount Melleray, *Eire.*

1946 — Dom Celsus O'Connell.

1948, 1950 and 1951 — Dom Celsus O'Connell.

9. COAT OF ARMS OF
The Right Reverend Abbot Eugene, O.C.S.O.
Our Lady of New Melleray Abbey
(For those who understand heraldry)

BLAZON

Impaled Arms. Dexter: Per fess dancette, azure and argent, in chief a cross botonny rayonnant or, between four mullets of the second, in base on a bar wavy of the first three fleur-de-lis of the second (Abbey of Our Lady of New Melleray). Sinister: Ermine, three bars gules, over all an eagle rising or, on the breast an inescutcheon azure charged with a crescent argent and a chief per pale of the first and of the last, on a chief azure, seme-de-lis of the third an inescutcheon bendy of six or and azure within a bordure gules (Abbot Eugene).

The Martin family of Ireland has a coat of arms consisting of an ermine field bearing three red bars.

The motto of Abbot Eugene, emblazoned at the base of his impaled arms, "Nihil amori Christi praeponere" is translated, "To prefer nothing to the love of Christ," and is taken from the Rule of St. Benedict, Chap. IV, "The Instruments of Good Works," Instrument No. 21.

10. CONDITIONS FOR ADMISSION TO THE CISTERCIAN ORDER.

"The choir monks, whose chief duty is the solemn and public discharge of the Holy Liturgy, are either priests or destined for the priesthood. Candidates for their ranks must, therefore, be free from any canonical impediments which would prevent their reception of Holy Orders. Young men from sixteen to about thirty-five years of age are received as postulants. Good recommendations must be presented from one's pastor or former Superiors. At least a high school education is recommended. Those who enter without this must complete their classical studies here in the monastery before receiving the holy Habit. Before their entrance, candidates are asked to procure certificates of their baptism and confirmation and parents' marriage certificate. Also it is required that one obtain a certification of good health from one's physician and have all dental needs taken care of.

"The postulantship ordinarily lasts one month, and is passed in one's civilian clothes. If the candidate shows evidence of a true vocation and the necessary aptitude, he is received into the novitiate at the end of this period. The two-year novitiate is followed by a three-year period of simple vows, then the solemn perpetual vows. In all, a little more than five years must elapse before the aspirant is permitted to bind himself irrevocably to this life. In the meanwhile, the young religious pursues his philosophical and theological studies, and begins to receive the sacred Orders sometime after his solemn profession.

"All that has been said for the admission, noviceship and profession of the choir monks applies also for the lay brothers. Their postulantship, however, lasts for six months, and the same educational requirements are not asked of them.

"Those seeking further information about the Order and about the life at New Melleray are cordially invited to correspond with THE RIGHT REVEREND ABBOT, Abbey of Our Lady of New Melleray, Dubuque, Iowa."

11. A MONK'S WILL.

Written by Abbot Bruno of New Melleray not long before he died in 1944, with the request that the document not be opened until after his death.

"Being weak in body but sound in mind, I make this my last will.

"In regard to worldly goods I have none whatever. Consequently, of the articles which I have been allowed to use, the Prior will dispose as, and when and where he may desire.

"Of spiritual goods I owe a tremendous debt. First to God for His mercies toward me and especially for having brought me into Religion, and for having enabled me to persevere therein until now. Next, the Blessed Virgin Mary I thank for the same.

"To the Archbishop and to all who offered masses, communions, sacrifices, or prayers for me, I return sincere and heartfelt thanks, and I promise them my poor prayers.

"To each in the Community I owe very much. There might be an objection to mentioning names; but how can I refrain from expressly thanking those who carried me up the stairs to the chapel so often to Mass and to Vespers! How can I refrain from thanking those who watched so patiently at my bedside, and deprived themselves of needed rest to assist me. To each and all I promise my lasting gratitude, and my poor prayers.

"If you would desire an advice from an old monk, here it is. Always value very highly your vocation, be grateful to God for it, and prove your gratitude by fidelity to Him, and to the ever Blessed Virgin Mary. Amen.

"BROTHER BRUNO, ABBOT."

SUFFIX

TRAPPISTS.

Postulants: Those who apply for admision to the Cistercian order. They are usually received into the Guest-House and then into the community for an initial period of trial, before the novitiate begins.

Novices: Aspirants to vows in the Cistercian order who have been canonically admitted to the prescribed course of training in the novitiate, that is, in that part of the monastery assigned to the aspirants as their place of residence and training.

Oblates: Lay-persons who desire to share, to some extent, in the life of prayer and the spiritual benefits of the Cistercian order. Oblates live in the monastery and lead the life of the monks but take no vows or other formal religious obligations.

Lay Brothers: Members of the Cistercian order who, though they make simple or solemn vows, remain technically laymen in the sense that they are not destined to the clerical state, or Holy Orders, or at least to the public celebration of the Divine Office. Lay brothers devote to labor the time that choir brothers or priests spend in prayer or study.—*Merton's Glossary.*

Choir Brothers: Members of the Cistercian order who are obliged to recite the Divine Office in common; or at least in private, even though not bound by Holy Orders.

Priests: Those members of the choir religious (choir brothers) who have received Holy Orders, that is, who have been ordained to the sacerdotal state.

VOWS

Solemn and perpetual religious vows are made publicly in the presence of representatives of the Church.

The Trappist monk makes five monastic vows:

226

Poverty, by which he relinquishes all right to exercise ownership over property;

Obedience, by which he transfers his will into the hands of a superior, his Abbot, who governs his life according to the Rule;

Chastity, by which he gives up even legitimate satisfactions of the flesh;

Stability, binding the monk to live and die in the monastery of his profession; and

Conversion of Manners, which imposes a special obligation upon him to strive always for Christian perfection.

THE CISTERCIAN REGULAR HABIT

127. The exterior habit of the Monks of our Order consists of a robe and scapular confined by a leather girdle, and a cowl with a hood attached to it.

128. All the garments shall be of a white woolen material, except the scapular, which shall be black . . .

129. We wear shoes such as are commonly worn in the country where we live.

130. All the Monks shall have their heads shaved every month, leaving only the circle of hair which is called the monastic crown.

177. The habit of the Lay Brethren consists of a robe, a scapular, a leathern girdle, and a cloak. All the garments shall be of brown woolen material. The novices shall not wear the cloak, but instead, a hooded cape covering only the shoulders and breast.

(From the Constitution of the Order of Cistercians of the Strict Observance.)

THE HOURS OF A CHOIR RELIGIOUS AT NEW MELLERAY

2:00 A.M.	Rise, little office of Blessed Virgin
2:30 A.M.	Mental Prayer
3:00 A.M.	The canonical hours of matins and lauds,* Angelus, private masses, interval
5:30 A.M.	Prime, chapter, frustulum (2 ounces of bread), interval
7:45 A.M.	Tierce, high mass, sext, work

* Canonical hour — any certain stated times of the day (now seven, viz., matins with lauds, prime, tierce, sext, nones, vespers and compline), appointed for the offices of prayer and devotion. The above is the winter schedule; there is a slight change in the summer hours. There are also some changes in the hourly duties assigned to the lay brothers.

10:45 A.M.   End of work, interval
11:07 A.M.   None, particular examen, Angelus
11:30 A.M.   Dinner, interval
 1:30 P.M.   Work
 3:30 P.M.   End of work, interval
 4:30 P.M.   Vespers, mental prayer
 5:30 P.M.   Collation, interval
 6:10 P.M.   Lecture, compline, Salve, Angelus, examen
 7:00 P.M.   Repose

SILENCE

There is no Trappist "vow of silence." Silence is a matter of strict rule in the Cistercian order, but it is not the object of a vow. The monks simply renounce pleasure of human conversation the better to dedicate their powers of speech entirely to the praises of God.

But the monks do not, as some are said to be foolish enough to believe, forget how to speak. If they did the recitation of the Office would soon have to be given up. In fact, besides reciting the Divine Office, they have occasion once or twice a day to speak to a superior, master-of-novices, or some other person, to whom they through necessity obtain permission to talk. Still, knowing by experience, that the more silent they are exteriorly, the more active they are in being interiorly raised to God, they avoid conversation except when absolutely necessary.

In most Trappist monasteries, the monks receive and write letters, ordinarily, several times a year, usually once in each quarter.

The peril of much talking has been the burden of advice of the sages of all races and all centuries. Fred L. Holmes found two hundred and four proverbs advising against too much talk, proverbs distilled from the experience of some twenty centuries, such as, among the Hebrews, "A fool's voice is known by a multitude of words," and among the Germans, "The more understanding, the fewer words."

VOCATION

There is perhaps no other matter of our Holy Religion that has been so beclouded with misinformation even among good and sincere Catholics as that of a vocation to the religious life. This applies to vocations to the Trappists as well as to other orders.

What is a vocation? Who has a vocation? How can one be sure? These are the questions that daily are troubling the soul who would join itself more closely to the gentle Christ. As in other matters of salvation we must look for the answer in the acts and words of our Savior. When He was on earth showing us the way to live, from the very beginning of His public life He chose close friends and faithful followers who were to live holy lives and help others to reach the kingdom of Heaven.

In this lies the essence of a religious vocation, to secure our own salvation, which of course is the life work of every Christian; it includes also a desire to aid in spreading the kingdom of God among our fellow men — a desire to live and work for God, to make others love and know Him, to share with other souls the joys, the peace, the blessings, that are ours. In a word, it is that a generous spirit, and a sincere desire to share our blessings, is a mark of the first seeds of a vocation.

This generosity of soul convinces one that more should be done for our Lord than the keeping of a law binding on all. To such Christ, our Lord, speaks as He did to the rich young man in the Gospel, "If thou wilt be perfect go sell what thou hast and give to the poor and come follow me."

THE TRAPPIST DAY

A day at New Melleray and at any Trappist monastery would find itself divided about as follows:

4 Hours for Divine Office and Little Office of the Blessed Virgin Mary.

2 Hours for Masses (though only one is of obligation by rule).

2 Hours for study and spiritual reading.

4 Hours for manual labor. Often the limits are from three to six hours but manual labor does not consist of heavy, prolonged field labor. The lay brothers have longer hours than the choir religious, and if by chance through some grave necessity the work is harder than usual, the rule prescribes that a greater allowance of food be given; but such extraordinary work is seldom necessary.

4 Hours for private devotions, reading and minor duties in the monastery.

1 Hour for meals.

7 Hours for sleep.

What is there in this to lure kings from their thrones, or young Americans from the world?

Good Will, a Vocation

and

The Grace of God.

THE TRAPPIST INSTITUTION IS A DEMOCRATIC ONE

The Cistercian vow of obedience whereby the monk transfers his will into the hands of a superior, his Abbot, who governs his life according to the Rule, might mislead the reader into believing that the order is entirely autocratic, or that its government in the ideology of today is purely "totalitarian." This is not true, for the monks, surprisingly to those who are unfamiliar with their organization, have a voice in many important matters.

1. Not only do the superiors of the various houses submit questions of importance to the votes and suggestions of the members of the communities, but certain matters of voting are absolutely *de rigeur* for the members. From the authoritative "Directoire Spirituel a l'usage des Cisterciens de la S.O." we take the following in regard to the important subject of admission of candidates to the order:

"Those who have a voice in Chapter are under the obligation of voting. Two questions are to be decided by them: Has the candidate a true vocation; has his past conduct been such as to offer hopes of his fidelity?"

2. At the election of an abbot all the monks of the monastery who are solemnly professed and are under stability in the community have the right to vote. An absolute majority of the votes is required. Titular priors are chosen in the same manner as abbots.

3. The supreme authority of the Cistercian order resides in the General Chapter which is composed of all the abbots, titular priors and provisional superiors of houses, who assemble every year at Citeaux on the 12th of September for deliberation, and when necessary, for elections. The Abbot General and the definitors must be elected by absolute majorities. For the deposition of an abbot or a titular prior two-thirds of the votes are required.

Further, at elections all votes are taken in secret.

VOX MONACHORUM VOX DEI!

BIBLIOGRAPHY

MANUSCRIPTS AND ORIGINAL SOURCES

I. New Melleray Abbey Archives:—
   The Narrative of the Foundation of the Monastery of New Melleray.
   Prior Clement Smith.
   Annals of New Melleray Abbey, 1849-1887.   Brother Kieran Mullany.
   Manuscript articles and biographies by Brothers Kevin, Patrick, Arsene
   and various others, some of them anonymous.
   Account books and letters.
   Visitation Cards from 1857 to 1950.

II. Other Archives and Libraries:—
   Letters and documents in Dubuque Archdiocesan Archives.
   Register of Religious in Mount Melleray Abbey, Ireland.
   Letters and documents in Mount Melleray Abbey, Ireland.
   Letters and documents in the following archives and libraries:—
      Propagation of the Faith Society, Lyons, France.
      Sacred Congregation of Propaganda de Fide, Rome.
      La Biblioteca Apostolica Vaticana, Rome.
      Irish College Library, Rome.
      Abbaye de la Grande Trappe, Orne, France.
      Abbey of Our Lady of the Valley, Rhode Island.
      Melleray Abbey, Melleray (Nantes), France.
      St. Augustine's Monastery, Nova Scotia, Canada.
      Mount Saint Bernard Abbey, Leicestershire, England.
      Mount Carmel Convent Archives, Dubuque, Iowa.
      Bureau of Indian Affairs, National Archives, Washington, D. C.
      Catholic Archives of America, Notre Dame University, Notre Dame,
      Indiana.
      Historical, Memorial and Art Department of Iowa, Des Moines.
      St. Louis (Mo.) Historical Society.
      Dubuque Public Library.
      Galena (Illinois) Public Library.
      Baltimore Archdiocesan Archives.
      New Orleans Archdiocesan Archives.
      New York Archdiocesan Archives.
      Omaha Archdiocesan Archives.
      St. Paul Archdiocesan Archives.
      Milwaukee Archdiocesan Archives.

PRINTED SOURCES

Actes des Chapitres Généraux de la Trappe. La Grande Trappe, 1872.

Anonymous, *Constitutions of the Order of the Cistercians of the Strict Observance,* Dublin, 1931.

Catholic Encyclopedia, The, 15 vols. New York, 1907.

Cistercian Monk, A, *History of the Cistercian Order with its Revival in England,* London, 1852.

De Cailly, Louis, *Memoirs of Bishop Loras and of Members of his Family,* New York, 1897.

Dickens, Charles, *American Notes,* New York, 1907.

Extraits des Actes des Chapitres Généraux de la Trappe, depuis L'Année, 1847. La Grande Trappe, 1866.

Garraghan, Gilbert J., S.J., *The Catholic Church in Chicago, 1673-1871,* Chicago, 1921.

———— "The Trappists of Monks' Mound." *Illinois Catholic Historical Review,* Vol. viii, October, 1925.

Gerow, R. O., *Cradle Days of St. Mary's, Natchez,* Natchez, Mississippi, 1941.

Gethsemani, a father of the Abbey of (M. Alberic), *Compendium of the History of the Cistercian Order,* Gethsemani, 1944.

Hoffman, M. M., *The Church Founders of the Northwest,* Milwaukee, 1937.

———— *Centennial History of the Archdiocese of Dubuque,* Dubuque, 1938.

———— *The Story of Loras College,* Dubuque, 1939.

———— "Clement Smyth, Second Bishop of Iowa," *Iowa Catholic Historical Review,* Vol. ix, February, 1936.

Holmes, Fred L., *The Voice of Trappist Silence,* New York, 1941.

Hughes, Carol, "Silent Sanctuary," *Coronet Magazine,* Chicago, October, 1951.

Luddy, M. Ailbe, *The Story of Mount Melleray,* Dublin, 1932.

Maguire, John Francis, *Father Mathew,* New York, 1864.

Mahan, Bruce, "A Day at New Melleray," *The Palimpsest,* The State Historical Society of Iowa, May, 1922.

Maynard, Theodore, *The Story of American Catholicism,* New York, 1942.

Merton, Thomas, *The Seven Storey Mountain,* New York, 1948.

———— *The Waters of Siloe,* New York, 1949.

Mount Carmel Convent, *In the Early Days, 1833-1887,* Dubuque, 1943.

Mullin, F. A., "The Chronicle of New Melleray Abbey," *The Iowa Catholic Historical Review,* Dubuque, Vol. vi, April, 1933.

New Melleray Abbey, A Priest of, *A Spiritual Directory for Religious,* translation of the *Directoire Spirituelle,* 2 vols., Westmalle, Belgium, 1932.

O'Rourke, John, *History of the Great Irish Famine of 1847,* Dublin, 1902.

Perkins, William Rufus, *History of the Trappist Abbey of New Melleray,* Iowa City, 1892.

Raymond, M., *Burnt Out Incense,* New York, 1949.

Religieux, Un, *Histoire de N.D. de la Grande Trappe,* Bordeaux, France, 1903.

Rothensteiner, John, *History of the Archdiocese of St. Louis,* St. Louis, 1928.

Ryan, M. V., *A Relation of the Sufferings of the Irish Monks of La Trappe.* (Translation from the French.) Limerick, 1832.

Schrepfer, Luke, O.S.A., *Pioneer Monks in Nova Scotia,* Tracadie, Nova Scotia, 1947.

Tallon, Clement, *Notices sur les Monastères de l'Ordre de la Trappe, en France, en Algérie, et en Amerique,* Paris, 1855.

Visitation, a Sister of, *Most Rev. Clement Smyth, Second Bishop of Dubuque.*
New Melleray, 1937.

Whalen, Charles, *The Trappist Way,* New Melleray, 1945.

The Dubuque *Times.*

The Dubuque *Globe-Journal.*

The Dubuque *Telegrah-Herald.*

The Dubuque *Witness.*

The Dubuque *Catholic Tribune.*

The Chicago *Tribune.*

The Chicago *Sun-Times.*

The New York *Freeman's Journal.*

The Denver *Register.*

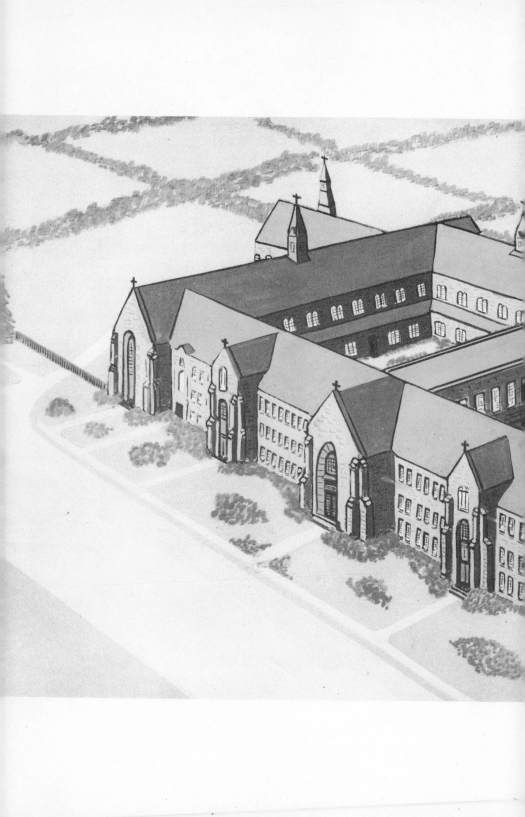